THE CAMBRIDGE SPY RING

THE CAMBRIDGE SPY RING

THE TREACHERY OF THE FIVE WHO GOT AWAY

SHAWNNA MORRIS

PEN & SWORD HISTORY

AN IMPRINT OF PEN & SWORD BOOKS LTD.
YORKSHIRE · PHILADELPHIA

First published in Great Britain in 2025 by
PEN AND SWORD HISTORY
An imprint of
Pen & Sword Books Ltd
Yorkshire – Philadelphia

Copyright © Shawnna Morris, 2025

ISBN 978 1 03610 868 7

The right of Shawnna Morris to be identified as Author of this work has been asserted by her in accordance with the Copyright, Designs and Patents Act 1988.

A CIP catalogue record for this book is available from the British Library.

All rights reserved. No part of this book may be reproduced, transmitted, downloaded, decompiled or reverse engineered in any form or by any means, electronic or mechanical including photocopying, recording or by any information storage and retrieval system, without permission from the Publisher in writing. NO AI TRAINING: Without in any way limiting the Author's and Publisher's exclusive rights under copyright, any use of this publication to "train" generative artificial intelligence (AI) technologies to generate text is expressly prohibited. The Author and Publisher reserve all rights to license uses of this work for generative AI training and development of machine learning language models.

Typeset in Times New Roman 11/14.5 by
SJmagic DESIGN SERVICES, India.
Printed and bound in the UK by CPI Group (UK) Ltd.

The Publisher's authorised representative in the EU for product safety is Authorised Rep Compliance Ltd., Ground Floor, 71 Lower Baggot Street, Dublin D02 P593, Ireland.
www.arccompliance.com

For a complete list of Pen & Sword titles please contact:
PEN & SWORD BOOKS LIMITED
George House, Units 12 & 13, Beevor Street, Off Pontefract Road, Barnsley, South Yorkshire, S71 1HN, England
E-mail: enquiries@pen-and-sword.co.uk
Website: www.pen-and-sword.co.uk

or

PEN AND SWORD BOOKS
1950 Lawrence Rd, Havertown, PA 19083, USA
E-mail: uspen-and-sword@casematepublishers.com
Website: www.penandswordbooks.com

Contents

Acknowledgements vi
Introduction vii
Cast of Characters x

Chapter One	From the Halls of Trinity	1
Chapter Two	The Brilliant Ringleader	7
Chapter Three	The Diplomat	16
Chapter Four	The Anti-Spy	24
Chapter Five	The Three Musketeers	35
Chapter Six	The Art Historian	44
Chapter Seven	Was He, or Wasn't He?	54
Chapter Eight	The World Heads to War	67
Chapter Nine	The Unholy Alliance	81
Chapter Ten	The Great Patriotic War	94
Chapter Eleven	A Shift in Focus	112
Chapter Twelve	A Precipitous Decline	123
Chapter Thirteen	The Unravelling	137
Chapter Fourteen	The Flight	155
Chapter Fifteen	The Fallout	170
Chapter Sixteen	The End of the Road	190

Bibliography 203
Notes 206
Index 219

Acknowledgements

I would first like to thank my commissioning editor, Sarah-Beth Watkins, for finding my obscure history blog online, and taking a chance on a new author. I would also like to thank my copyeditor, Sarah Hodder, for her patience with my learning process. I am grateful for the talent of Jon Wilkinson, who created an amazing book cover from my simple sketches. I would also like to thank the entire production team at Pen & Sword Books for making my dream a reality.

Most of all, I want to express my sincere gratitude to my family. I would like to thank my mother, Valerie DeLuca, for her positivity and enthusiasm. Thanks to my brother, Todd DeLuca, for helping me to organise my most challenging project. Thanks to my daughter, Natalie Graham, for her encouragement and technical advice. I would like to thank my son, Benjamin Morris, for understanding how much this project means to me, even as it ate up so much of our time. I would like to express my deepest love and gratitude to my husband, Tim Morris, who always believed in me.

Introduction

What is it about the Cambridge Spy Ring that continues to fascinate, more than seven decades after its existence came to light? Is it the mythology of the well-dressed, glamourous secret agent, which is credited with inspiring spy thrillers by Ian Fleming and John le Carré? Is it the sheer volume of the material handed over? Is it the fact that none of the five spies were ever prosecuted? Or is it simply the slow release of information, dragged out over decades, that leaves us hungry for more?

When Cyril Connolly published *The Missing Diplomats* in 1952, it was the first written account of the dramatic disappearance of suspected Soviet agents Donald Maclean and Guy Burgess. Connolly knew both suspects personally, having worked with them at the Foreign Office. His brief analysis, first printed as a two-part feature in *The Sunday Times*, underlined their common alma mater, Cambridge University. Both diplomats had been active in communist circles during their time at Cambridge, and both had disavowed those associations before entering the Diplomatic Service. By pointing out the Cambridge connection, Connolly was the first author to touch upon the existence of a Soviet spy ring originating from the prestigious university.

As the years passed, more secrets leaked out, drip by drip. Rumours of a third man in the spy ring, who helped the first two in their escape, began to circulate almost immediately. Once the third man was revealed as Kim Philby, the hunt for a fourth man was soon underway. Even after the public unmasking of Anthony Blunt in 1979, and that of John Cairncross shortly afterwards, the story wasn't quite finished.

The 1980s brought forth a slew of books written by journalists and retired intelligence officers alike, offering their own version of events, and their own theories surrounding the spies' motivations. The fall of the Soviet Union at the end of 1991 ushered in a new era of the Cambridge Five canon, promising more information from the files of the KGB. Western publishers were inundated by retired Soviet intelligence officers, desperate for income once their pension, like their government, ceased to exist. Some of these books are reliable; most are not.

With the exception of the *Mitrokhin Archive*, the KGB files remain unavailable. The British Intelligence Services have released selected files to the public only occasionally. The CIA is slightly more transparent, due to America's Freedom of Information Act. Alas, only part of the story involved the United States.

In an attempt to control their own legacy, some of the spies wrote memoirs. Kim Philby's autobiography, *My Silent War*, is a largely self-serving composition, exaggerating his own stories for dramatic effect, while failing to reveal anything new. John Cairncross, on the other hand, took pains to minimise his role in spying for the Soviets. In his memoir, *The Enigma Spy*, published posthumously by his widow, he insists that he was not even a member of the Cambridge Spy Ring. Anthony Blunt started to write his memoirs, then quit in frustration, leaving them unfinished and unpublished. Guy Burgess and Donald Maclean chose not to write memoirs at all.

Many wonderful individual biographies have been published within the past two decades, but there has been no comprehensive account of the full saga of the Cambridge Five. Portions of the story are scattered throughout a broad catalogue of books; not just biographies of the five spies, but also biographies of supporting members of the spy ring, like James Klugmann and Michael Straight. Histories of the British Intelligence Services shed light on flaws in the institutions that enabled the spies. Books by former Soviet controllers, though often factually inaccurate, nonetheless offer compelling insights into their personalities. Biographies of their unwitting accomplices, like those of James Angleton, add yet another dimension to the story.

In my attempt to piece together a complete narrative of the Cambridge Five, I have happily delved into all of these secondary sources. Due to the ongoing secrecy surrounding many of the historical events involved, some mysteries remain unsolved to this day. Accounts of specific events often differ slightly, even among respected historians. I have pointed out incidents where there is conflicting or unreliable information. In these cases, I have generally deferred to the most recent publications.

Introduction

A few notes before we begin: the British Intelligence Services are organised under the abbreviation MI, for Military Intelligence. Domestic security is ensured by MI5, and foreign intelligence falls under MI6, which is commonly called the Secret Intelligence Service, or SIS. Both abbreviations are used interchangeably. Similarly, in the United States, the Central Intelligence Agency, or CIA, handles foreign intelligence, leaving domestic security to the FBI (Federal Bureau of Investigation).

In the interest of simplicity, the Soviet Intelligence Service, which was organised under many different names in its history (NKVD, OGPU, NKGB, etc.,) will be referred to as the KGB, its final and most familiar title. Its headquarters are sometimes referred to as Moscow Centre, or simply The Centre. The KGB stations located within foreign embassies were commonly known as Rezidenturas, and the head of station was called the Rezident.

This book will not bring forth any shocking new revelations, nor will it be the final word on the Cambridge Five. Instead, it will serve as an overview of the complete history of the Cambridge Spy Ring, for those readers who would like to find it all in one place. It brings together the lives and adventures of each spy, and the many points at which their stories intersect with one another, against the backdrop of some of the most important events in twentieth century history.

Cast of Characters

The Cambridge Five

Kim Philby: The first spy recruited to the Cambridge Spy Ring. Approached by Arnold Deutsch in 1934. Code named SÖNCHEN, later STANLEY, possibly ELLI.

Donald Maclean: Recommended by Kim Philby. British diplomat, and most valuable to the KGB. Code named WAISE (ORPHAN), LYRIC, STUART, and HOMER.

Guy Burgess: Discovered the spy ring, and forced his way in. The first spy to infiltrate MI6. Code named MÄDCHEN, later HICKS, sometimes PAUL.

Anthony Blunt: Art Historian and MI5 officer. Recruited by Burgess as talent spotter for the Cambridge Spy Ring. Code named TONY.

John Cairncross: Linguist, literary expert. The last spy recruited. Denied he was the fifth man in the Cambridge Spy Ring; many still believe him. Code named MOLIÈRE, LIZT, and CARELIAN.

The Spy Handlers

Arnold Deutsch: The mastermind behind the Cambridge Spy Ring. Code named OTTO. Active in London 1934–1938.

Boris Kreshin: Real name Boris Mikhailovich Krötenschield. Also called Krechin, or Krotov. Served in London approximately 1944–1947.

Theodore Maly: Agent handler in 1935, assisting Deutsch. London Rezident, 1936–1937. Code named THEO.

Grigori Grafpen: London Rezident during 1938.

Anatoly Gorsky: London Rezident, 1940–1944; Washington DC Rezident, approximately 1944–1948.

Kitty Harris: Donald Maclean's handler and lover in London and Paris, approximately 1938–1940. Code named NORMA, later ADA.

Yuri Modin: The last London handler for the Cambridge Five, approximately 1948–1951. Code named PETER.

Vladimir Pravdin: Donald Maclean's first handler in the United States; served briefly in New York while waiting for Gorsky's arrival in 1944. Sent the telegram to Moscow which led to Maclean's eventual exposure.

Alexander Orlov: London Rezident in 1935; supervised Arnold Deutsch.

Supporting Actors

Eric Kessler: Journalist and casual boyfriend of Guy Burgess. Used his position as Swiss Embassy press attaché to gather intelligence.

James Klugmann: Close friend of Donald Maclean and schoolmate at Gresham's. Credited with Maclean's conversion to communism. Friends with Guy Burgess, Anthony Blunt, and John Cairncross. Recruited John Cairncross.

Leo Long: Member of the Cambridge Communist Party, recruited by Anthony Blunt.

Michael Straight: American undergraduate student at Cambridge, recruited by Anthony Blunt to infiltrate the Roosevelt administration.

Goronwy Rees: Close friend of Guy Burgess. Recruited by Burgess, then changed his mind about spying. They remained friends, but Burgess always feared exposure by him.

Andrew Revoi: Also known as Andrew Revai. Journalist and casual boyfriend of Guy Burgess.

Spouses, Partners, and Family

Evelyn Bassett: Mother of Guy Burgess.

John Bassett: Stepfather of Guy Burgess.

Nigel Burgess: Brother of Guy Burgess.

Alec Cairncross: Also known as Sir Alexander Cairncross, economist and older brother of John Cairncross.

Gabrielle Oppenheim Cairncross: First wife of John Cairncross.

Gayle Brinkerhoff Cairncross: Second wife of John Cairncross.

Melinda Dunbar: Donald Maclean's mother-in-law.

John Gaskin: Anthony Blunt's partner.

Jack Hewit: Long term partner of Guy Burgess. Engaged in a year-long affair with Anthony Blunt.

Alan Maclean: Donald Maclean's younger brother. Worked in the Foreign Office Press Department before becoming private secretary to Gladwyn Jebb, British representative to the United Nations.

Sir Donald Maclean: Father of Donald Maclean. Liberal Party politician and President of the Board of Education.

Lady Gwendolyn Maclean: Mother of Donald Maclean.

Melinda Marling Maclean: Wife of Donald Maclean.

Harriet Marling: Sister-in-law of Donald Maclean, Melinda's favourite sister.

Peter Montgomery: Occasional boyfriend of Anthony Blunt.

Nancy Maclean Oetking: Donald Maclean's sister.

Aileen Furse Philby: Kim Philby's second wife, mother of his five children.

Dora Philby: Kim Philby's mother.

Eleanor Brewer Philby: Kim Philby's third wife.

Litzi Friedmann Philby: Kim Philby's first wife.

Rufina Pukhova Philby: Kim Philby's fourth wife.

St John Philby: Kim Philby's father, eminent Middle East expert.

Peter Pollock: Boyfriend of Guy Burgess.

Esther Whitfield: Personal secretary to Kim Philby. Had an affair with Philby, then later a relationship with Guy Burgess.

Cast of Characters

Friends and Associates

James Angleton: Head of Staff A of the CIA's Office of Special Operations. Close friend and unwitting accomplice of Kim Philby.

Julian Bell: Student and Apostles member at Cambridge; briefly dated Anthony Blunt. Close friend of Guy Burgess.

Clarissa Churchill: Niece of Winston Churchill, close friend and possible girlfriend of Guy Burgess.

John 'Jock' Colville: Friend and co-worker of John Cairncross at the Foreign Office.

Cyril Connolly: Foreign Office colleague of both Donald Maclean and Guy Burgess. Wrote first account of their disappearance.

Miles Copeland, Junior: American CIA agent in Beirut station; close friend of Kim Philby.

John Cornford: Communist Party activist at Cambridge, friends with Burgess, Maclean, and Blunt.

Felix Cowgill: Head of Section V of SIS; supervisor and friend of Kim Philby.

Jack Curry: MI5 officer. After retirement came to MI6 to reactivate Section IX, which Philby would head.

Maurice Dobb: Created first communist cell at Cambridge University, converted Guy Burgess to communism.

Nicholas Elliott: Officer at MI6, close friend of Kim Philby.

David Footman: MI6 officer; recruited Guy Burgess to help spot communists working at the BBC.

Graham Greene: Author and journalist, briefly served in MI6 under Kim Philby during the Second World War, where he met John Cairncross. Remained a close friend of Cairncross the rest of his life.

David Haden Guest: Communist Party activist at Cambridge University.

Edith Tudor Hart: Illegal agent and close friend of Litzi Friedmann. Introduced Kim Philby to Arnold Deutsch.

Tomás Harris: Art dealer who served with MI5 during the Second World War. Friend of Kim Philby.

Jim Lees: Coal miner on scholarship to Cambridge University. Friend of Kim Philby and Guy Burgess.

Guy Liddell: Director of MI5's B Division. Supervised Anthony Blunt. Friend of Burgess and Philby.

Tim Milne: Kim Philby's oldest friend, schoolmate from Westminster. Officer at MI6.

Jack Macnamara: Conservative member of parliament, employed Guy Burgess as his personal assistant.

Louis MacNeice: Poet and playwright. Anthony Blunt's oldest friend; classmate at Marlborough.

Lees Mayall: Foreign Office staffer, worked under Donald Maclean in Cairo.

Tess Mayor: Colleague, friend, and roommate of Anthony Blunt. Later married Victor Rothschild.

Hector McNeil: Labour MP, Minister of State at the Foreign Office, Vice President of United Nations General Assembly. Employed Guy Burgess as his personal assistant.

Stuart Menzies: Head of MI6, 1939–1952. Oversaw Kim Philby's tenure at MI6.

Bernard Miller: American medical student, unwittingly used by Guy Burgess as an alibi for his defection.

Malcolm Muggeridge: Journalist; briefly worked under Kim Philby at MI6 during the Second World War.

Harold Nicolson: Labour MP; close friend and mentor of Guy Burgess.

Dennis Proctor: Officer at the Treasury and later Permanent Secretary at the Ministry of Power. Cambridge Apostle, friend of Burgess and Blunt.

Patricia Rawdon-Smith: Briefly dated Anthony Blunt at Cambridge, later became his roommate.

Cast of Characters

Victor Rothschild: Cambridge Apostle and close friend of Guy Burgess, Anthony Blunt, and Kim Philby, though not a communist. Briefly served with MI5 during the Second World War.

Flora Solomon: Philanthropist and Zionist activist. Close friend of Kim Philby.

Philip Toynbee: Journalist and close friend of Donald Maclean. Shared in Maclean's alcoholism.

Valentine Vivian: The first head of Section V of MI6. Recruited Kim Philby to MI6.

Enemies

Meredith Gardner: American linguistics specialist, assigned to the US Army Signals Intelligence top secret Venona project. Decoded KGB cables; was instrumental in the exposure of Donald Maclean.

Walter Krivitsky: Soviet illegal agent and defector; revealed clues to the identity of the Cambridge spies.

Robert Lamphere: FBI agent; worked closely with Meredith Gardner to find Soviet agents through the Venona project.

Robert Mackenzie: Head of Security for the British Embassy in Washington DC. Disliked and distrusted Guy Burgess.

Arthur Martin: MI5 officer; investigated prominent spy scandals during the early Cold War.

Vladimir Petrov: KGB agent; defected in 1954 while serving in Soviet Embassy in Australia. Revealed the extent of Burgess and Maclean's espionage.

Jim Skardon: Head of MI5's Special Branch. Deeply involved in the investigations of the Cambridge Spy Ring.

Erich Vermehren: Defector from the German Abwehr. Revealed the existence of an anti-Nazi and anti-Soviet German resistance movement to MI6, which Kim Philby then reported to the KGB.

Konstantin Volkov: KGB agent in Turkey, attempted defector. Promised to unmask three double agents working in the SIS but disappeared before he could be interviewed.

Dick White: The only person to serve as both Head of MI5 (1953–1956) and Head of MI6 (1956–1968). Began to suspect Kim Philby after the defection of Maclean and Burgess.

Peter Wright: MI5 officer, worked with Arthur Martin to interrogate John Cairncross and Anthony Blunt.

Chapter One

From the Halls of Trinity
The Spymaster Plants the Seeds

Espionage is a crime nearly as old as time itself. Spies are first named specifically in the Old Testament's Book of Numbers, but the oldest known spy report survives from the court of Babylonian King Hammurabi, 400 years earlier. In the cheeky title of his book on the history of secret agents, author Phillip Knightley called espionage *The Second Oldest Profession*. In matters of war and diplomacy, information about the opponent is critical. For every person, or nation, who has a secret, there is someone else who wants it.

The ancient art of recruiting a spy follows a time tested formula. First, a person with access to sensitive information must be located. Next, they must be assessed for vulnerabilities. Financial troubles, marital difficulties, or dissatisfaction with their job can make someone ripe for the picking. Finally, the recruiter must get close to his mark and befriend him. Once trust is established, the source must be convinced to betray his country.

And what kind of person would betray their country? Some are motivated by love, others by greed, and a few by fear. Maybe they feel unappreciated by their employer. Perhaps they have secrets of their own, and are open to blackmail. The best spies, though, are idealists; true believers in a cause for which they are willing to risk everything.

In the 1930s, a Soviet case officer named Arnold Deutsch turned the conventional process on its head. Instead of infiltrating a government and peeling off impressionable civil servants, he scoured an elite university to find young radicals with the potential for high achievement. He then instructed them in the dark arts of spycraft before sending them, like poisoned pills, into the world of influence and power.

Luckily for Arnold Deutsch, the climate at England's Cambridge University had shifted in his favour by the time he arrived in 1934.

The university students had grown up during the political unrest of the interwar period. At the end of the Great War, the British Empire had reached the apex of its power. With control over twenty-four per cent of the world's land mass, and twenty-three per cent of its people, it was now the largest empire in history. However, cracks were beginning to emerge at the seams.

The tumultuous epoch began with an unemployment crisis among veterans returning home from the Great War. Taxes, first levied to fund the war effort, remained high long after Armistice Day. Economic stagnation crippled the manufacturing sector. The first general strike in British history, in support of underpaid coal miners, paralysed transportation and heavy industry for nine days in 1926.

America's stock market crash of 1929 rippled throughout the entire developed world, and the United Kingdom suffered its own subsequent crash in 1931. A looming deficit triggered a run on gold. The Labour Government, unable to fund its raft of welfare expansion policies, sought to borrow from overseas. The loans could not be secured, though, without deep budget cuts. An irreconcilable divide formed within the party over proposed cuts to unemployment benefits, leading to the resignation of the Labour Government in August 1931. Prime Minister Ramsey MacDonald was forced to form a coalition government with the Conservative and Liberal Parties. For his efforts, he was branded a traitor and ousted from his own Labour Party, which refused to participate in the new government.

At Cambridge University, a cloud of disillusionment settled over the student body. Great Britain was in the throes of economic depression, and the ostensible champion of the working class, the Labour Party, had utterly failed to address it. Those fortunate enough to attend a prestigious university could not ignore their pangs of guilt as they witnessed the suffering of their fellow countrymen. Some leading intellectuals interpreted the economic fallout as the failure of capitalism. Seeing the widespread poverty at home, they looked to the new experiment in the Soviet Union with hope. The Soviet Union, due more to its economic isolation than its central planning, had not been affected by the Great Depression. Reports of the Soviet gulag system and the ongoing famine in Ukraine were largely suppressed, making it easy for outsiders to believe in the promise of a worker's paradise.

Furthermore, the rising menace of fascism had begun to cast its dark shadow over Europe. From its inception in Italy, the totalitarian system had spread to Germany, where the Nazi Party took control with the appointment of Adolph Hitler as chancellor in early 1933. Fascist parties threatened to take power in Austria, Portugal, and Spain.

At Cambridge University, the Marxist philosophy captivated many students, as well as a few professors. The promise of economic and racial equality appealed to those students who were disenchanted with the British class system and the old colonial order. Furthermore, the Soviet Union declared itself as the only bulwark against the threat of fascism. By 1933, a fascination with communism had taken hold at Cambridge, creating the perfect conditions for the machinations of Arnold Deutsch.

Arnold Deutsch arrived in London in 1934 with an impressive history. He was born to a Czech Jewish family in what was then Austria-Hungary. A brilliant student, Deutsch received a PhD in chemistry at the age of 24, after only five years of study at the University of Vienna.

Deutsch became a member of the Communist Party while attending university. He was recruited by the Communist International (Comintern), the Soviet organisation dedicated to the formation of a worldwide Soviet Republic by revolution. Arnold Deutsch and his wife, Josefine, both worked as couriers for the Comintern in Europe and the Middle East.

In 1932, Deutsch was transferred to the Soviet KGB. He was trained in Moscow as an illegal agent, then sent to France, where he established clandestine border crossings into the Netherlands, Belgium and Germany.

Deutsch was part of a generation of Soviet spies known in Moscow as the Great Illegals. A certain romance is associated with these spies who operated in the 1930s. They were talented, multilingual agents who moved in and out of countries with pseudonyms and forged passports. They often were not Russian, but hailed from the countries of Eastern Europe. In the era before strict KGB protocols were established, these operatives were given wide latitude to exercise their own creativity in espionage and recruiting. This permissive style of management, combined with the lenient security of their target countries, allowed the Great Illegals to play largely by their own rules.

When Deutsch received his second posting, this time to England, he broke protocol and entered the country under his real name. He had a special mission this time, which would be aided by his academic credentials. Deutsch enrolled as a graduate student of psychology at the University of London, which enabled his mingling in academic circles. Deutsch's plan required his infiltration, not of a government, but of a world class university.

Arnold Deutsch was uniquely suited for the recruitment of brilliant young radicals. He was an intellectual with diverse interests and a true believer in the utopian vision of a communist future. He was also a sexual revolutionary, styled after the culture of the early years of Bolshevism, which championed the rejection of monogamy and the traditional family. Deutsch was a follower and collaborator of Dr Wilhelm Reich, a former protégé of Dr Sigmund Freud, who believed in the compatibility of Marxism and psychoanalysis. Reich founded the Sex-Pol movement (Association for Proletarian Sexual Politics), which opened birth control clinics for Vienna's working class, as well as a publishing house for Reich's books and pamphlets. Dr Reich, through the Sex-Pol movement, asserted that sexual repression was synonymous with political oppression, and that breaking free from traditional sexual mores would ignite political revolution, as well. Deutsch's rejection of traditional sexual morality endeared him to potential recruits at Cambridge, where a small cell of sexual revolutionaries already existed.

Deutsch first met Harold Adrian Russel 'Kim' Philby on 1 June 1934 on a bench in Regent's Park. Kim Philby had already graduated from Trinity College at Cambridge University, and had just returned from Austria, where he had been helping communist refugees to escape from Hitler's Nazi Germany. On that fateful day in Regent's Park, Deutsch, using his code name, OTTO, invited Philby to take his cause to a new level. He suggested that Philby could do clandestine work in the fight against fascism. Arnold Deutsch appealed to Philby's sense of reason. As a member in good standing of the bourgeoisie, Deutsch argued, Philby could fight fascism from a position of power. Though he didn't say it outright, Deutsch hinted that Kim should spy for the KGB.

Philby was enchanted with Deutsch's intelligence, humour, and sensitivity. Although Deutsch was only eight years older than Philby, he gave him the affectionate code name, SÖNCHEN (German for 'Sonny'), perhaps as a tacit nod to Philby's complicated relationship with his father.

And so, by enticing the romanticism of a young leftist, Arnold Deutsch set in motion a plan that would result in the most catastrophic breach of British and American intelligence for the next forty years. Deutsch is credited by the KGB files with the recruitment of twenty agents during his four years in London.[1] None, however, were as notorious as those whom the Soviets later dubbed 'The Magnificent Five'.

At Deutsch's request, Philby provided a list of names, fellow Cambridge students who might be receptive to his plan. The most impressive of these candidates was Donald Maclean, the handsome, intelligent son of cabinet minister, Sir Donald Maclean. Then in his final year at Trinity Hall, the strapping rugby player and editor of the student magazine was interested in a career in academia. He was hoping to continue his education and earn his PhD, or possibly teach English in the Soviet Union.

Muscling his way into the conspiracy was the wily Guy Burgess, mutual friend of Philby and Maclean. Burgess became suspicious when his two friends cut ties with their associates in the Cambridge Communist Party (which was the standard practice for newly recruited Soviet agents). He relentlessly needled Donald Maclean, until Maclean grudgingly revealed his and Philby's new vocation. Burgess insisted on being included.

It is a credit to the creativity and open-mindedness of Arnold Deutsch that the gossipy and flamboyantly homosexual Guy Burgess was not disqualified from service. A traditional case officer might see these traits as a serious liability, but Deutsch saw instead a social butterfly with connections in many diverse circles. Burgess was intellectually gifted, if not reaching his full potential. He was in his fourth year at Trinity College, working on his thesis, which he would never finish.

Upon Deutsch's instruction, Philby, Maclean, and Burgess abandoned their career plans and entered professions which would best facilitate their access to useful intelligence. Kim Philby took a job as a journalist, giving him ideal cover to travel, to speak with important people, and to gather sensitive information. Maclean completed his Civil Service exams and entered into His Majesty's Diplomatic Service, becoming the first of the Cambridge Five to enter government. Burgess took a temporary job as personal assistant to minister of parliament, John Macnamara. When his posting ended, Burgess secured a position as a producer at the BBC (British Broadcasting Corporation).

Privately, they called themselves 'The Three Musketeers'.

It was not until 1937 that the quintet was completed. In January, Guy Burgess set up a meeting between Arnold Deutsch and Anthony Blunt. Blunt had already graduated from Trinity in 1930 with a first class degree and was now a Trinity College fellow, doing postgraduate research.

Later in the year, Anthony Blunt, acting in his new role as Deutsch's talent spotter, recommended his brilliant French literature student, John

Cairncross. Unlike the other four, Cairncross was a Scotsman from a working class town. Cairncross had already spent time at Glasgow University and the prestigious Sorbonne in Paris before entering Trinity on a scholarship in modern languages.

After graduation, the profoundly intelligent Cairncross impressed his proctors with two first place rankings on his Civil Service exams. He promptly received a posting with the British Foreign Office.

Kim Philby, Donald Maclean, Guy Burgess, Anthony Blunt, and John Cairncross were known in Moscow Centre as The Magnificent Five, but were revealed much later in the west as the Cambridge Spy Ring, or simply the Cambridge Five.

Their exploits led to the most devastating exposure of secret intelligence in British history.

Chapter Two

The Brilliant Ringleader
The Duplicitous Kim Philby

What's in a name? New parents take great care in selecting a name for their new baby, for many believe that a child will be shaped by the name bestowed upon him or her. They will always be seen by others through the lens of that name, perhaps bringing to mind a political figure, a religious saint, a famous personality, or a character in a story who bears the same moniker. Assumptions and judgements will be made and the child will react accordingly, gradually building their identity around others' perception of them.

But what about a nickname? A nickname carries even more weight in the minds of those around; after all, they must have done something to earn it.

Such was the case with Kim Philby.

Born on an auspicious day to a beautiful mother and a powerful father, great things were expected from this firstborn child and only son. Harold Adrian Russell Philby was born in British India on New Year's Day, 1912. His father, Harry St John Bridger Philby, an administrator in the Indian Civil Service, was stationed in the Punjab in the city of Ambala. Like many children with busy parents of that time and place, the boy was cared for by his Indian nanny. Naturally, he picked up some Punjabi. When St John found his 3 year old son in the kitchen, chatting up the staff in their own language, he called him 'Little Kim'.

St John, as he was called, was referring to the title character in Rudyard Kipling's novel, *Kim,* about an orphaned boy named Kimball O'Hara, who acted as a spy in the first Afghan War. Like his namesake, little Kim Philby was a dark haired child who, with his immersion in the local culture, could be mistaken for an Indian boy. He could move between two worlds and become two different people.

St John Philby could not have known how appropriate the appellation would later become.

St John was himself a fascinating and controversial man. Born in British Ceylon to a tea planter, he was educated first at Westminster School, then at Trinity College, Cambridge. After earning a degree in modern languages, he joined the Indian Civil Service in 1908. He was stationed in Lahore, Punjab, where he met Dora Johnston, a fetching redhead who was the daughter of a railway engineer. They were married in 1910, and Kim, as he was later called, came along in 1912. They later had three daughters – Helena, Diana, and Patricia.

While little Kim was still a toddler, the Great War broke out in Europe, eventually spreading to the Ottoman Empire. By late 1915, St John was assigned to the British forces, fighting the Turks in Mesopotamia.

St John soon became involved in the British effort to persuade the Arabs to rise up and fight their Ottoman rulers. He was sent on a mission to meet with Bedouin chieftain Ibn Saud, not unlike T. E. Lawrence, who met with the rival sheik, Faisal bin Al-Hussein. Just as T. E. 'Lawrence of Arabia' was forever changed by his exposure to Arab culture, so too was St John. He could not forgive the betrayal of the Sykes-Pekoe agreement, in which the self-determination promised to the Arabs was revoked, and their land divided between the victorious great powers. He formed a lasting friendship with the future Saudi king and turned against the colonial policies of the British. St John became a career Arab expert, as well as an explorer. He later became the first European to cross the Rub al Khali, the largest part of the Arabian Desert.

When St John first left India for his posting in Baghdad, Kim and his mother, Dora, moved to England with St John's mother, May. With his father overseas for long periods, and his mother frequently gone to visit him, Kim was looked after by his grandmother. St John's distance afforded him a mythological status in the eyes of little Kim, who heard of his many adventures from his grandmother. He went years at a time without seeing his father, and even his mother was sometimes like a stranger to him.

In order that Kim may fulfil the destiny set forth by his father since the day of his birth, St John and Dora enrolled him at Aldro Preparatory School, an elite boarding school close to the English Channel in Sussex. St John hoped for Kim to earn a scholarship to Westminster, followed by a scholarship to Trinity College, just like he had. Kim rose to the challenge. He excelled in academics as well as sports, playing cricket, football, rugby, and boxing. He became Head Boy and House Prefect and delighted his father by winning multiple academic awards.

When Kim was 12 years old, he followed in his father's footsteps and became a King's Scholar at London's Westminster School. St John had since moved to Jeddah, Saudi Arabia, on a permanent basis. Kim's feelings toward his father during this period whipsawed between admiration and resentment. As St John earned recognition and awards for his diplomatic work in the Middle East, he took numerous lovers overseas, and made no effort to hide it from Dora. In fact, he often bragged about his conquests in letters home.[1] While St John dined with the Saudi king and explored the Arabian Desert by camel, Dora struggled to pay the heating bill and buy groceries for the children.

Kim rarely answered St John's letters, which nagged him relentlessly about his performance in school.[2] St John had made a lasting mark as an outstanding student at Westminster and Kim struggled in his shadow. Unlike at Aldro, where he could forge his own path, Kim found it hard to stand out while being constantly compared to his father, and usually coming up short. He lost much of his interest in sports, not returning to cricket until 1927. He was afflicted with a stutter from early childhood, which now exacerbated under stress. His atheism, drilled into him since birth by St John, made unbearable the Christian instruction at Westminster, and drew harassment from his teachers. In contrast to the convivial Kim Philby of adulthood, his oldest friend and fellow King's Scholar, Tim Milne, remembered him as solitary and detached.[3]

Later in life, Kim claimed to have suffered a nervous breakdown at Westminster.[4]

St John often expressed disappointment with Kim in his letters home to Dora, worrying that Kim would not make the cut for Trinity College, his own alma mater.

At the age of 15, Kim's housemaster, the Reverend Kenneth Luce, wrote to St John that Kim had developed the habit of lying, which was a grave offense at Westminster. After his reprimand, Kim wrote an essay and sent it to his father. He flattered St John by mimicking his writing style, and by expressing unconventional views that were similar to his own. St John was impressed with Kim's free-thinking, unorthodox mind set, which reminded him of his younger self. The incident may have marked the first recorded display of Kim Philby's notorious capacity for charm and duplicity.[5]

Despite St John's worries, Kim performed exceedingly well at Westminster. Through grit and hard work, he overcame a rough start and clamoured to the head of his class by the end of the sixth form. He graduated at 17 years old with not one, but two scholarships: one to Christ Church at Oxford and the other to Trinity College, Cambridge. Naturally, he chose to fulfil St John's ambition by selecting Trinity.

After a long summer holiday in Spain, Kim Philby arrived at the University of Cambridge in the autumn of 1929, where he had more shadows than his father's to contend with. The ancient university, dating back to the eleventh century, has been central to some of the most seismic changes in history, including the Protestant Reformation and the Great Migration of Puritans to New England. Trinity College, founded by King Henry VIII in 1546, is the most prestigious college within Cambridge and has produced the highest number of Nobel Laureates at Cambridge, as well as six British prime ministers. Its alumni include such luminaries as Francis Bacon, Isaac Newton, Niels Bohr, A.A. Milne, Vladimir Nabokov, and Bertrand Russell. Nestled near the centre of Cambridge among the oldest colleges, the Great Gate, featuring a statue of Henry VIII, leads to Trinity Court, the largest enclosed courtyard in Europe.

Kim settled into his room at 8 Jesus Lane and quietly set about his studies in history. He kept mainly to himself during his first year, eschewing sports for solitary evenings at home listening to records. He made friends with some students, Harry Dawes and Jim Lees, former coal miners on a Workers Education Association scholarship, who described him as egalitarian, unconcerned with anyone's class status.[6]

Although it is tempting to credit his associations with working class students or his summer motorcycling through Spain as the impetus for his turn to communism, Philby himself pointed to the 1931 collapse of the Labour Government as the beginning of his radicalism.[7] He was already interested in politics and joined the Cambridge University Socialist Society (CUSS) in 1929. He later served as its treasurer from 1932 to 1933. There, he was exposed to left wing ideas by witnessing contentious debates on the issues of the day.

Philby's growing attraction to communism mirrored its rise in popularity at Cambridge. Maurice Dobb, an economics lecturer, had been a member of the Communist Party since 1920. Dobb had visited the Soviet Union with renowned economist John Maynard Keynes in 1925 and established the first communist cell at Cambridge in 1931. He wrote numerous books and pamphlets in support of Marxism, and gave frequent lectures on the topic, at least one of which was attended by Kim.

The cell was soon taken over by a dashing student, David Haden Guest. Guest had just returned to Cambridge from a year studying mathematics at Germany's University of Göttingen, where he had been arrested at an anti-Nazi student demonstration. He dramatically recounted his brave ordeal to his awestruck classmates, which helped to fuel a robust drive for membership. He transformed Dobb's quiet and theoretical discussion group into a boisterous crowd of revolutionaries. They criticised CUSS for being ineffectual and shouted down their opponents during debates, a practice previously unheard of at Cambridge. When a flank of the 1932 Hunger March passed through Cambridge, Guest led a delegation of students out to meet with the marchers, and join them in their protest against the government means test for welfare benefits.

Kim Philby, still a member of CUSS, supported the marchers by organising food and lodging for them. Although he sympathised with the plight of the working class, Kim hesitated to join the Communist Party. He clung to a tenuous thread of hope that conventional socialism could remedy the stark inequality of British society. Suspecting that the problem owed something to the rigid British class system, he decided to visit other countries to see how their people fared.

During summers off, Kim travelled throughout Europe, sometimes accompanied by his old Westminster chum, Tim Milne, who was now attending Oxford. In addition to France, Hungary, and the Balkans, they went to Germany, where they were alarmed to witness a huge rally at which Adolph Hitler spoke to an enthusiastic crowd. Shocked by the violent rhetoric, Philby made up his mind that the Soviet Union, staunchly opposed to Germany, must be defended at all costs.

On his last day at Cambridge University, Kim Philby finally made the decision to become a communist. He approached Maurice Dobb to find out the best way of joining the Party.[8] Curiously, instead of sending Kim to London's Communist Party headquarters on King Street, Dobb consulted a Comintern group in Paris, most likely the International Organisation for Aid to Revolutionaries (IOAR). Dobb wrote a letter of recommendation to the Head of IOAR, Louis Giberti. Giberti, an old friend of Dobb's, happily wrote his own letter of recommendation to the Austrian Committee for Relief from German Fascism, another Comintern front group in Vienna. Under the guise of improving his German, which was required for the Foreign Service, Kim headed to Austria.

Austria was then in the midst of a tumultuous political upheaval. The former Hapsburg Empire, after its defeat in the Great War, was reduced to a population of six million and confined to the Alpine and Danube crownlands. Its economy suffered hyperinflation, as well as trade embargoes by neighbouring Italy, Hungary, Czechoslovakia and Yugoslavia. Austria's conservative country peasants were pitted against the Social Democrats in the cities. Tensions culminated in the 1927 July Revolt, a massive riot that resulted in a fire in the Palace of Justice, followed by police firing into the crowds, killing eighty-nine protesters. The leftist uprising led to a consolidation of power by the conservative elements, and the 1932 election of the far right Engelbert Dollfuss as chancellor. Dollfuss promptly suspended the constitution and cracked down hard on leftist elements. By the time Kim Philby arrived in 1933, Austria was on the brink of civil war.

Upon his arrival in Vienna, Kim rented a room with Israel and Gisella Kohlman, a Jewish couple friendly to the anti-fascist cause. Also in the home was their attractive 20 year old daughter, Alice Friedmann, who usually went by Litzi. A member of the Austrian Communist Party, Litzi was worldly for her age. She had already been married to the Zionist activist Karl Friedmann, divorced a year later, and had been briefly imprisoned for her communist activities. Litzi was currently head of the International Organisation for Aid to Revolutionaries (IOAR) in her district. Kim soon fell for her. They began a passionate love affair almost immediately, fuelled by the intensity of their political work.

Kim joined Litzi's division of the IOAR, which officially made him a part of the communist underground. The IOAR, which was subordinate to the Comintern, was operating illegally in Austria. However, the Austrian Committee for the Relief from German Fascism was perfectly legal, so it was used as a front group for the IOAR.

Kim was appointed treasurer, though most of his work fell into the category of fundraising. In his halting German, he called clients on the telephone to solicit donations to help the refugees. He also wrote pamphlets, which were translated into German by other members, then printed on a small printing press owned by the IOAR. He also helped to distribute gloves, socks, or cash to German refugees.

With his British passport, Kim was able to travel freely around Europe in ways that Austrians could not. He was soon employed as a courier, carrying mysterious brown packets to partner organisations in Budapest and Prague. His signal was ridiculously obvious – he carried a small spray of mimosa flowers, so that his contact could easily identify him. Worse still, his contacts were nearly always men. Philby would spend hours on a train, knock on a door, then hand the wilted little bouquet to a sceptical Eastern European man, who would then invite him inside to deliver the package.

In February 1934, Kim and Litzi were sitting at home when the power abruptly went out. Kim soon learned, through a journalist friend, that the workers in the power plant were on strike. The workers were protesting a search of the Hotel Schiff in Linz, Austria by the fascist paramilitary group, the Heimwehr. The hotel was a property owned by the Social Democratic Party (SDP). Members of the illegal Schutzbund, the paramilitary wing of the SDP, resisted the Heimwehr, triggering a violent skirmish which spread to other cities, culminating in the Austrian Civil War. Dollfuss' government attacked the offices of trade unions, newspapers, and welfare offices. Armed conflict between the groups ensued for several days.

Kim and Litzi prepared to take up arms in Vienna. They met with a communist leader at a café, where they were asked to man a machine gun that was already set up in the city. They agreed enthusiastically, but the machine gun never materialised.

The battles, which had begun with the 12 February search for arms at the Hotel Schiff, finally died down on 16 February. Several hundred people were killed and more than one thousand were injured. Chancellor Dollfuss declared a state of emergency and imposed martial law, allowing his government to arrest 1500 people and to execute nine Schutzbund leaders. The Social Democratic Party was banned, as were the trade unions. A new constitution created a one-party fascist state, modelled on that of Mussolini's Italy.

Kim and Litzi sprang into action, helping to smuggle communists out of the country to Czechoslovakia.

In the face of the failed uprising, Kim worried for Litzi's safety. She was both a communist and a Jew, and had already spent time in jail for her political activities. He married her on 24 February at Vienna Town Hall. Although it was true that he married Litzi in order to move her out of the country, it also appears that they were truly in love. It is not clear why they waited until May to move to London, given the deteriorating situation in Austria.

Upon their arrival in England, the newlyweds stayed with Kim's mother, Dora, in West Hampstead. In a letter to St John, Dora expressed her displeasure with the union, as well as with Kim's fascination with communism. She didn't care much for Litzi's assertive personality and worried that Kim's politics were becoming too extreme.[9] St John, for his part, was untroubled by Kim's beliefs, seeing communism as simply an outgrowth of his own Fabian socialism, which was once considered quite radical.

Kim and Litzi soon moved into a shabby communal flat with fellow comrades. Kim stalled for a while, unable to find work, and unsure of how to help the anti-fascist cause from London. He struggled with boredom after the danger and excitement of his work in Vienna. Kim had applied for the British Foreign Service before leaving for Austria, but quickly withdrew his application. His economics tutor, Dennis Robertson, did not wish to write him a letter of reference, telling him that his politics were too leftward.[10] Kim attempted to officially join the Communist Party upon his return to London, but incredibly, was rejected for being too bourgeois.

Philby's fortunes turned one day when Litzi received a phone call from an old friend, Edith Tudor Hart. Edith, like Litzi, had been a member of the Austrian Communist Party. She had also married a Brit, Alex Tudor Hart, and fled to London to avoid persecution as a communist, and as a Jew. Unlike Litzi, Edith was not just a member of the communist underground; Edith and her husband were agents of the KGB. Edith offered to introduce Kim to a man who would change the course of his life forever.

The mysterious figure waiting for Kim in Regent's Park was Arnold Deutsch, the celebrated illegal agent who was already Edith's handler. Philby was told to call him by a pseudonym, OTTO, and did not learn his real identity until many years later.

Sitting on the bench, Philby and Deutsch held a long conversation in German. Philby told him about his background, his education, his political views, and his work in Vienna. Near the end of their conversation, Deutsch made a dramatic pitch. He commended Kim for his courage in Austria, and for his commitment to communism. He then shifted gears, arguing that his bourgeois status was an advantage. Rather than waste time distributing pamphlets on the street, Kim could make a real difference. With his education and background, Philby would be able to penetrate the corridors of power and fight fascism from the inside.[11] Deutsch was careful not to say explicitly that Philby would now be working directly for the Soviet Intelligence Service.

Philby jumped at the chance to do something important. He was perhaps just as excited to engage in work that was clandestine and dangerous.

Later in life, Philby spoke of Deutsch in glowing terms. He was struck by the way Deutsch gave his undivided attention to whomever he spoke with and his transparent love of people. He was enthralled with Deutsch's knowledge of, and passion for, the tenets of Marxism, as well as the writings of Vladimir Lenin. Philby admired his authenticity and true belief in revolutionary ideas.[12]

Deutsch was well educated in psychology and he had a preternatural ability to read people, to know what they needed. In addition to meaningful work, and perhaps a little danger, Philby needed affection and acceptance from a male mentor. His father, St John, was absent for years at a time during Kim's childhood. He sometimes showed great pride in his only son, but his approval was often dependent upon Kim's achievements, and on his willingness to hew to the course laid out for him. Deutsch deftly stepped into the role of father figure. In case of any confusion, he gave Kim a German code name that properly set the tone for their relationship: SÖNCHEN, which translated loosely into English as 'Sonny'. Of course, in dispatches to Moscow Centre, he was referred to in the Russian form, SONYEK.

While Kim was convinced that he was recruited because of his bravery in Austria, KGB files indicate otherwise. He was pegged as a valuable asset due to his father's position in the Near East and his own intention to enter the British Foreign Service (they were unaware of the withdrawal of his application).

Deutsch instructed Philby to break off all contact with his former communist associates, so that he could appear to outgrow his youthful dalliance with the far left. Kim did so without fanfare, quietly letting old friendships wither on the vine.

One of Philby's first assignments was to write up a concise biography of everyone he knew, including (especially) his father's contacts. A naturally gifted writer, Philby made short work of the task. Over the course of his career, he continued to create and maintain thick files on nearly everyone he met.

His next assignment was to visit his alma mater, Cambridge University, to enlist more high achievers with a radical bent like himself. He returned to Arnold Deutsch in late September 1934 with a list of seven men, complete with short biographies, analyses of strong and weak attributes, and Kim's estimation of their value to the cause.

At the top of his list was Donald Maclean.

Chapter Three

The Diplomat

Donald Maclean, Operating in Plain Sight

Donald Duart Maclean was accustomed to high expectations. His middle name was that of Duart Castle, the ancient thirteenth-century keep of the Clan Maclean, located on the Scottish island of Mull. Donald's father was only one generation removed from the Maclean lands on the west coast of Scotland, with Donald's grandfather hailing from the island of Tiree. The name Duart honoured a proud family history stretching back centuries.

And his first name, Donald? Well, it was the name of his father, Sir Donald Maclean, whose legacy was nearer, and more daunting.

Young Donald's father, Sir Donald Maclean, had risen above his humble roots to become a towering figure in British politics. The son of a Scottish shoemaker in Wales, Sir Donald trained to become a solicitor at the age of 19, and opened a law practice in Cardiff soon afterward. Sir Donald spent his adult life in public service and philanthropy. He served as vice president of the Cardiff Free Church Council, and was deeply involved with the National Society for the Prevention of Cruelty to Children. He was first elected as a Liberal member of parliament in 1906, lost his seat in 1910, but ran in a different constituency, which returned him to parliament. He was appointed a privy counsellor in 1916 and was knighted in 1917.

Sir Donald was a deeply religious man, in the low-church 'Chapel' tradition of the Welsh Presbyterian Church. He was strongly averse to alcohol and tobacco and raised his children with inflexible standards of behaviour. His faith was not limited, however, to superficial quirks. It informed his every decision. He was not a radical, but a nonconforming liberal who championed progressive causes such as women's suffrage, old age pensions, and free trade. By all accounts, Sir Donald was a man of integrity and unimpeachable character.

On 2 October 1907, Sir Donald married Gwendolyn Margaret Devitt, a beautiful woman who was sixteen years his junior. Though not as religious as her husband, Lady Maclean was pleased to strictly enforce his rules for the children. Her outspoken and dominant personality earned her the nickname 'Queen Bee'.

In 1908, Margaret gave birth to Ian, followed two years later by Andrew. Young Donald was born on 25 May 1913. A younger sister, Nancy, was born in 1918, and the youngest brother, Alan, was born in 1924. Like many middle children, Donald found it easy to fly beneath his parents' radar, leaving youthful rebellion to his older brothers, and clinging neediness to his younger siblings. Though close with his mother for his entire life, Donald felt an impenetrable distance from his father, who had children later in life and was often preoccupied with his service in government, his law practice, and his charity work.

The Maclean household was one of temperance, daily prayer, and Sunday service at the Presbyterian church, where Sir Donald was an elder and occasional lay preacher. Sir Donald worked diligently in parliament, in a sincere endeavour to help the working class and the less fortunate. He had an unambiguous view of the world, seeing right and wrong in stark moral terms. At home, Sir Donald was generally intolerant of differing viewpoints. His middle son, young Donald, would acquire the same unbending moral compass, though his needle would point in a different direction.[1]

Young Donald went away to school at Gresham's, a boarding school in Holt, Norfolk. Handpicked by his father, Gresham's was unlike many of the better-known public schools near London. It was a smaller than average school, with a lesser emphasis on sports. Gresham's boasted of a robust science curriculum, and claimed to encourage free thought in their pupils. Its remote location served as a buffer against the influence of the elite schools closer to the city.

Gresham's was run by Headmaster J. R. Eccles, who imposed a strict moral code on his students. Smoking, swearing, dishonesty, dirty talk, and other impurities were strictly forbidden. As a progressive Methodist who opposed corporal punishment, Eccles meted out more humane consequences, like writing essays, or running a few miles. To enforce his policies, he relied on a method called the Honour System, which encouraged students to police and report on one another. By delegating supervision to the students, Eccles felt that he was cultivating an environment of trust. The students, by contrast, felt that he had created a culture of paranoia.[2] Young Donald, who was used to keeping his true thoughts and impulses to himself at home, simply continued this practice at school. Many of his hallmark personality traits, such as his alcoholism, leftist politics, and occasional homosexual dalliances, did not publicly surface until he went away to university.

Still, there were a few outward signs of his blossoming radicalism. During the General Strike of 1926, which Sir Donald opposed, the two oldest Maclean sons took temporary strike breaking jobs. Young Donald did not.

While at Gresham's, Donald became close friends with a fellow classmate, James Klugmann. The son of an upper middle class Jewish family, Klugmann would later go on to Cambridge, like Donald, and would join the Communist Party while there. It would be a stretch to call their group of friends at Gresham's a communist cell, but Klugmann claimed to have become a communist while there, and Donald later credited Klugmann with his own conversion to communism.

Donald did well in both sports and academics at Gresham's. He played cricket, rugby, and hockey. Though he never became Head Boy like his brother Ian, he did become House Prefect, and rose to the rank of Lance-Corporal in the Officer Training Corps. He showed an aptitude for foreign languages, and was sent abroad by his father to France and Germany during the summers to improve his skills. Upon graduation, Donald was offered a scholarship in modern languages to Trinity Hall, Cambridge.

Unlike the neighbouring Trinity College, Trinity Hall was smaller and less prestigious. Tucked quietly between Trinity College and King's College, Trinity Hall had only around 100 undergraduates. It was an intimate atmosphere, and Donald thrived there. At roughly 6 feet, 4 inches tall, with light hair and classic good looks, Donald stood out in this smaller crowd.

His old Gresham's schoolmate, James Klugmann, attended Trinity College. Together they joined the Cambridge University Socialist Society (CUSS), and both were soon elected to its governing committee. Two years behind Kim Philby in school, Donald had arrived at the pivotal moment of Cambridge's sharp turn leftward. Still mindful of his father's influence, Donald was careful to hide his political activities from his father. In one close call, Donald was arrested while participating in the 1932 Hunger March, which had escalated into a clash with the police. He was not charged with a crime, but his mother had to pick him up from jail. Mercifully, Sir Donald was away from home on parliamentary business.

Young Donald was so committed to his secret life that he admitted, in an interview with a student magazine, to having not one, but three personalities.[3] He even gave names to his alter egos: Cecil, the poet and artist; Jack, the easy-going rugby player who just wanted to have a good time; and Fred, the intellectual workaholic with ambitious plans for his future. Of course, all of these personae served as window dressing for the real Donald, who remained a mystery to nearly everyone.

In spite of his membership in several student political associations, playing rugby, cricket, and tennis, and writing for student publications, Donald had few close friends. Those who knew him best described him as a lonely figure who never dated women, and kept male acquaintances at arm's length. His own mother, though she adored Donald, admitted that he had never liked social gatherings.[4]

Women seemed as much a mystery to Donald as he was to them. Although he was tall and attractive, his features were somewhat feminine. Coupled with his higher-pitched voice, this made him seem more 'pretty' than handsome. His shyness may have been mistaken for aloof snobbery, which certainly didn't help.

Donald's membership in the CUSS led to the fateful friendships that would change his life forever. He met Kim Philby, who would later introduce him to Arnold Deutsch. He also met Guy Burgess, a charming and funny binge drinker who was openly gay and quite promiscuous. The two men were nearly total opposites, excepting their radical politics and increasingly problematic drinking. Never hesitating to kiss and tell, Burgess claimed to have seduced the reserved and inhibited Donald Maclean.[5]

Meanwhile, another life changing event took place back home.

After the Labour Government crisis of 1931, Sir Donald Maclean was appointed to Ramsey MacDonald's coalition National Government as President of the Board of Education. He had reached the pinnacle of his political career with a seat in the cabinet. Unfortunately, he would not have much time to enjoy the moment. On 15 June 1932, Sir Donald Maclean suffered a massive heart attack and passed away.

After a quarter of a century in government service, Sir Donald had touched the lives of many people. Members of the House of Commons issued kind statements about him, and glowing obituaries appeared in the newspapers. Lady Maclean received a telegram from the King expressing his condolences.[6]

Young Donald sincerely grieved the passing of his father, a man whom he simultaneously loved, resented, admired, and feared. While at odds with his father's politics, he shared many of his character traits – a strong work ethic, an unbending sense of morality, and a stubborn certainty in the righteousness of his own cause. However, with the sudden absence of Sir Donald's watchful eye, young Donald was freed from his constant secrecy. He became more outspoken, more politically involved, and more comfortable with himself. He began wearing shabby clothes, presumably to show solidarity with the working class. Upon Hitler's rise to power in 1933, Donald officially joined the Cambridge Communist Party. Having already rejected the religion of his father, young Donald simply replaced it with Marxism, a dogma that he could truly believe in. His interior conflict, for the moment, was resolved.

With his newfound freedom, Donald began to display not only his radical politics, but also a surprising amount of anger. On Armistice Day, the CUSS led an anti-war march toward the town's war memorial, in order to lay upon it a wreath carrying the message, 'To the victims of the Great War, from those who are determined to prevent similar crimes of imperialism'. The protest was intercepted by throngs of rugby players and oarsmen from the university, incensed by their disrespect for the fallen soldiers. Fisticuffs ensued, requiring the police to break up the brawl. Maclean wrote two blistering diatribes about the incident; one in the form of a poem, and one as an editorial, both of which were published, anonymously, in the *Silver Crescent*, a student magazine.[7] His editorials and book reviews in various student publications became increasingly unhinged, as if a lifetime of bottled up rage was finally uncorked.

As graduation approached, Maclean began to plan for his future. He was torn between two options. He considered applying for a Cambridge fellowship, so he could earn his PhD writing a thesis on Jean Calvin's role in the rise of the bourgeoisie. He also considered moving to the Soviet Union to teach English. He talked it over with his mother, who was supportive but quietly disappointed. Lady Maclean had hoped that Donald would enter the Diplomatic Service, as his late father had wanted.

After graduating with a Bachelor of Arts with honours, and a first class degree in French and German, Maclean joined two of his Cambridge friends on holiday to the northern coast of France. While there, he engaged in a fling, likely his first, with a local married woman whose husband was away with the Garde Mobile (the French equivalent of the Army Reserve). The adventure was not to last. Word soon got back to her husband, who immediately headed home. Maclean and his friends cut their visit short, beating a hasty retreat back to England. Though it was a minor episode in Maclean's life, it is a revealing early indicator of his surprising penchant for thrill seeking.

In August 1934, Kim Philby surprised Donald with a dinner invitation to his modest flat. Maclean knew Philby, though not very well, from their common membership in the CUSS. Philby was impressed by Maclean's commitment to communism, and even more so by his likelihood of passing the Foreign Office exams. Philby went straight to the point, asking if Maclean would like to do some 'special work' while at the Foreign Office. Donald's ears perked up at the suggestion. Casting aside any polite euphemisms, he asked Kim whether he would be working for the Comintern, or for the KGB.[8]

Philby, faced with Maclean's bluntness, became coy. He assured Donald that the people he worked for were very serious, that they were anti-fascist, and that they might have some ties to Moscow. Donald, who would very much have liked to work for the Comintern, hesitated. He was still loyal to his own country and the idea of spying for a foreign nation gave him pause. After some thought, Donald asked Kim if he could talk it over with his old friend James Klugmann, who was currently working for a Comintern front group in Paris.

Philby demurred, warning that if Donald shared their conversation with anyone else, the offer was off the table, and it would be as if their talk had never taken place. Maclean, eager to be involved in important, covert work in the service of communism, gladly agreed to take a meeting with the mysterious OTTO.

In December 1934, Donald Maclean walked into a London café carrying a book with a bright yellow cover. This signal was recognised by none other than Arnold Deutsch. Deutsch did not need to convince Maclean, he had already made his decision. Philby had shamelessly plagiarised nearly all of Deutsch's talking points when he had first approached Donald in August. Maclean then spent the next few months rationalising a way to betray his own country. In the end, he concluded that bringing the communist revolution home to the United Kingdom would be beneficial to the British people. In his own mind, he would not be hurting his country, he would be helping it.

Deutsch bestowed on him the code name WAISE, the German word for ORPHAN (in Russian, the word is SIROTA).[9] The name spoke not only to the recent death of Donald's father, but to Donald's overall feelings of solitude and alienation, of feeling like an outsider in his own family, as well as his own class.

It is not clear at which point Maclean abandoned his plans to earn his PhD or move to Russia, and to apply for the Foreign Office instead. It would appear that Kim Philby or Arnold Deutsch had pointed him in that direction, but the timeline does not add up. Lady Maclean reportedly breathed a sigh of relief when Donald returned from his French holiday in July 1934 and told her of his decision to apply for the Foreign Office. Around the same time, he wrote a letter to Trinity Hall fellow, Owen Wansbrough-Jones, advising him that he would not be continuing his education at Cambridge.[10] Furthermore, according to Philby himself, Maclean had already submitted his application to the Foreign Office when he first met with him in August 1934.[11]

Soon, Donald began to pull away from the Cambridge communist scene and left the Communist Party. To the casual observer, he simply appeared to be growing out of a youthful phase. He settled in for months of rigorous study at Scoones, a school which specialised in preparation for the Foreign Service exams. In addition to economics and history, Donald also brushed up on his French and German.

Maclean's intellect and capacity for hard study prepared him for the final exams, but when it came to the interview, his family name and connections carried the day. One member of the interview board was family friend Lady Violet Bonham Carter, and the board was chaired by Sir Horace Rumbold, the father of Donald's friend, Anthony. Other members included minister of parliament, Edgar Granville, and future prime minister, Clement Atlee. Even those board members who were not personally connected to Maclean surely knew of his famous late father, Sir Donald.

Only one tense moment interrupted the clubby reunion that the interview became. One board member brought up Donald's strong and openly communist opinions that he held while at Cambridge, and asked, point blank, if he still held such views. Maclean, stunned for just a moment, swiftly recovered. With confidence, and a plausible display of frankness, he volleyed back his answer.

'Yes, I did have such views – and I haven't entirely shaken them off.'[12]

The board members all smiled and nodded, pleased with his apparent honesty. In this moment, Maclean was technically telling the truth, if perhaps not the full truth. It was one of many half-truths and rationalisations that would allow him to live in two separate realities, without sacrificing his principles. He could serve his own country, fulfil the hopes laid out by his father, and make his family proud, while also serving the Soviet Union and furthering the mission of worldwide communist revolution. Maclean saw no conflict and his conscience was at peace.

Donald Maclean's brief period of outward radicalism was over, and his double life was resumed.

Chapter Four

The Anti-Spy
The Colourful Guy Burgess

'Do you think that I believe even for one jot that you have stopped being a Communist? And do you think that you can convince me of that? Me? You're simply up to something! I know you, you old liar and sneak. You expect me to believe that you would betray yourself?'[1]

In this manner, Guy Burgess pestered Donald Maclean mercilessly when he found out that he had left the Cambridge Communist Party, according to an account given later by Kim Philby. Guy knew when he was being lied to, and would stop at nothing to get to the truth. He wanted to know all of the gossip and all of the secrets. Guy Burgess wanted to get to the centre of everything. If something shifty was going on, he wanted to be a part of it.

In many ways, Burgess had spent much of his life in this way, on the outside, trying to get in. In spite of his respectable background and numerous achievements, he was not satisfied until he was accepted by everyone.

Guy Francis de Moncy Burgess came from a family of military officers. His father, Malcolm Kingsford de Moncy Burgess, was born in Aden in 1881 while Malcolm's father, Colonel Henry Miles Burgess, was stationed there with the Royal Artillery. Young Malcolm entered the officer training school, Britannia Royal Naval College, also known as Dartmouth, in 1894 at the age of 14.

In 1898, Malcolm entered the British Royal Navy as a midshipman. His early years were marred by a collision between his own ship, the HMS *Thrasher*, and another, the HMS *Panther*. A 1902 court of inquiry admonished him, but did not issue harsh discipline in light of his inexperience. Though his reputation never fully recovered, Malcolm was promoted to Lieutenant in 1903, and eventually rose to Commander in 1916. His career was marked largely by mediocrity; he spent the First World War at port, servicing submarines. However, simply being a naval officer granted him a measure of esteem in the community.

While an officer in the world's largest Navy commanded a certain amount of prestige, the family money most likely came from Guy's mother, Evelyn Mary Gillman. Born in 1884 in Portsea Island, Evelyn began her life in a family of privilege and good standing. Her father, William Gillman, was a partner in a small bank based in Portsmouth. The bank, Grant, Gillman, and Long, was sold to Lloyd's in 1903, leaving him a small fortune. Now free to pursue other interests, William served as director of both the Portsmouth Gas and Water Companies, and volunteered as a magistrate. Evelyn's mother, Maud Hooper, had her own money, having come from a wealthy Canadian family.

Malcomb met Evelyn while he was stationed at Portsmouth and married her there in 1907. Their first born son, Guy Francis de Moncy Burgess, was born on 16 April 1911, in the nearby naval town of Devonport. His younger brother, Nigel, came along in 1913. Guy's father was mostly away at sea during his early childhood, leaving his mother to spoil him. Their household was a comfortable one, with housemaids and a cook. The boys' early education was most likely provided at home by a governess. At the age of 9, Guy was sent away to Lockers Park, a boarding school in Hertfordshire.

Lockers Park was one of the earliest and most prestigious preparatory schools in England. Founded in 1874, Lockers Park soon became known as a feeder for some of the best public schools, like Rugby, Harrow, Winchester, and Eton. Notable Lockers alumni include two members of the royal family, Prince Maurice Battenberg and Louis Mountbatten (the last Viceroy of India), as well as Sir Keith Joseph (MP), Sir Robert Laycock (Governor of Malta), numerous government officials, and a long list of cricket captains.

Despite some initial difficulty adjusting to the all-male environment, Guy was a responsible student. He received high marks, finishing second in his class when he left in 1923. He also played for the First XI football team, and took piano lessons. He showed talent as an artist and he developed a love of automobiles that lasted his entire life.

Guy was academically advanced as a child and had finished the top form at Lockers Park a full year early, at the age of 12. His parents had planned for Guy to attend Dartmouth, like his father, but he could not be admitted until he was 13½ years old. For the intervening school year, he was sent to Eton College.

Eton was, and still is, the largest and most famous of the British public schools, housing over 1000 students. Founded by King Henry VI in 1440, its distinctive red-brick buildings sprawl outward from College Chapel, an imposing Gothic-style sanctuary whose spires can be seen from miles away. Eton, just a stone's throw across the Thames from Windsor Castle, has educated some of Great Britain's most successful and famous men, including George Orwell, John Maynard Keynes, Ian Fleming, several members of the royal family, and no fewer than nineteen prime ministers.

Guy lived in a house of forty boys, which included a few former classmates from Lockers Park. He had his own private room. As a first year student, he was required to cook and clean for the older boys. His school day began at 7:30 am, and classes continued until 5:00 pm. A heavy emphasis was placed on sports; three afternoons per week were reserved for practise and games.

Guy, younger than most of his classmates, flourished in his new environment. He breezed through much of the curriculum, earning good marks and recognition for his artwork. He approached his days with good humour and conscientiousness, determined to get along in his new school.

At the end of Guy's first term, tragedy unexpectedly struck the Burgess family. On 15 September 1924, Guy's father, Commander Malcolm Burgess, suffered a massive heart attack and died at the age of 43. The reported circumstances of his death are somewhat controversial, as the only account came from Guy Burgess himself, who often fabricated stories for his own amusement.

As an adult, Burgess told others that his father had gone into cardiac arrest whilst engaging in marital relations with his wife. Guy, 13 years old, was allegedly awakened in the night by his mother's cries for help. Upon his discovery of her predicament, Guy was forced to drag his father's body off of his mother. When recounting the incident, he sometimes pointed to the traumatic episode as the cause of his homosexuality. Neither his younger brother, Nigel, nor the house servants have corroborated Guy's version of events.[2]

In any case, Malcolm's untimely death shocked and devastated his wife and his young sons, who lost their father at such a crucial age in their formation. Compounding matters further, they returned to school only one week later.

Three months later, the moment he reached the minimum age of 13½, Guy was pulled from Eton and enrolled at Dartmouth, his late father's alma mater. In the early days, Dartmouth students had been housed in two ships, the HMS *Britannia* and the HMS *Hindostan*, which were moored in the River Dart in Devon. By the time Guy arrived, Dartmouth had moved their students out of the old moored wooden hulks, and placed them into new buildings overlooking the Dart River. Though the classes no longer were held on board a ship, the school was run as if they were. The students, called cadets, wore Navy uniforms and were expected to salute their officers. The cadets' dormitories were referred to as 'gun rooms', and the officers slept in 'cabins'. Each class was divided into two sections, 'port' and 'starboard'.

Discipline was a top priority at Dartmouth, and like most other boarding schools of the era, corporal punishment was employed, albeit with above average enthusiasm. Caning, whether public, private, over the trousers, or bare-bottomed, was imposed with some regularity by both the staff and the older students.

At Dartmouth, Guy did well in academics, sports, and drill, and was considered good officer material.[3] He won prizes for his essays on geography, history, and naval operations. Unfortunately, Guy soon had to withdraw from Dartmouth due to poor eyesight, which would have hindered his future career in the Navy. In the decades hence, historians have questioned that diagnosis. His later Civil Service medical exam did not report any visual problems, and, most obviously, no photographs of Burgess exist in which he is wearing glasses.[4] At the time, some rumours circulated that he was accused of theft, and speculations have persisted that 'poor eyesight' was some kind of polite euphemism referring to his homosexuality.[5] It is also possible that Burgess simply hated Dartmouth, and wanted out. Nonetheless, he received an honourable discharge and praiseworthy recommendations and returned to Eton in autumn 1927.

Having realised that he wasn't really cut out for the Navy anyway, Guy must have been relieved to join his younger brother, Nigel, and some of his old friends at Eton. He gladly adapted to an environment with a different uniform (black suit, silk top hat, and bow tie), different titles (Mr, Lord, and Sir instead of Lieutenant, Commander, or Captain), and an entirely different social protocol. The customs and rituals were just as rigid, but were designed to induct pupils into an exclusive segment of society.

Guy's second tour at Eton was even more impressive than his first. Surprisingly athletic, he ran, rowed, swam, and won his house colours in football. He joined the Officer Training Corps, and rose to the rank of Lance Corporal. His love of history blossomed, documented in his extraordinary essays. He nurtured his talent for drawing, particularly cartoons and caricatures, which won him several awards.

According to one of his mentors, history instructor Sir Robert Birley, Guy began his political turn leftward at Eton.[6] He was influenced by Birley's passion for social justice and began reading more radical books. Like many of his leftist contemporaries, Burgess claimed that his interest in politics began in earnest with the election of the Labour Government in 1929.

Guy's desire for belonging drove him to join nearly every club available to him. Only one membership eluded him: Eton Society, known casually as 'Pop'. An elite cadre of two dozen of Eton's most popular boys, Pop members acted as prefects for the entire school. Pop conferred certain privileges on its members. They were permitted to wear a waistcoat in the colour of their choosing and to carry an umbrella. More importantly, they could order around and cane fellow pupils who were not members of Pop.

Burgess yearned to gain entry into Pop, this exclusive little self-elected clique, which would have added the phrase 'with distinction' to his career at Eton. He was recommended several times by his friends in 1929, only to be repeatedly rejected.

Descriptions of Burgess at Eton varied greatly from person to person, with some classmates remembering a strange loner, others recounting a kind young man with a disarming sense of humour.[7] Due to his ability to compartmentalise his associations (and indeed, his own personality), Guy had a rather polarising effect on those around him. People either loved him or hated him. In the same vein, some of Guy's fellow pupils knew of his homosexuality, while others had no idea, though there is no record of him actively hiding it.

Burgess was popular enough, however, to have forged many friendships that would last his whole life. In today's common parlance, Guy's wide circle of acquaintances would be called a network. Eton's alumni, called Old Etonians, many of whom rose to the upper echelons of society, formed the foundations of Guy's extensive and diverse connections.

Though personally opposed to the elitist British public school system, Burgess maintained a special affection for Eton, and for his classmates. He often spoke with fondness for his time there, and could frequently be seen wearing his Old Etonian school tie. By January 1930, Burgess was ranked second in the sixth form and was awarded the Gladstone Memorial Scholarship in History to Trinity College, Cambridge.

Cambridge, an imposing symbol of the insularity and exclusionary privilege of the British upper class, was beginning to catch the fever of communism. Its broad collection of clubs, societies, high flyers, and intellectuals was developing into a groundswell of populism and sexual freedom. In this era of contradictions, Guy Burgess finally found an outlet for both sides of his personality. He was the outsider who was now on the inside. Naturally, he flourished.

Upon his arrival at Trinity College, which was smaller and even more exclusive than Eton, Burgess set about gaining entry to as many clubs and societies as he could. He joined the University Pitt Club, an undergraduate social club located at 7a Jesus Lane, where Guy drank a bottle of white wine every day with lunch. Founded in 1835, notable Pitt Club alumni include Kings Edward VII, George V, and later, Charles III, economist John Maynard Keynes, novelist E. F. Benson, and, of course, fellow Cambridge spy Anthony Blunt. He joined the Cambridge Amateur Dramatic Club (ADC), which was known as a starting point for many of the United Kingdom's most famous actors and directors. Burgess designed the set for *Captain Brassbound's Conversion,* a production starring future film legend Michael Redgrave in the title role. Guy's membership in the ADC facilitated a new circle of friends and associates completely separate from the crowd of old boys he knew in academia. Burgess loved to name-drop the growing list of famous actors and directors he met through the ADC, but the drama club provided something else for him, as well. Through his friendship with director George 'Dadie' Rylands, Guy entered a close-knit community of gay men who accepted him as he was.

Possibly through Michael Redgrave, who was a mutual friend, Burgess met Anthony Blunt in 1931. Though put off at first by Guy's incessant gossip and indiscretion, Blunt was soon impressed by his intelligence and wide range of interests. The admiration appears to be mutual. A portrait of a young man sketched by Burgess, published in a magazine showcasing Etonian talent, bears a strong resemblance to Blunt. They were probably lovers for a while, but they were close friends for life.

It was Anthony Blunt who brought Burgess into the Apostles, originally founded in 1820 as a secret university society, similar to Yale's Skull and Bones. The official name was simply the Society, though it was informally called the Apostles, presumably because there were twelve founding members. It was an intellectual discussion club that had included such luminaries as Bertrand Russell, G. H. Hardy, and E. M. Forster. In the early 1900s, when the Society became dominated by future psychoanalyst Lytton Strachey and economist John Maynard Keynes, it developed a reputation as a fashionable homosexual coterie. This dubious distinction hung on through the 1930s, somewhat unfairly. It was, however, an increasingly radical body, and the sexual revolution was simply another facet of the rising tide of leftism then sweeping Cambridge writ large.

In 1933, Burgess prepared for part two of the Tripos, the final exams for his degree. In 1932, he had scored a first in part one, and was expected to repeat his success in the second part a year later. He was instead awarded an aegrotat, an unclassified degree usually given to students unable to complete the exam due to illness. The aegrotat implies that the student would have passed the exam, had they been able to take it. His unknown illness on exam day has since led to some speculation. Some believe that he had simply collapsed after cramming all night, others have suggested that said collapse was caused by the use of amphetamines or alcohol. Some of his friends suspected that he had staged a nervous breakdown because he had not studied at all.[8]

In spite of the debacle surrounding his final exam, Burgess earned his bachelor's degree and returned to Trinity as a graduate student. He further immersed himself in the political scene that had captivated him since his first year as an undergrad.

At the end of his first term, Burgess had been elected to the Trinity Historical Society, which was made up of only twenty-five of the brightest history students. Another member, one year ahead of Guy, was Kim Philby. Guy's already leftward politics were pulled farther along by a fellow student named Jim Lees, whom he met through the Historical Society. Unlike most of his classmates in the privileged enclave of Cambridge, Lees came to Trinity from the working class city of Nottingham, by way of a trade union scholarship. He had left school at the age of 14 to become a coal miner, and he educated Burgess and Philby on the harsh realities of life for so many Britons who suffered through the brutal economic conditions of the post-war years. Along with Professor Maurice Dobb and classmate David Haden Guest, Burgess later credited Lees as a primary influence on his evolution from socialism to communism.[9]

Burgess met David Haden Guest through his membership in the Cambridge University Socialist Society (CUSS). Guest, who had taken over the small Marxist study group founded by Maurice Dobb, had formed a communist wing within the CUSS. At the urging of Guest, Burgess began reading Marx and Lenin, though it was Dobb who recruited him to the Communist Party, which Guy officially joined in 1933.

Guy's membership in CUSS led to his friendships with Kim Philby, James Klugmann, and Donald Maclean. He also made the acquaintance of another young radical, John Cornford. Together with Klugmann and Guest, Cornford helped to transform the Cambridge Communist Party from a theoretical study group into a force for action. Cornford led the notorious Armistice Day march of 1933, which was memorialised in Donald Maclean's anonymous poem. Burgess played a more active role in the protest than Maclean. He rode with his friend, Julian Bell, in Bell's car, the outside of which they had tied on mattresses, as armour. As they were pelted with tomatoes, Julian used his vehicle as a battering ram to get through the blockade of counter-protestors several times before they were ordered by police to leave.

In summer 1934, Guy began one of his closest friendships with a young Oxford fellow, Goronwy Rees. They were both guests at a dinner party hosted by future American Supreme Court Justice, Felix Frankfurter, a visiting professor at Oxford. The dinner was also attended by the philosopher and future diplomat, Isaiah Berlin, the future American FBI agent and politician, Fred Ayer, and the Oxford don and literary critic, Maurice Bowra. Burgess and Rees immediately took a liking to one another, and began discussing the finer points of Marxism. After the party ended, they chatted late into the night over a bottle of Jameson scotch whiskey. As he did with nearly all young men, Burgess propositioned Rees. Rees politely demurred, being a confirmed heterosexual. No offense was taken and they soon became great friends.

Many students from Cambridge, disenchanted with their own country, visited the Soviet Union during the 1930s. They were given tightly managed tours of collectivised farms, efficient factories, and state of the art elementary schools. Tour guides sang the praises of the Five Year Plan, and ordinary citizens were carefully concealed from the passing tour groups. Tourists were filed into the newest factories and shown the most impressive architecture, but never left free to wander the slums or take a train to the country, lest they see any sign of poverty, disease, or oppression.

Goronwy Rees organised a long holiday trip for his new friend, Guy, to visit the Soviet Union. Though Rees was unable to come along, Guy was accompanied by another Oxford communist, Derek Blaikie. Burgess and Blaikie sailed to Leningrad before boarding a train into Moscow. They were led on a heavily supervised tour by representatives of the Comintern, and were introduced to Party officials and English expats living in Russia. Burgess may have met the Russian revolutionary Nikolai Bukharin, the former Secretary of the Comintern and editor of *Pravda* magazine.[10] Generally, Burgess was unimpressed with Moscow. He had expected a more cosmopolitan city, but found it to still be somewhat primitive. He complained that it was, '…just a Balkan town, you know. Pigs in the trams'.[11]

Upon his return, Burgess reported what he saw to his fellow Cambridge communists. Though he found the housing deplorable, he lauded the lack of unemployment. He felt that the Soviets would not go to war any time soon, as they were more focused on domestic issues. Guy claimed to have been reprimanded by a member of the militia for walking on the grass in the Park of Rest and Culture. Derek Blaikie later reported that Guy had actually been rebuked not for stepping onto the grass, but for his public drunkenness.[12]

Afterward, Burgess spent a tense holiday at home with his family. His relationship with his mother, which had always been warm, began to show signs of strain. He wasn't getting on with his stepfather, retired Navy Colonel John Bassett, whom his widowed mother had married while Guy was still at Eton. Colonel Bassett had never liked his oldest stepson, and Guy, now a grown man, spent a ridiculous amount of energy retaliating through passive-aggressive provocations. His mother Evelyn, who rather enjoyed having two men squabble over her attention, did nothing to diffuse the antagonism between them. Guy's relationship with his brother Nigel, who was also attending Trinity College, was cordial but chilly. The boys had little in common and were simply not very close.

Burgess returned to Cambridge for his fourth year, ostensibly to continue work on his doctoral thesis, *Bourgeois Revolution in the Seventeenth Century*. Unfortunately, he had discovered the previous March, it had already been done. A new book by Basil Willey, *The Seventeenth Century Background*, published in March 1934, provided an exhaustive study of the very topic Burgess had spent months researching. Guy wrote an admiring review of Willey's book for *The Spectator*, as an expert historian. The review itself earned praise for Guy, placing him on the map in journalistic and publishing circles. For Burgess, though, Willey's comprehensive and eloquent manuscript was a crushing blow to his own academic plan. Fearing that he could not possibly best Willey's effort, Guy abandoned his original thesis. He instead settled on the Indian Mutiny of 1857, but eventually withered on that topic as well.

Burgess entered a period of aimless idle. Having lost a sense of career purpose, his research floundered as he drank and chain smoked. He worked occasionally as a teaching assistant and tutor to younger students, but mainly threw himself into political activities, like organising pickets to support striking bus workers, and encouraging the waiters at Trinity's dining hall to go on strike.

Unbeknownst to Burgess, a greater purpose was about to find *him*. His friend, Kim Philby, had submitted his name for consideration to Arnold Deutsch. Their mutual friend, Donald Maclean, had already agreed to work for the Soviets, and was preparing to enter the Foreign Office.

Deutsch equivocated for months on the pros and cons of recruiting Burgess as an agent. His drawbacks were many. For one thing, he was too conspicuous to get along in the world of clandestine work. Guy was a dreadful gossip who talked too much at the wrong time. He also drank to excess. While Donald Maclean had worn threadbare clothing as a costume to fit in with the working class, Guy looked unkempt due only to his dreadful personal hygiene. His promiscuous homosexuality could have left him open to blackmail, were he not so proud of it. Philby appeared to have his doubts, as well. On his list of recommendations, Guy Burgess fell dead last.

And yet, his name *was* on the list. Deutsch discussed the matter with his superior, the new head of the illegal Rezidentura in London, Alexander Orlov. Burgess was well connected, from the aristocracy to academia, to the world of fine arts, to the coal miners of Nottingham, all the way down to the male prostitutes of Soho. He belonged to the most fashionable social clubs, and his charm and good looks had a way of putting people at ease.

Also, as Orlov pointed out, Guy's profligate homosexuality could actually serve as an asset to the secret work of espionage.[13] The illegality of homosexual relationships in 1930s England forced gay men to keep a part of themselves a secret. They formed a tightly knit underground network of their own, protecting one another from exposure. Members of the gay community came from every walk of life, including government and the Diplomatic Service. Burgess could easily operate as a mole within this select group, either as a honey trap or just as a friend who shared a secret.

Ironically, Guy's over-the-top flamboyance, public drunkenness, and dishevelled appearance would serve as a cover for his clandestine work for Moscow Centre. Who would suspect that this walking disaster could actually be a Soviet spy?

As Deutsch and Orlov were coming around to the idea of an unconventional operator, Burgess was figuring things out on his own. He became suspicious when his friend, Donald Maclean, left the Communist Party. Burgess knew Maclean well and did not believe for a moment that he had simply stopped believing in communism. Every time they met, Burgess would harass Maclean, whether privately or in public. His attacks were unavoidable. Maclean finally broke down.

'Listen, shut up, damn you! All right, I am still who I was. But I can say no more, I don't have the right.'[14]

Burgess directly accused him of working for the Soviets, which Maclean denied, unconvincingly. Burgess, satisfied that he had cracked Maclean, insisted on being included. Philby and Maclean both knew that they had a problem on their hands. Fearing exposure by Burgess, Philby went to Deutsch. They came to the conclusion that Guy must be recruited, and soon.

Maclean made the initial offer to set up a meeting between Burgess and Deutsch sometime in early 1935. Deutsch, the amateur psychologist, created a personal profile for the Centre. His analysis was spot on, as usual. In his report he described Burgess as 'a very temperamental and emotional man and he is easily subject to mood swings. The Party for him was a saviour. It gave him, above all, an opportunity to satisfy his intellectual needs'.[15] Deutsch praised his ability to befriend nearly anyone, citing this as his primary asset. Keeping with the familial theme for his new recruits, he gave Guy the suggestive code name MÄDCHEN, which in German means, 'Little Girl'.

Like his two friends before him, Burgess was ordered to break from the Communist Party. Unlike Kim Philby, who quietly receded into the background as he let old friendships fade, Burgess announced his departure with great fanfare.

For his first assignment, Deutsch asked Burgess to make a list of all of his friends and associates. He returned with over 200 names. As they say, it's not *what* you know, it's *who* you know.

Chapter Five

The Three Musketeers
Exceeding Expectations

Arnold Deutsch was playing the long game. He made it clear to his young prodigies that his immediate requests were minimal. The new recruits were asked to obscure their communist backgrounds, learn the espionage tradecraft, and get themselves into an influential position. The collection of useful intelligence would come later.

Donald Maclean was the first to enter the corridors of power. His acceptance to the Diplomatic Service came at a pivotal moment in history, and granted the young spy ample opportunities to prove himself to his new handler. Italian Fascist Dictator, Benito Mussolini, invaded Abyssinia in October 1935, just as Maclean was entering the Foreign Office for the first time. Hitler would send troops to occupy the Rhineland in 1936, and the Spanish Civil War would break out later that same year.

Managing relationships with Switzerland, the Netherlands, Portugal, Spain, and in particular, the League of Nations, the Western Department of the Foreign Office afforded Maclean an ideal vantage from which to gather intelligence on the most important global events of the day. As history has repeatedly demonstrated, security concerns are always reactive, and almost never proactive. When Maclean arrived at the Foreign Office, no massive breach of secrecy had yet happened, and therefore, no security measures existed. Maclean happily filled his briefcase with documents nearly every day, and none of his colleagues batted an eye when he took them home to 'work' on them.

After leaving the office, Maclean would meet with Deutsch, who would bring the files to a secret location to be photographed. A few hours later, he and Maclean would meet again, and Deutsch would return the papers. Donald's natural industriousness, coupled with his enthusiasm to help the Soviet Union, drove him to collect massive amounts of documents and files, so many that Deutsch asked him to slow down, because his photographer could not keep up.[1] Deutsch asked if Maclean would please bring fewer papers on weekdays, and more on Fridays, so the photographer might have an entire weekend to work on them. Finally, another illegal agent, Theodore Maly, was enlisted to help.

Theodore Maly, like most illegals of his era, had a fascinating backstory. As a newly ordained Catholic priest, he had joined the Austro-Hungarian army as a chaplain during the Great War. He was wounded and captured by the Russians in the Carpathians, and endured horrific conditions as a prisoner of war. Having lost his faith, and never forgiving the Czarist Empire, he joined the Bolshevik revolution upon his release. By 1921, Maly had become an operative for the KGB. Now in London under the alias 'Peters', he claimed to be a businessman with a Dutch textile company. Any attempt to blend in was futile; Maly was over 6 feet tall, always dressed in black, and several of his front teeth were capped in gold.

Back at Cambridge, Guy Burgess was finishing up the lent term of 1935, where he continued to attend meetings of the Cambridge Apostles. Unlike Kim Philby, Burgess used no finesse while changing his political philosophy. His about face on communism upset many of his friends within the CUSS, who openly called him a traitor.

The following June, Deutsch encouraged Burgess to attend London University's Institute of Slavonic Studies to learn Russian. Additionally, he could meet fellow classmates, some of whom might be secret intelligence officers. Burgess did not officially enrol, but did sign up for a private lesson with an instructor named Elizabeth Hill, who shared a treasure trove of information about the program. She confirmed that the institute was attended by many MI6 officers, and that the school's director was himself retired from the Secret Intelligence Service (SIS).

Meanwhile, Burgess occasionally visited the home of Victor Rothschild, a friend and fellow Apostles member. Victor's mother, Rózsika, was so impressed with Guy's knowledge about markets and current events that she paid him for his investment advice. He had correctly predicted the nationalisation of railways in Latin America and had recommended that she sell her stocks in the railroad industry. She kept him on retainer for several months as an investment advisor.

Burgess also met MP (Minister of Parliament) Harold Nicolson, who became an important mentor to him, and with whom Guy probably had an affair. Nicolson likely introduced Guy to Colonel John Macnamara, a retired Army officer and Conservative MP. Macnamara hired Burgess as his personal assistant in late 1935. While not an anti-Semite, Macnamara was a strong supporter of Germany as a bulwark against communism. He was heavily involved in the Anglo-German Fellowship, an organisation dedicated to improving British relations with Germany. Burgess joined the Anglo-German Fellowship, and brought in Kim Philby, as well.

As Orlov had predicted, Guy's homosexuality opened the door to a high level secret network. Like Burgess, Macnamara was gay and belonged to just such an underground alliance. Macnamara brought Burgess with him on fact finding missions to Germany and France, where he came into contact with another well-placed homosexual, Edouard Pfeiffer. As private secretary for French War Minister Édouard Deladier, Pfeiffer provided Guy with a great deal of background in Franco-German relations. Burgess later entertained his friends back home with outlandish stories of orgies in the gay brothels of Paris and Cologne. Since he was prone to exaggeration and outright fabrication, it is not known whether these fantastical tales were true. It is possible that they were just a red herring to distract from Guy's espionage.[2]

As Donald Maclean's parallel careers as a diplomat and a Soviet agent soared upward on their double trajectory, his drinking problem advanced right alongside them, the third leg in the triad of his personality.

In the summer of 1936, Maclean met a kindred spirit and began an intense friendship that would bring devastating consequences in the years to come. Donald was sitting at the edge of the dance floor at a debutante ball, drinking to get through yet another performative social ritual of the kind he hated. He was spotted by Philip Toynbee, a hard drinking writer who had been the first communist president of Oxford's student union. Though Donald had publicly moved away from communism, he told Toynbee that he still believed in Marxism, but now considered it a lost cause. As the conversation progressed, it came to light that Maclean and Toynbee knew many of the same people and they talked about the women in their shared circle that they admired. After a few drinks, Donald felt comfortable enough to confess his crush on a man, Jasper Ridley. Toynbee, himself bisexual, encouraged Donald to pursue Ridley.

Maclean and Toynbee soon piled into a taxi together and headed to a local night club, still dressed in white ties and tails. After a bottle of gin, they swam together in the Serpentine, a narrow lake winding through Hyde Park. They ended up passed out at Maclean's flat. Their eventful first night together set the tone for all of their future meetings, each more volatile than the last.

Meanwhile, as Maclean was methodically pilfering the Foreign Office files between drinking binges, and Guy Burgess was carousing with Nazi sympathisers, Kim Philby waited impatiently for an important mission, or at least a well-placed posting. As he waited, he was asked to commit his first act of betrayal. Orlov was convinced that Kim's father, St John, was a secret British Intelligence agent. There is no evidence to bear this out, but Orlov never let go of his suspicion. In June 1935, while St John was on a visit home to London, Philby was instructed by Deutsch to search his flat and photograph any important papers. Nothing useful was gained in the exercise, other than proof of Kim's loyalty to Moscow and his willingness to betray his own family.

Deutsch then asked Philby to exploit someone closer to the levers of power. Surveying Kim's list of acquaintances, he settled upon one of Kim's old Westminster classmates, Tom Wylie. Now private secretary to Sir Herbert Creedy, permanent head of the War Office, Wylie was also resident clerk at the War Office. He had an apartment on site so that he could be available for any after-hours business. This kind of access to sensitive information was exactly what Deutsch was looking for.

Philby reconnected with his old school chum and joined him for his weekly game of fives (a sport similar to squash). Afterwards, they would head to the pub, or back to Wylie's apartment for drinks. Philby attempted to discuss Wylie's job, but Wylie was thoroughly uninterested in discussing his work, or politics, or even current events.

Philby and Deutsch considered their options. Recruitment was out of the question. Wylie was no communist sympathiser. He was impervious to bribery, being financially well off. Deutsch raised the possibility of blackmail, threatening exposure of Wylie's homosexuality. Kim didn't believe that Wylie would bend to any threats. His only real weakness was his heavy drinking.

On one of his visits to Wylie's apartment, Kim watched him unlock a safe, retrieve a bottle of whiskey from inside, and return it after pouring. He then locked the safe, tossing the key onto his desk.

Deutsch and Philby concocted a plan to look inside the safe and see what was else was in there. Deutsch gave Philby a pill to knock out Wylie for a little while, so that Philby could unlock the safe and have a look. Kim wrapped the pill in tissue paper and carefully concealed it in his pocket.

That evening, having won their fives match, Philby and Wylie celebrated by crawling several pubs, imbibing more than usual. Retiring to the apartment, Wylie unlocked the safe and poured two glasses of whiskey, leaving the safe wide open. After draining his tumbler, Wylie passed out drunk on the couch. The knockout pill, now completely unnecessary, remained in Kim's waistcoat pocket.[3]

Kim anxiously explored the open safe, excited to uncover his first intelligence coup. Unfortunately for Kim, the safe contained only one official document; it was a simple memo from the British Embassy in Italy, summarising a routine meeting. Crestfallen, Kim recommended to Deutsch that perhaps Guy Burgess should be introduced to Tom Wylie, so that Guy could work his own charms on him. Burgess deployed his powers of seduction, and capitalised on his position in Macnamara's office. Wylie, in turn, allowed Burgess to look at many of the papers which crossed his desk, and gladly tagged along on Macnamara's half-business, half-pleasure tours of Germany and France.[4]

Philby changed course, focusing now on his own career. Having withdrawn his application for the Foreign Service, Kim was encouraged by Deutsch to enter the British Secret Intelligence Service. The problem was, the SIS did not officially exist, and therefore had no human resources department at which to apply for a job. Employment in the SIS was by invitation only. Kim needed to be discovered, and then recruited. On the recommendation of Deutsch, Philby pursued a career in journalism. While not immediately obvious, Deutsch knew that the SIS often plucked talent from the news services, particularly foreign correspondents. Journalism requires a skill set which is remarkably similar to that of secret intelligence – cultivating contacts, tireless investigation, and, of course, discretion, make desirable experience in a prospective agent.

Kim's father, St John, helped him to get a job at *Review of Reviews*, where he wrote features from a right-wing point of view. In doing so, Philby was not just placing his foot in the door, he was slowly expunging his communist past, one article at a time.

At the invitation of Guy Burgess, Kim joined the Anglo-German Fellowship. As a newly established writer, Philby was offered a full time position to start a trade journal, funded by the German Propaganda Ministry. Philby made several trips to Berlin in pursuit of this venture, and even met with Ambassador Joachim von Ribbentrop, the future German Foreign

Minister. Although plans for the new publication eventually collapsed, Kim was able to issue occasional reports to Moscow about Anglo-German relations. The Soviets were keenly interested, because they feared an alliance between the British and the Germans.

Burgess was trying to break into the news business, too. Near the close of 1935, the British Broadcasting Company (BBC), seeking staffers for its Talks Department, wrote to the Appointments Board at Cambridge University. On a short list of only three candidates, Guy Burgess was the most highly recommended, owing to his amiability, his extensive social connections, and his interest in politics and current events.

In spite of glowing references and a heavily embellished resume (Guy counted his adolescent tenure at Dartmouth College as two years of service in the Royal Navy),[5] Burgess was not immediately selected after his first interview with the BBC. He instead took a probationary job as sub-editor at *The Times* for one month, but he was not hired permanently.

After some back and forth among the management at the BBC, Burgess was finally hired as an assistant producer in the Talks Department in October 1936. His duties included the procurement of interesting guests to be interviewed for the broadcast, which proved easy for Guy. He scheduled Kim Philby's father, St John, to talk about the history of Mecca. He invited his former co-worker from *The Times*, Roger Fulford, to discuss his forthcoming book on King George IV. He invited his good friend, Anthony Blunt, to talk about art. His close friend and mentor, MP Harold Nicolson, made frequent appearances on the program.

Guy's Oxford friend, Goronwy Rees, became Assistant Editor at *The Spectator* and moved into a London apartment just a few blocks away. Burgess continued to meet for lunches and drinks with Harold Nicolson, as well as his former employer, John Macnamara. It was during this period that Guy met a young chorus dancer, Jack Hewit. Jack became Guy's steady, though not monogamous, partner for the next fourteen years. Hewit, only 19 when he met Burgess, has condescendingly been described as Guy's 'houseboy', or his personal valet. He might better be characterised as his long-suffering housewife, or rather, house husband – cooking, cleaning, and pressing Guy's shirts, while Burgess worked, partied, and philandered.[6]

Somehow, Burgess caught the attention of David Footman, head of Section I of the SIS. Responsible for analysing political information, Footman approached Burgess to help him sniff out suspected communists working at the BBC. Of course, Guy's cooperation was strongly encouraged by Deutsch. Footman eventually introduced Guy to his own supervisor, Valentine Vivian. Burgess spent the following year doing small freelance assignments for MI6, while simultaneously passing information to his Soviet handlers. He was the first of the Cambridge spies to penetrate the SIS.

Kim Philby's fortunes began looking up in July 1936. A partially successful military coup against the duly elected Popular Front government ignited the Spanish Civil War. Within days, Adolph Hitler and Benito Mussolini sent aid and arms in support of General Franco's fascist Nationalist forces. The Soviet Union seized on the opportunity to use the Spanish Civil War in their propaganda. The conflict came to represent themes like class struggle and social reform. The Soviets promoted the war as the front line in the fight against fascism.

The Soviet Union sent materiel to the Loyalist Republicans. Elsewhere, the Comintern began organising the International Brigades, an all-volunteer force of 5000 foreign men who travelled to Spain to support the Republican government now under siege. As a cause célèbre among the left intelligentsia, the International Brigades drew volunteers from the educated class. From Trinity, John Cornford, Julian Bell, and David Haden Guest joined the International Brigades.

The Soviets needed intelligence on the movements of Franco's Nationalist troops. Theodore Maly, now taking over as Kim's handler, decided that Philby would report from the battle front as a journalist, covering the Nationalist forces. Moscow Centre at first wanted to send Philby to assassinate Franco, but Theodore Maly knew that Kim was no killer. Even if he could get close enough, the young man would be unable to carry out the order.[7] Maly quickly talked his supervisors out of the outlandish idea. Philby would instead infiltrate Franco's troops as a reporter.

As any aspiring journalist seeking employment would do, Kim hustled. He first obtained credentials from the London General Press, and in early 1937, headed to Spain as a freelancer. Next, Philby began sending numerous articles to *The Times*, unsolicited, about developments in the war. Finally, one of his pieces providing careful analysis of the situation in Spain was published. The article impressed not only the editors, but also St John Philby. Once again, Kim was assisted by his father. St John, on a visit home to London, invited the assistant editor of *The Times*, Robin Barrington Ward, out to lunch. Ward was an old friend from St John's Westminster days, and in May 1937 a position was secured for Kim as *The Times* correspondent with the Nationalist forces from their headquarters in Seville.

When Kim went to Spain, he left Litzi behind. It hardly made sense for a young reporter to bring his wife to a country in the midst of a violent civil war. His departure also served to initiate the beginning of their permanent separation. After all, Kim could not reasonably establish a right-wing cover for himself and continue living with a communist woman.

On a related subject, Kim began the first of his many adulterous affairs during his time in Spain. Through another correspondent, Kim was introduced to Frances Doble, an alluring brunet ten years his senior. Frances was a Canadian-born actress who had spent much of the previous decade performing on London's West End stage. Though divorced from Sir Anthony Lindsay-Hogg, she continued to use her title, Lady Lindsay-Hogg. She was fascinated with royalty, and was good friends with the exiled King Alfonso XIII of Spain. The royal family was allied with Franco, and Lady Lindsay-Hogg was staying in Spain to support the Nationalists in any way she could. She adored Kim, and the two of them carried on with their tryst until Kim left Spain in 1939.

Spain in those years was a dangerous place for journalists, let alone a Soviet spy. Philby had several close calls. He could have been killed near battle zones, or imprisoned and killed for being a Soviet agent. Years later, Philby opened his memoir with a compelling story of the dangers he faced in Spain.

Just a few short weeks after arriving in Seville, Kim had gone to Cordoba to see a bullfight. In the middle of the night, he was allegedly dragged from his hotel room by Franco's security forces, who were always suspicious of foreign tourists. They accused him of entering the city without a travel permit. According to Kim, he had a tiny scrap of rice paper with a cypher code in his pocket. Before his clothing was searched at the police station, he distracted the officers by tossing his wallet onto a table. While the officers scrambled to grab it, Kim pulled the paper from his pocket and ate it. Kim was released from custody without incident, and Guy Burgess was promptly dispatched to meet him in Gibraltar with a new codebook.[8]

Philby's passport stamp reveals that, if his story was true, it didn't happen quite the way he remembered. Philby had been in Cordoba a month prior to the alleged incident and obtained his visa while there. He obviously did not enter the city illegally.

He need not have fabricated such a tale. Philby *was* placed directly in harm's way later that year, in a more frightening episode with numerous witnesses. In late December 1937, Franco granted permission for a convoy of reporters to travel to the mountains of Aragon, where the Republican forces besieged the walled city of Teruel. In an ill-advised strategy, General Franco pulled troops from his Guadalajara offensive and sent them to Teruel, during the coldest winter in twenty years. Anticipating an easy victory, Franco allowed the journalists to travel to Teruel, hoping for favourable coverage in the international press.

On 31 December, Philby rode with the escorted convoy departing from Saragossa. The Spanish officers pulled over for a break in the village of Caude to get out and stretch their legs. Philby and his fellow reporters remained in their vehicle, sheltering from the extreme cold. They first heard a shell fire about a half mile away. Seconds later, an enormous blast shook the vehicle; they had been fired on by the Republican Army, using Soviet artillery. Of the four journalists in the vehicle, one was killed on impact, another died later that evening, and a third succumbed to his injuries two days later. Philby, suffering only a superficial head wound, was treated at a field hospital and driven back to Saragossa. The following day, 1 January 1938, he sent a telegram to his parents assuring them that he was only slightly injured in the deadly impact. It was Kim's birthday, and he was only 26 years old.

Philby dutifully sent a dispatch to *The Times* on 2 January detailing the events, as well as the unfortunate news that the Nationalists in Teruel had surrendered to the Republicans, despite Franco's reinforcements. In a bizarre scene, Kim, the Soviet mole, was awarded the Red Ruby Order of Military Merit for the events at Caude. The award was pinned on his lapel by the fascist General Franco himself.

Less than three years after their initial recruitment, the Three Musketeers, as they called themselves, had exceeded all expectations in their espionage careers. Maclean was submitting massive amounts of classified documents from the Foreign Office, Philby had successfully infiltrated Franco's army, and Guy Burgess had been recruited by MI6.

Somehow, during the rapid advancement of his career, Burgess managed to find time to recruit more spies to the successful Cambridge Spy Ring. The first of these was Anthony Blunt.

Chapter Six

The Art Historian
Anthony Blunt, the Reluctant Spy

Anthony Blunt would never have been a spy, had it not been for Guy Burgess. In fact, he might not even have been a communist.

Anthony Frederick Blunt was a minister's son. He was born on 26 September 1907 in Bournemouth, England, the youngest of three boys. His father, Stanley, was vicar of Holy Trinity Church, an evangelical congregation of the Anglican Church.

Stanley was himself the son of a minister, Frederick LeFevre Blunt, who served as the first Bishop of Hull and had served as chaplain to Queen Victoria. Stanley's older brother, Walter, had followed in their father's footsteps, becoming the vicar of the parish of Ham. When Walter died unexpectedly of scarlet fever in 1898, Stanley took over his position. Stanley was never a towering figure like his father, the archbishop, nor was he a gifted and charismatic speaker, like his late brother, Walter. Rather, Stanley was more approachable and easy going and was admired as a steady presence for his flock.

In 1900, when Stanley was 30 years old, he married the then 20-year-old Hilda Master. Hilda was the daughter of Jonathan Master, a magistrate from the Indian Colonial Service. When Jonathan retired, he returned to England with his wife, Gertrude, and their children.

Though they never boasted, the Masters took pride in their connections to the royal family. Hilda's second cousin was the Earl of Strathmore, whose daughter, Elizabeth, would later become the Queen Mother. The Masters were also close friends with the Duke and Duchess of Teck, whose daughter later became Queen Mary, through her marriage to King George V.

Hilda struggled socially well into her adulthood. Her relationship with her demanding mother was difficult. She had often been sick as a child and was unable to participate in games or group activities. Making things worse, a botched surgery had rendered her deaf in one ear. When Hilda married Stanley Blunt, her parents considered it a step down, which only confirmed her standing as an outsider in her own family.

Stanley and Hilda had in common their puritanical sensibilities around their religion, and a passion for serving the less fortunate. Both grew up feeling like the odd one out in their families, and together they took pride in their quiet nonconformity. Hilda was deeply devoted to Stanley, and their marriage was, indeed, a happy one. Their oldest son, Wilfred, was born in 1901, followed by Christopher, in 1904. In 1906, Stanley was appointed vicar of Holy Trinity. The Blunt family moved to Bournemouth, where Anthony was born one year later.

The Blunts lived a modest life of genteel poverty and social consciousness. Hilda kept their home in the church rectory clean, cold, and scantly furnished.

This all changed in 1912, when Anthony was 4 years old. Stanley was appointed bishop of St Michael's, which ministered to the British Embassy in Paris. The Blunt family moved into a grand mansion in Paris, where they often hosted parties for diplomats. Anthony and his two older brothers cheerfully adapted to their new palatial home in the large cosmopolitan city. The boys learned how to speak French fluently, and were exposed to some of the world's greatest works of art. Anthony's father, Stanley, appreciated the classics and imparted their historical importance to his sons. Anthony later credited his early years in Paris as the impetus for his love of art, which inspired his eventual career path.[1]

The family's idyll was shattered in 1914, as German troops invaded France. As the Germans threatened to take Paris, the British Embassy was evacuated to Bordeaux. For their safety, Hilda Blunt sent her three boys to Warwickshire, England, to stay with her sister. Hilda and Stanley stayed behind to help stranded tourists get home to England.

After Paris was secured, the Blunts moved back to their residence. Wilfred and Christopher were sent to a boarding school. Anthony, the youngest, returned to Paris to live with his parents. Stanley signed on as an Army chaplain, and opened a club for British soldiers in the ballroom of their Paris residence. There the soldiers could relax, socialise, play billiards, and perhaps see a concert. Around 40,000 meals were served there per month, while volunteers wrote letters for the soldiers, or gave tours of the city. At war's end, Stanley was awarded the Order of the British Empire for his service to the troops.

Anthony never quite got on with his father, and his two brothers similarly failed to connect with him. Though he was a good father and a hardworking, decent man, he kept his sons at arm's length. Conversely, all three boys were very close with their mother. They admired Hilda for her integrity and her quiet strength. As the youngest, Anthony was clearly her favourite.

In 1920, young Anthony was awarded a scholarship to Marlborough College, as had both of his brothers before him. Established in 1843 for the sons of Anglican clergy, Marlborough College is located in the county of Wiltshire, in southwestern England. The most obvious feature of the campus at Marlborough is a man-made hill standing 60 feet tall, like a tree-covered layer cake. The Mound, as it is called, once served as the motte for the medieval Marlborough Castle, elevating the Norman fortification above the plain. The castle no longer survives, but the ancient Mound, dating back to 2400 BCE, continues to cast its Pagan shadow over the Christian school.

By all accounts, Anthony's first two years away from home were miserable. Just over twenty miles from Stonehenge, another ancient monument, Marlborough College was somewhat isolated in its rural environs. In the years after the Great War, the food was scarce and usually unpleasant. Growing boys lived on one hot meal a day for lunch, supplemented by bread and tea for the other meals. The rooms were cold and the beds uncomfortable. Discipline was borderline abusive, with both the teachers and the older prefects caning the younger boys.

Anthony had a fair amount of trouble adjusting to life away from home. He was very shy, rather skinny, and much of his education up to that point had been at home. Having spent his early childhood in Paris, he didn't know any of his classmates, most of whom had friends that they knew from prep school. Sports were heavily emphasised at Marlborough, and Anthony hated sports and games. He spent the first two years at school alone, and often bullied. In spite of it all, he managed to score high marks in class. He specialised in mathematics, but also excelled at modern languages, and won numerous prizes for his academic work.

It was not until his third year that Anthony began to make friends. He found a small group of boys who considered themselves intellectuals and proudly differentiated themselves from the so-called 'hearties', the athletes and bullies who dominated the school's social culture. In finding his niche, Anthony became comfortable with his own personality; it was now fine to love art, to speak fluent French, to be apart from the normal rough and tumble of a boys' school. His little clique of aesthetes enjoyed rebelling against the establishment and even started a magazine, *The Heretick*, in 1924, for the purpose of criticising their school. Anthony's first published article, defending modern art, was printed in the premier issue. The tone of his article was quite condescending; he denigrated the general public as too ignorant to appreciate the *avant garde* movement.[2] He was 16 years old.

Young Anthony also became disenchanted with the religion of his childhood. He found his parents' puritan, teetotaling, threadbare style of faith to be bland and empty. He only found true transcendence in art, filling the void left behind by the rote worship imposed daily at school.

He formed his closest friendship at Marlborough with Louis MacNeice, a fellow minister's son and future poet. MacNeice was also an outsider, due to his own childhood isolation, and the fact that he was Irish. Unlike Anthony, Louis broke through the social rejection by playing rugby, which he loved. Blunt had created his own little art appreciation group, calling it the Anonymous Society, which MacNeice joined in 1924. MacNeice, who was heterosexual, had a gregarious and outgoing nature, which made a nice contrast with Anthony's brooding sensitivity and closeted homosexuality. MacNeice's extroverted personality made Blunt feel safe to be himself. As long as Louis was funny, emotional, and clever, Anthony was free to be quiet, pensive, and rational. Their friendship, which began at the age of 16, continued long after they graduated from Marlborough in 1926. They stayed in touch through their letters when MacNeice left for Oxford, and Blunt for Cambridge.

It is unknown whether Blunt had some type of homosexual experience at Marlborough. Schoolboy crushes there were common and something of an open secret, but were rarely consummated. There is no record of any love affair, short of unrequited affection.[3] However, Blunt could be very private about these things. His own mother, with whom he was very close, never knew of his homosexuality.

When Anthony arrived via scholarship to Trinity College, he reverted into the same apprehensive schoolboy that had first walked into Marlborough. He had to begin once more, learning how to make friends and find his way all over again. He spent the first year depressed and alone, with only MacNeice's letters to look forward to. He travelled back to Marlborough to declare his feelings to a younger student, only to be rejected. His troubles were exacerbated at year's end when he received a second, instead of a first, in his part one mathematics exams. He changed his major to modern languages in his second year.

Though modern languages did not carry the same intellectual weight as mathematics, it dovetailed nicely with Blunt's interest in French art and literature. Art history, his true passion, did not yet exist as an official discipline at Cambridge, but his new field of study allowed him to explore it more freely.

He also entered into his first romantic relationship with a wealthy and well connected young undergraduate named Peter Montgomery. Through Peter, Anthony finally made a small circle of friends, who were impressed by his intellect and charmed by his impeccable manners. As much as he had rebelled against the popular crowd in his youth, Blunt still wanted desperately to belong.

Since his teens, Blunt had been fascinated by the Bloomsbury Group, a loosely organised ensemble of intellectuals, writers, and artists, most of whom had attended Cambridge. Clive Bell, John Maynard Keynes, Lytton Strachey, and Leonard and Virginia Woolf were some of the more famous names on Bloomsbury's roster. Not only did the group advocate for literature and the fine arts, they influenced popular opinion in areas like economics, politics, and social issues. Dadie Rylands, a young Cambridge don and director at the Cambridge Theatre, took a shine to Anthony, and gladly brought him into the world of Bloomsbury. The reticent young man found himself attending parties at Rylands' home, surrounded by his boyhood heroes.

In May 1928, Blunt was elected into the Apostles, further confirming his acceptance into the elite echelon of Cambridge society. Unlike the more political atmosphere of the early 1930s, the subjects of discussion when Blunt first joined were of poetry, literature, and philosophy. He was disdainful of politics at this point in his life.

In the spring of 1929, Blunt's friendship with Louis MacNeice was under considerable tension. After a life of abstinence, MacNeice finally discovered alcohol and it had begun to wreak havoc upon him. A few months earlier, Blunt had set up a meeting with Leonard Woolf in order to get MacNeice's poetry published by Hogarth Press. MacNeice never showed up, having crashed his car into a tree on the way over. Making things worse, Louis had recently become engaged to a woman named Mary Ezra, whom Anthony despised.

Still needing a friend to confide in, Blunt became close with Julian Bell, the son of art critic Clive Bell. Anthony had met Julian through the Bloomsbury Group, and inducted him into the Apostles. By May, the two had become a couple, shocking everyone, not least because Julian was heterosexual.

Over the summer, Anthony's father, Stanley, became gravely ill and was diagnosed with cancer. Hilda asked that her sons not come to visit him, fearing their presence would alert him to the fact that he was dying. He passed away in November 1929. Anthony never spoke publicly of his father's death, and it does not appear that he told either of his two closest friends, Julian Bell or Louis MacNeice. Just as Hilda tried to protect Stanley from his own impending death, Anthony protected his friends, and perhaps himself, from his own complex feelings toward his father.

To be fair, both of these friendships were struggling at the time. His affair with Julian was coming to an end. He continued his battle with Louis over his relationship with Mary Ezra, whom Louis married anyway the following June. Anthony did not attend the ceremony, nor did either of the couple's parents. Blunt soon took up with a new friend, the wealthy and exciting Victor Rothschild. A descendant of the prominent Rothschild dynasty, Victor was a fellow member of the Apostles. A brilliant eccentric, he collected rare paintings and books, and drove a Bugatti. He remained friends with Anthony long after graduation.

In June 1930, at the end of his last term at Trinity, Blunt earned a first in part two of his Tripos, and was granted a fellowship. His thesis would be on Nicholas Poussin, the French Baroque painter. The previously awkward young man was now a Cambridge bachelor don, who had earned the respect of his peers and ran in the most elegant circles.

In the autumn of 1930, a force of nature called Guy Burgess landed upon Trinity College. A more determined social climber even than Anthony Blunt, Burgess inserted himself into all of the fashionable clubs and societies. Like most shrinking violets, Anthony was drawn irresistibly to chaos, and it was only a matter of time before Blunt and Burgess found each other.

The exact nature of their relationship, at least in the early stages, remains a topic of debate. They most likely slept together at some point, if only because Burgess slept with nearly everyone. Their friendship was never really about that, however. They shared a common interest in art, and Burgess had a formidable intellect, which impressed Blunt. Guy's humour always seemed to pull Anthony out of his quiet, stewing moods. Anthony lived vicariously through Guy's ridiculous exploits, while remaining his dignified and courteous self. Guy's mother, who disliked most of Guy's boyfriends, simply adored Anthony. Nigel Burgess found Anthony easier to get along with than his own brother, Guy.

Meanwhile, Blunt's academic career began to take off. He discovered that Poussin, the subject of his dissertation, was heavily influenced by the Italian writers of the Renaissance period; so much so that Poussin's own writings bordered on plagiarism. He included his discovery in his dissertation, and this finding earned him another four-year fellowship to study the roots of Italian classicism in French art. His research on the topic would later contribute to his first book, *Artistic Theory in Italy, 1450–1600*. Blunt was invited to be a guest lecturer at the Courtauld Institute of Art in London, and he was hired by *The Spectator* as an art critic. In 1933, he was granted a one year sabbatical to work in Rome.

Blunt finally developed an interest in politics, evidenced by an article he wrote in 1934, critical of the fascist response to modern art. He complained that the Nazis had removed modern art from public view, while the Italians had simply adopted futurism as the official art of Italy, using it as a vehicle to promote fascism.[4]

Blunt visited his brother, Wilfred, in Munich in May 1934. He was still in Germany on 30 June, the Night of the Long Knives, when Adolph Hitler ordered the arrest and execution of his rivals. Like most foreign tourists, Blunt was shocked and horrified by the events. It is possible that he was impacted by the homophobic nature of some of Hitler's rhetoric, but it is more likely that he was influenced by the persecution of his friend and mentor, Walter Friedlaender. Shortly after receiving an award for his scholarship in art history, Friedlaender was removed from his professorship at Freiburg because he was Jewish.

While Blunt was away, Cambridge fell under the communist spell. When he returned to Cambridge, he discovered that many of his friends, including Guy Burgess, had joined the Communist Party. Blunt found that nearly everyone in his social circles talked mostly about left wing politics. Anti-fascism had become a fashionable topic of conversation among the intelligentsia. The rising popular tide of communism at Cambridge was due mostly to the work of David Haden Guest, James Klugmann, and John Cornford. Klugmann, who had been a student of Blunt's, was the pragmatic intellectual, while Cornford and Haden Guest were the emotional radicals, the true believers who made communism such a glamorous cause.

James Klugmann began to educate Blunt on the principles of Marxism. He was not an absolutist, but instead embraced the new Soviet strategy of the United Front, which advocated partnership with non-communist left and liberal groups, working together in the fight against fascism.

The next stage of Blunt's conversion was becoming a rite of passage for blossoming communists in the west. Just as Anthony's parents had once made a religious pilgrimage to the Holy Land, Anthony, joined by his brother Wilfred, made a 1935 pilgrimage to the socialist utopia of Soviet Russia. Although Anthony was impressed with the art collection on display at the Hermitage (there were a few Poussins), he was somewhat disappointed in the architecture in Moscow and with the newer Soviet paintings. Predictably, he had little interest in the output of the factories, or the alleged crop yield.

Though Blunt's notes did not reflect an enchantment with the New Experiment, it does appear that his trip had initiated a slow change of viewpoint within him. His articles began to take on a political edge, as he peppered his critiques with Marxist lingo. He adopted the Soviet line in favour of realism, sneering at anything abstract – unless, of course, its purpose was to rattle the bourgeoisie. He wrote three articles praising the overtly political murals of Diego Rivera, and nearly twisted himself into a pretzel defending Moscow's denunciation of surrealism.[5]

In March 1936, Blunt travelled to Spain with his old chum, Louis MacNeice. MacNeice's wife, Mary, had recently left him, and he was badly in need of a friend. Though Spain was at the precipice of civil war, Blunt was as lukewarm as always when it came to current events. He insisted that he was interested mainly in seeing the works of the great Spanish art masters. He did, however, express hope for a communist revolution in Spain, which might eventually spread to England, revitalising the art scene. MacNeice, though sympathetic, was not persuaded by the heady fantasy of communism.

Shortly after their visit, in July 1936, the Spanish Civil War erupted.

Meanwhile, Arnold Deutsch was hoping to recruit more spies from the fertile grounds at Cambridge. Though delighted with the performance of his Three Musketeers, they were long since gone from Trinity College. He needed a new scout to find and recommend suitable high flyers to work for the Soviets. At first blush, Anthony Blunt didn't seem to be ideal for the job. He had not the passion of Guy Burgess, nor the devotion of Kim Philby. Though accomplished in his own area of expertise, he really didn't have the tireless work ethic of Donald Maclean. But Anthony did have something that the others no longer had – he had access. He was still on the campus, among the 'Peter Pans', as MacNeice called his naïve students. He was teaching and so could determine which undergraduates held the highest potential. Critically, he was mingling in leftist circles, ideally positioned to divine the true believers from the hangers on. Blunt was great at keeping secrets, and he kept even his closest friends at a distance.

It was his friend, Guy Burgess, who recognised that Blunt had the personal qualities of a good agent. Burgess recommended Blunt for the job of talent spotter, and it was Burgess who made the first approach. There is no record of the exact date, but Blunt later placed their first conversation in either late 1935 or early 1936, shortly before the start of the Spanish Civil War.[6] He didn't agree to work for the Soviets until almost a year later.

Burgess, with his persistence and gift for persuasion, convinced Blunt that the most effective way to fight the spread of fascism was to support the Soviet Union, which was the only government actively working to stop it. The British were looking the other way as Hitler sent tanks and troops to the demilitarised zone near the Franco-German border. Furthermore, the British had enacted a policy of non-intervention in Spain.

Like many other young leftists, the Spanish Civil War was the deciding factor in Blunt's decision to put his idealism into action. While committed intellectuals and writers laid down their pens and took up arms to defend the Republicans against Franco's Nationalists, Anthony Blunt chose to spy for the Soviet Union. He agreed to meet with the legendary OTTO in January 1937, days after hearing of the death of John Cornford, the inspirational force who led so many Cambridge students to communism, while fighting in Spain. Blunt was captivated by the intellect of Arnold Deutsch, and particularly by his work with the Sex-Pol movement.[7] Unlike his clever and familial code names for Philby, Maclean, and Burgess, Deutsch bestowed on Blunt a somewhat disappointing code name, TONY.

In many ways, Blunt's decision was easy. He did not have to commit fully to the principles of Marxism, or learn the finer points of dialectical materialism. He was free to practise a 'cafeteria' communism, selecting the bits that he liked, ignoring the rest. He wouldn't have to publicly disavow the

Communist Party, because he had never joined it. He wouldn't have to die on the front lines in Spain, like his former boyfriend, Julian Bell. He could remain sheltered in the safe, affirming cocoon of Cambridge University, basking in the admiration of young undergraduates as he cracked off angry diatribes against the surrealist movement. All he had to do was locate high achieving students who were more committed than he was.

In return, Anthony could be satisfied that he was doing something constructive, playing his small part in the noble fight against fascism. He would be granted the thrill of keeping a secret, as he whet his lifelong appetite for danger – vicariously, as usual, through someone else more courageous.

Blunt's first target was Michael Straight, an American student who had travelled to Moscow with Anthony's group in 1935. Straight, a trust fund beneficiary of the prominent Whitney family, had joined the Cambridge Communist Party under the mesmerising influence of John Cornford. He had been introduced to Blunt in 1935 by Guy Burgess and James Klugmann. Thereafter, Blunt had asserted himself as Straight's mentor, advising him on his career path, and his complicated love life. Blunt approached Straight in early 1937, while Straight was in a highly vulnerable state.[8] He was dating a ballet dancer while pursuing Belinda Compton (whom he would later marry), all the while fighting off the advances of Victor Rothschild's wife, who had taken a liking to him. He was also grieving the death of his good friend, John Cornford.

According to Straight, Blunt exploited his shaky emotional state to suggest that he return to America to work for the international bank, in order to advise the Soviets of America's economic movements. Blunt allegedly invoked John Cornford's ultimate sacrifice to sway him. Straight cut ties with the Communist Party, and boarded a ship bound for the United States after graduation. He took a job with the Department of the Interior in the Roosevelt administration, and in 1938, established contact with his new Soviet handler, Iskhak Akhmerov, alias Michael Green.[9]

Anthony Blunt's second recruit was a 23-year-old man named John Cairncross.

Chapter Seven

Was He, or Wasn't He?
The Elusive John Cairncross

From the beginning, John Cairncross was different.
While the first four Cambridge spies professed their solidarity with the working class, Cairncross had lived their reality and was trying to rise above it.

Unlike the other four spies, John Cairncross wasn't English. He was born in the small coal mining town of Lesmahagow, Scotland, just twenty-seven miles southwest of Glasgow. Johnny, as he was called, was born 25 July 1913, with an unruly shock of red hair, perhaps a warning of his temperament. He was the youngest of eight children: four boys and four girls.

His father, Alexander Cairncross, ran the family business, Cairncross and Menzies, an ironmongery inherited from his own father. His obligation to the shop, which he ran with a business partner, precluded the furthering of his own education, but his talents were obvious. Along with a natural acumen for business, he was skilled with numbers and arithmetic. The people in town often asked for his advice in preparing their taxes.

Alexander married a local schoolteacher named Elizabeth Wishart. One of the many values they held in common was education. Though Alexander was unable to attend university due to his responsibilities running his business, both parents imparted to their children a heavy emphasis on education. In Scotland, scholarships were available to any student who performed well up to the age of 11, making secondary education essentially free. A generous scholarship program was also available at university level. Alexander and Elizabeth encouraged their children to take advantage of this opportunity, and five of them did, earning university degrees. Two of Johnny's sisters continued their education and became schoolteachers like their mother, and three of the boys became university professors, including, eventually, himself.

Even when the children were young, Elizabeth worked hard to cultivate a love of learning in her children. Though her formal teaching days were over, her four boys and four girls formed a virtual classroom in her home. A powerful intellect ran in the Cairncross family, and Elizabeth did her best to nurture it, instilling a love of reading in the children. Young Johnny purchased his first book, an illustrated selection from *Arabian Nights*, at a local store when he was 6 years old. With no radio, and only rare outings by train to Glasgow, reading books became an escape for him, a way to travel beyond his insular little town. He later credited his appreciation of literature and interest in travel to his early love of reading.[1] Elizabeth also embraced a permissive style of teaching, allowing her children to follow their own curiosities, wherever they may lead. If their school curriculum did not cover a topic that interested them, the child was encouraged to seek instruction outside of school.

John Cairncross admitted that, while his father was a good man, their relationship was rather distant. As an adult, John attributed this lack of intimacy to their age difference; Alexander began having children later in life, and little Johnny was the youngest, making Alexander 'old enough to be my grandfather', as John liked to say.[2] Alexander was also a product of his generation, focusing most of his attention on his business so that he could support his large family. Though he expressed pride and affection when Johnny brought home good marks from school, most of the warmth and nurturing was left to Elizabeth.

John was closest with his brother Alec, and would remain so well into adulthood. Only two years older than young Johnny, Alec was an ideal playmate and role model. John later described feeling like he was always in Alec's shadow, though never in a negative way.[3] Alec would later be recognised as Sir Alexander Cairncross, a highly regarded economist. John would follow his brother to the University of Glasgow, and later still, to the University of Cambridge.

A sharper contrast could not be drawn between the privileged English public school education afforded to the other Cambridge spies, and the grammar school experience of John Cairncross. At 5, he entered the Lesmahagow infant school at Turfham, which consisted of one large room containing about seventy students. He later advanced to Lesmahagow Higher Grade School, before finally attending Hamilton Academy. Unlike Philby, Maclean, Burgess, and Blunt, John's schooling was coeducational and most of the teachers were women. Though not completely free from the tedious distinctions of the British class system, John's school included all of the children in the village. The sons and daughters of coal miners, farmers, shopkeepers, and ministers all learned side by side in the classroom. Unlike the four English spies, who were sent away to boarding schools, the Cairncross children returned every afternoon to their crowded home.

Even outside of the school, the townspeople of Lesmahagow mingled easily among the different classes. The town's Presbyterian history and rural location fostered a cohesive community spirit. Cars were almost unheard of, milk was delivered by horse and cart, and children often hitched a ride on hay wagons during the harvest. Though John bristled as an adult when anyone called him working class (he considered himself lower middle class), he had lived much of their experience. Little Johnny spent time as a child helping to milk the neighbour's cows and attended the local Boys Brigade alongside the miner's children. Kim Philby, on the other hand, never saw a coal miner in his life until he went to Cambridge, where he encountered the small group of miners on scholarship.

During Great Britain's General Strike of 1926 the coal miners in Lesmahagow faced desperate circumstances. Unlike in London, however, there was no violence, only one peaceful protest at the town hall. John's father, Alexander, offered a store discount to anyone who produced a union card. After all, these were his neighbours.

Alexander was a religious man who took his family to church every Sunday, and led them in prayer before dinner every evening. Both John and his brother, Alec, though obedient, were sceptical of religion from a fairly young age. John would later reject the puritan moral strictures of his Presbyterian upbringing, being drawn instead to the looser sexual mores of the French Renaissance. Even so, John developed an interest in exegesis interpretations of the gospel, and looked back fondly on his religious education as foundational in his appreciation for the English language.

When Alec graduated from Hamilton Academy, he earned a scholarship to the University of Glasgow. At first, he took a train back and forth from Lesmahagow every day, but soon moved into a house in the city with a friend, Ian Smith. When John graduated from Hamilton a year ahead of schedule, he joined his brother at Glasgow in 1930, moving in with Alec and Ian. Their scholarships were awarded by the Carnegie Trust, established by Scottish-American steel magnate Andrew Carnegie in 1901 to help deserving Scottish students to further their education.

The ancient University of Glasgow, founded in 1451, played a critical role in the Scottish Enlightenment of the eighteenth century, educating such luminaries as economist, Adam Smith, and philosopher, Francis Hutcheson. Other famous alumni include four Nobel Laureates, three British prime ministers, and three Scottish first ministers. Originally located near the gothic Glasgow Cathedral, the university was moved in 1870 to the West End of Glasgow, where its prominent clock tower rises above the city's skyline.

While Alec studied economics, John entered the honours degree course in modern languages, which required students to spend their third year studying abroad. Excited at the prospect of spending a year in France, John threw himself into the study of French and German. At the end of his first year, he won prizes for both. He took a course in economics and studied the Scottish Enlightenment. John took a special interest in the philosopher David Hume, probably due to his own religious scepticism. He was deeply influenced by Hume's *Treatise of Human Nature*, which emphasised the need for empirical evidence in arguments, as well as the need for lived experience when explaining human behaviour.

John's studies of French literature led him to the seventeenth-century French playwright, Molière, falling in love with his literary style and forward-thinking social commentary. His comedic plays were used to poke fun at the orthodoxies of his time, whether they be religious, traditional, or political.

John's interest was piqued by the Scottish Nationalist movement and he attended a few meetings. He also attended lectures hosted by the Rationalist Free Press Association, whose speakers covered topics on atheism, art, feminism, and science. He did not join any political parties, due to his strong individualism. He was, however, a free speech absolutist, a rationalist, and something of a sexual libertine, if only in theory.

At the end of his second year, Cairncross embarked on his first journey outside of his hometown and Glasgow. He boarded a ship bound for the Continent, travelling by bicycle through Belgium, Germany, and Austria, staying at youth hostels and meeting the local townspeople. It was the summer of 1932, and John already sensed a stirring among the unemployed and angry young men in Germany. He observed, uncomfortably, the growing support for Adolph Hitler, as well as the crude anti-semitism expressed openly by ordinary Germans. Everywhere he went, young men expressed bitterness at Germany's treatment after the Great War, as well as predictions of a new war on the horizon.

In Austria, he met an older Jewish man named Rosenberger, who showed him around Vienna. Cairncross admired the architecture, viewed paintings from the German and Italian masters, and attended a performance of *Faust*. Rosenberger introduced John to his family and friends, who accepted him warmly, and complimented him on his German. Cairncross enthusiastically immersed himself in Vienna's vibrant Jewish community. He listened with growing concern as they shared with him their fears of being scapegoated for Germany and Austria's economic problems. Some predicted a civil war, which in fact came to pass two years later. Another young Jew he met in the hostels told John of how he had been attacked and beaten in the street in Frankfurt by a crowd of Nazis. In spite of his usual political apathy, John was able to see and understand the rising Nazi threat.

By summer's end, Cairncross, the 19-year-old boy who had never left Scotland, was now better travelled, more worldly, and awakened to world events. He was ready to start his first year of study abroad. John had been offered a job as a teaching assistant in Clermont-Ferrand, but he really wanted to study in Paris. His parents generously offered to subsidise his lodging, enabling him to study at the Sorbonne.

Cairncross was captivated by Paris, charmed by its culture, art, and history. For the first time in his life he tried wine, and found that he enjoyed it. John had looked forward to indulging in the carnal delights of Paris, but was disappointed to learn that he was forbidden from bringing women into the dormitory. He would remain frustrated, for the time being. Even so, John so loved Paris that he had his scholarship transferred to the Sorbonne, so that he could spend not one, but two years in the City of Light.

During his second year at the Sorbonne, the situation in Germany had become even more precarious. Hitler had seized power in 1933, and the university was inundated with Jewish refugees, hoping to finish their degrees. Paris had become a magnet for the burgeoning anti-fascist movement; German Jewish refugees, exiles from fascist Italy, socialists, communists, and, of course, Comintern agents, converged on the city. For the first time, Cairncross saw the need for some kind of organised opposition to fascism.

Meanwhile, John's older brother, Alec, had graduated from Glasgow in 1932, and had begun a PhD program in economics at Trinity College, Cambridge. He encouraged John to apply and join him at the prestigious university. Due to John's excellent performance on his entrance exams, combined with his degree from the Sorbonne, he was allowed to skip the first year and begin straight away on his second year of studies at Cambridge University. Alec, again looking out for his younger brother, moved in with John to keep him company.

John arrived at Trinity in 1934, as a fascination with communism had taken hold of the student body. John, like his brother Alec, was amused at the radicalism of these privileged youths and their alleged camaraderie with the working class. Many students at Glasgow were middle or working class, and were mostly either conservative or liberal, but not communist. They might have been surprised by these students claiming to know what was best for them.

For his part, John was largely disenchanted with the repressive culture at Cambridge. The students were required to wear their gowns to class and had an eleven o'clock curfew. These impositions didn't go over well for a young man who had bicycled through Europe alone as teenager, before living in the bohemian environment of Paris. He was surprised and appalled to learn that women were excluded from study at Cambridge. Glasgow had offered equal education to women since 1892. Embittered by his unsated desires, he derided the all-male atmosphere at Cambridge as 'distinctly homoerotic'.[4]

Despite the stifling atmosphere, Cairncross flourished academically. He was pleased with the numerous plays and concerts available, and the brilliant and fascinating people he met there. He studied German philosophers voraciously and began writing poetry. He even stumbled upon the little-known theories of Wilhelm Reich, founder of the Sex-Pol movement, and mentor to Arnold Deutsch.

John Cairncross found an important mentor of his own at Cambridge. His French tutor, Professor Henry Ashton, shared John's affinity for Molière. Ashton encouraged Cairncross to research the historical context of Molière's plays, insisting that literature and history were inextricably linked. Ashton was instrumental in Cairncross' later scholarly work on French Renaissance literature.

Contrary to Anthony Blunt's account, Cairncross claimed that he was never taught by Blunt,[5] though he knew him from the Modern Languages club, and lived upstairs from him at Nevile's Court. Unlike some of his less educated peers, he was unimpressed with Blunt's knowledge of French literature, and he disagreed with his interpretations of Renaissance art. Although many younger students were in awe of Blunt's social position at Cambridge, Cairncross had no reverence for such hierarchies. Rather, he was somewhat put off by Blunt's social climbing.

Cairncross did make friends with James Klugmann, who also lived in his building. Unlike John Cornford, the communist firebrand who converted so many students, Klugmann was calm, rational, and pragmatic. He spoke at length with Cairncross about Marxism, which Klugmann saw as a conglomeration of the best ideas from all institutions: religious, economic, industrial, and educational. He presented Marxism as a philosophical and intellectual pursuit, rather than the quasi-religion embraced by the likes of David Haden Guest and John Cornford. His approach intrigued, but did not convince, Cairncross.[6]

As a headstrong nonconformist and free speech advocate, Cairncross was largely unpersuaded by the inflexible tenets of Stalinist communism. He preferred Keynesianism, a more moderate form of government intervention, to the rigid central planning of the Soviet Union. Growing up in a fairly egalitarian community made him likewise impervious to the rhetoric of class struggle. He did not romanticise the working class, because he had lived and worked alongside them. Overall, John Cairncross was a bad fit for ideological Marxism.

However, he had been awakened to the threat of fascism, and in particular, Nazism, in 1932, long before most of the Cambridge student body. His empathy for the plight of Germany's Jews caused him to react with anger at the British government's refusal to take seriously Hitler's rise to power. The Communist Party, for all its flaws, was the only political party taking a stand in the fight against fascism. Cairncross decided to attend their meetings, though he never formally joined. According to his own memoir, he went along as a fellow traveller in the anti-fascist movement.[7]

Upon graduation, Cairncross was hoping for a research fellowship from Cambridge. In spite of his degree with first class honours, he was not offered one. He chalked this up to his inability to fit in with the academic community at Cambridge. Cairncross chose instead to pursue a career in the Civil Service. With his natural gift for language, his desire to travel, and his newly discovered awareness of rapidly shifting world events, Cairncross felt drawn to the foreign services, and felt that he could secure a position in the Foreign Office.

Unlike Donald Maclean, Cairncross could not afford to enrol in a specialised school like Scoones to prepare for the exams, and so had to study on his own. He somehow obtained a copy of the previous year's exam, which gave him some direction. Though the questions changed year to year, he was able to get a general idea of the format and topics which would be covered on the exams. Cairncross hunkered down in a small London flat and set about cramming for the next three months.

After taking the written portion of the exams, Cairncross travelled to Berlin to visit a family whose son he had once tutored. While there, he received a telegram from his parents announcing his impressive scores on the exams. He had come in first place on both the Civil Service and the Foreign Office exams. Back home in Scotland, his achievement was printed in *The Glasgow Herald*.[8] He returned to London to sit for the interview board.

Cairncross worried that he had tripped up on some questions, perhaps being too frank in his opinion concerning the situation in Germany, about which he had strong feelings. In any case, he performed well enough to pass the boards, and was appointed Third Secretary of the American Department at the Foreign Office in October 1936.

Everyone must start at the bottom, but Cairncross felt especially low in his new position among the established cadre of bureaucrats in the Foreign Office. As seismic events erupted across Europe, he was relegated to dealing with minor territorial disputes in places like British Honduras and Venezuela. As a newcomer to the department, he was also tasked with making tea for his superiors.

Cairncross found himself at a disadvantage when it came to the unspoken etiquette and customs of the upper crust into which he had broken. His Scottish accent flagged him immediately to his colleagues as coming from a lower class, and they treated him accordingly. He was reportedly reprimanded for leaving a cupboard door open in the first month of his employment. His own personality contributed to the situation, as well. Cairncross could be stubborn, blunt, and outspoken at times when it would best serve him to be quiet. He was unable to supress his displeasure at official British policies. Furthermore, in spite of his impressive education, Cairncross lacked simple administrative skills, and wasn't eager to learn or obey official procedures. He failed to fit in, due partly to the snobbery of his co-workers, and partly to his refusal to try.[9]

In early 1937, as the Spanish Civil War escalated, Cairncross was transferred to the Western Department, which oversaw Spain. This was likely due to his proficiency with the Spanish language. He found himself sharing an office with Donald Maclean, who had been appointed to the Foreign Office a year earlier. The two had little in common and never became very friendly. Cairncross later stated that he never knew of Maclean's clandestine activities on behalf of the KGB, and Maclean rarely discussed his own political views with him.[10]

Cairncross, an avowed anti-fascist, was deeply disturbed by Britain's non-interventionist policy in Spain. Senior officials at first refused to believe reports of German and Italian support for Franco, which frustrated Cairncross. He found it difficult to keep his opinions to himself, which led to friction with his superiors.

One of his important duties in the Western Department involved negotiating the release of British prisoners held by Franco, which usually involved an exchange for prisoners held by the Republican Loyalists. In February 1937, a Hungarian-born Comintern agent named Arthur Koestler was captured by Franco's troops in Spain. Koestler, like Kim Philby, had been working undercover as a journalist in the conflict. He served as a foreign correspondent for London's *News Chronicle,* covering the Nationalist rebels. Koestler has been credited as the first journalist to find evidence of Italian and German collusion with Franco. Koestler had been exposed as a communist in 1936, forcing him to flee Franco's headquarters in Seville. He unwisely returned to Spain to do further reporting, and was in Malaga when Mussolini's troops invaded the city. Koestler was arrested and sentenced to death. He was imprisoned for several months before the British Consul intervened on his behalf. A prisoner exchange was arranged by the Foreign Office, and John Cairncross was involved in the negotiations for Koestler's release. Arthur Koestler soon broke with the Communist Party during Stalin's purges of 1938. After the publication of his 1940 anti-totalitarian novel, *Darkness at Noon,* Koestler became a world famous anti-communist activist.

Confusion has surrounded the timing of Cairncross' recruitment as a spy for many decades. It was first assumed that he was recruited while still attending Cambridge, like his fellow Cambridge spies. After all, Cairncross changed his plans to continue an academic career in favour of a posting in the Foreign Office, just like Donald Maclean had done. It would make sense that Cairncross might have made this decision at the urging of Arnold Deutsch. It was not until the fall of the Soviet Union, and the release of a portion of KGB files, that it was confirmed that Cairncross was not approached until he was settled in at the Foreign Office.[11]

Working as Arnold Deutsch's new talent spotter, Anthony Blunt recommended Cairncross as a suitable prospect. Guy Burgess was entrusted to approach him. Cairncross had finally begun attending parties associated with the Foreign Office and had seen Burgess around a few times. As usual, Burgess proved to be a fascinating conversationalist, chatting up Cairncross on French history, art, and literature. He flattered Cairncross by introducing him to interesting and famous people, plucked from his wide circle of friends. One evening, Burgess, learning of his passion for poetry, invited Cairncross to a gathering at Anthony Blunt's apartment to meet the poet, and Blunt's best friend, Louis MacNeice.

After the party, on the train ride back to London from Cambridge, Burgess asked Cairncross how he felt about the international situation. Cairncross was frank in his assessment of the developing crisis in Europe. He expressed his frustration with Britain's non-intervention policy toward Spain, as well as his certainty that a war with Germany was inevitable. Cairncross also expressed worries that England was unprepared for such a war, and felt that an alliance with Russia would be necessary. Burgess was impressed with him.

When Cairncross mentioned that he would soon be spending a few days in Paris, Burgess said that he would also be in town and suggested they meet up. Cairncross grudgingly agreed, annoyed with having his holiday interrupted. Burgess then made a rare misstep; he told Cairncross to meet him in Paris at a café called *Le Sélect*. Upon further investigation, Cairncross discovered that *Le Sélect* was a popular hangout for the gay community in Paris. Repulsed, Cairncross simply failed to show up. Though Cairncross considered himself something of a sexual libertine, he was far less open minded when it came to homosexuality. He later claimed, incredibly, that he had not realised that Burgess was gay.[12]

The botched attempt at recruitment led to a breach of KGB protocol. Burgess had been the best choice to make the first approach to Cairncross, and he had failed. Maclean did not have a close friendship with Cairncross, and risked exposure himself if the attempt went south. Anthony Blunt, whom Cairncross actively disliked, was out of the question. As for Kim Philby? He didn't know Cairncross at all.

In a report filed with Moscow Centre, Burgess expressed some reservations about Cairncross, noting that he had never been a party member in the full sense. He was concerned that Cairncross didn't fit in and that his work was mediocre. Still, he felt Cairncross was worth the risk, citing his intellect and sincere desire to thwart fascism. It was Burgess who recommended that Cairncross be approached by an open party member.[13]

There was one committed communist, someone who knew Cairncross well, someone who could be trusted by both Cairncross and by Soviet Intelligence. James Klugmann would have to be recruited.

By 1937, Klugmann was an important figure in the Communist Party of Great Britain (CPGB). He had sacrificed a promising career in academia to work for the Comintern. After graduating from Trinity College, he became Secretary of the World Student Association, a communist front organisation based in Paris. Klugmann travelled around the world, working tirelessly to help build what became known as the Popular Front, a coalition of support in the struggle against fascism. He was on the leading edge of the movement, which moved away from rigid party discipline to form alliances with other groups on the left, without demanding that they sign on to the full program of communism.

John Cairncross had stayed in touch with Klugmann after leaving Cambridge. Cairncross occasionally saw Klugmann on his regular trips to Paris, and they would usually meet during Klugmann's visits home to London. Cairncross trusted and respected his old Cambridge friend, even if he did not fully agree with all of his communist philosophies. Percy Glading, a CPGB organiser (and a Soviet Spy himself), set up a meeting between Klugmann and OTTO.

Arnold Deutsch carefully broached the topic with Klugmann, who was reluctant to participate in the scheme. Klugmann considered himself a man of integrity, and saw clandestine work as a betrayal of his personal ethics. He had worked with the party long enough to know that the Soviet Union had an extensive espionage network, but he considered it counterproductive to the open advocacy and organising in which he was engaged. Working for the KGB posed a considerable risk to himself, as well. In the end, his own loyalty to the Communist Party was the deciding factor. He insisted that he would only approach Cairncross under direct order from the party. Harry Pollitt, General Secretary of the Communist Party of Great Britain, was summoned. Pollitt gave the order, and Klugmann had no choice but to comply.[14]

In May 1937, during the period in which Cairncross was working on the Koestler case, Klugmann invited Cairncross to join him for an evening stroll at Regent's Park. At seven o'clock, they met at the park entrance and headed inside. Upon reaching a secluded cluster of trees, Arnold Deutsch emerged. Klugmann introduced him as OTTO, and promptly retreated, leaving the two strangers alone together.

Deutsch talked about the looming threat of Hitler, and spoke with concern about the British policy toward Germany. He stressed the need for all people to unite against fascism, and in particular Nazi Germany. Deutsch was careful to stay on message, appealing to Cairncross' anti-Nazi convictions, never mentioning espionage. He used instead the word 'cooperation'. He even dangled the possibility of Cairncross receiving a top posting in the Diplomatic Services, should the communists gain power in Great Britain. Cairncross, shocked by the implied overture, agreed to meet with Deutsch again, but would not commit further.

Without explicitly agreeing to work for Deutsch, Cairncross continued to meet with him over the next four months. He was deeply conflicted at the time, and Deutsch played masterfully upon his insecurities. Cairncross wasn't getting on with his colleagues, and Donald Maclean had reported to Deutsch that his reports were sloppy. Cairncross clearly had the desire for advancement, but lacked the specific skills and connections to get ahead. He was becoming frustrated not only with his own career, but with Great Britain's *laissez-faire* diplomatic policies toward Spain and Germany. A disgruntled employee like John Cairncross presented an opportunity for Deutsch.

At the same time, Cairncross felt that he was being subtly blackmailed.[15] After being approached by Deutsch the first time, he should have reported the incident to his superiors in the Foreign Office. Such a report would naturally have triggered an investigation, which would likely have uncovered his own communist ties from his days at Cambridge. Donald Maclean, who had a more open and committed connection with the party during his college days, was able to brush it off as youthful dalliance. Maclean also knew people in high places who were willing to vouch for him. Cairncross had no such old boys' network to back him up. His social isolation in the workplace, coupled with his lacklustre performance, might seal his fate. Furthermore, every additional meeting he took with Deutsch after failing to report the first added to his own culpability.

As he got to know Cairncross, Deutsch developed a genuine affection for the Scotsman. Deutsch appreciated his humble upbringing and the experience that it gave him. He admired Cairncross' modesty, as well as his intellect. Deutsch felt that Cairncross would make a good agent, and assigned to him an appropriate code name: MOLIÈRE.

While he waited patiently over the summer for Cairncross to decide on his future path, Deutsch continued to groom him as Donald Maclean's replacement in the Foreign Office (Maclean was scheduled for a promotion to the Paris Embassy). Deutsch suggested that John move to a larger apartment in a more fashionable neighbourhood, which would enable him to meet and befriend more people. The move was subsidised with funding from the KGB, which made more difficult the possibility of John backing out. As a gesture of friendship, Deutsch invited the Francophile to join him in Paris for the International Exposition. Though he was not yet smuggling documents from the Foreign Office, Cairncross was being trained by Deutsch in the art of spycraft. Deutsch provided a sympathetic ear as Cairncross complained of his problems at work, and of his growing apprehension at the rise of Nazi Germany. As he became ever more incensed by the apathy of his superiors, his conscience gnawed at him, imploring him to do something about it.

In September 1937, as John Cairncross was finally coming around to the idea, Arnold Deutsch was called back to Moscow, never to return.

Chapter Eight

The World Heads to War
The Purge, the Appeasement, and a Deadly Compromise

The Spanish Civil War, which galvanised young communists to take up arms and join the fight against fascism, would eventually end in defeat for the Republicans. In the process, some of the brightest lights from Cambridge were snuffed out in the bloody conflict. John Cornford was killed near Cordoba in late 1936. Julian Bell, who dated Anthony Blunt and drove with Guy Burgess in the Remembrance Day protest, was killed by bomb shrapnel in the summer of 1937. David Haden Guest, the student responsible for transforming the Cambridge Communist Party, was killed by a sniper in July 1938 as he read a newspaper. Of all of the Cambridge communists who chose to take action in service of the Soviet cause, The Cambridge Five were among the most fortunate.

What they did not yet know was that the regime of Soviet Leader Joseph Stalin had entered one of its darkest periods, the Great Purge. After his break with Leon Trotsky, who was now living in exile, Stalin was driven to paranoia by the assassination of his ally, Sergei Kirov, by enemies within his own government. Stalin made it his mission to eliminate any suspected Trotsky allies within the Soviet government. Many of his victims were the foreign agents, those Great Illegals, who were serving in postings abroad. One by one, they were summoned to Moscow, never to return. Those who refused the call were tracked down and assassinated.

By the time Theodore Maly received his notice in June 1937, he knew his time was up. Though he knew his odds of survival were not good as a former priest, he willingly obeyed the summons. Maly was allowed to work in Moscow for nearly a year before facing trial. He was sentenced to death, and executed in September 1938.

Arnold Deutsch was recalled to Moscow in September 1937, but managed to avoid imprisonment or execution. However, he was not allowed to travel abroad until 1942, when he disappeared for good. The final fate of Arnold Deutsch remains a mystery to this day.

Grigori Grafpen, sent to London in April 1938 to replace Deutsch and Maly, was himself recalled to Moscow in December 1938. He was sentenced to five years in the gulag. Stability was temporarily restored to the London Rezidentura with the appointment of Anatoly Gorsky in 1939.

Stalin had a particular distrust of communists fighting in the Spanish Civil War. Alexander Orlov, who had been transferred to Spain to hunt down and execute Stalin's Trotskyist enemies, eventually fell under suspicion himself. Orlov took note as his friends and colleagues began to disappear. When Orlov received orders to board a Soviet ship, he instead defected to Canada. He left a letter for Stalin, threatening to expose large numbers of Soviet spies working abroad if he was targeted.

Donald Maclean, unaware of Stalin's terror, continued to show up for his clandestine meetings. He was confused when his handlers, week after week, failed to appear. Finally, an attractive dark haired woman, code named NORMA, met him with the agreed upon recognition signal. Donald was issued a new code name, LYRIC, alluding to his love of poetry.

NORMA's real name was Kitty Harris. A Canadian child of Polish immigrants, Kitty was older than Donald, with a solid working class background. She had worked in a cigar factory, then later as a seamstress in a clothing factory in Winnipeg. Kitty came to the Communist Party through her association with the labour union. She was married to Earl Browder, who would go on to become the Secretary of the Communist Party of the United States (their marriage was likely invalid; Browder already had a wife and child living in Russia). Grigori Grafpen, the current Soviet Rezident, had pulled Kitty from Shanghai, China, where she had been working as a courier for her husband, to come to London. Grafpen felt that a woman meeting with Donald one or twice a week would arouse less suspicion than a man. A meeting of two men, after all, looked like business. A meeting between a man and a woman just looked like a date.

Somehow, Grafpen did not predict the most natural consequence of two good looking people spending a great deal of time together. Donald, lonely and isolated in all of his secrets, fell in love with the woman who shared them. Against all KGB rules, they began a passionate love affair.

In September 1938, Maclean's hard work at the Foreign Office earned him a promotion. He was appointed Third Secretary at the British Embassy in Paris. Donald's advancement was good news for the KGB, too. He would presumably continue to produce huge volumes of documents, but would have access to more important files. Still enthralled with his Soviet handler, Donald asked that Kitty be transferred to Paris as well. In an unusual move, his request was approved.

Deutsch, before his recall to Moscow, had originally planned for John Cairncross to replace Donald Maclean as First Secretary of the Western Department. After his numerous failures though, Cairncross was instead transferred to the Central Department, which oversaw Germany. At first blush, the new position appeared to be a better fit for him, as a German speaker with knowledge of the culture. Cairncross, still naïve to the ways of government, may have thought he would be in a better position to influence British policy on Germany, which was quickly overtaking Spain as the top priority. The Soviets would have appreciated more inside information, as their old nemesis, Germany, threatened to expand further east. Unfortunately for Moscow, Cairncross was out of KGB contact after the recall of Deutsch. He was also about to lose his position in the Central Department. Cairncross, passionately opposed to Chamberlain's strategy of appeasement, found it impossible to keep his feelings to himself. His outspokenness began to create the same workplace issues that had dogged him at the Western Department. Having exhausted the patience of the staff at the Foreign Office, he was transferred to the Treasury Department in December 1938.

Soviet leader, Joseph Stalin, chose an unfortunate time to liquidate his spy network. A resurgent Germany threatened the safety of the Soviet Union, and the major European powers were so far unwilling to stop them. Adolph Hitler had already annexed Austria in March, and was now eyeing the Sudetenland of Czechoslovakia, a mountainous region where most of the population was composed of ethnic Germans. After the horrors of the Great War, in which Great Britain suffered 880,000 deaths, and France a staggering 1.4 million, the British and the French were desperate to avoid another war with Germany. Adolph Hitler, on a mission to lead Nazi Germany to world domination, gladly exploited their vulnerabilities.

Despite the tumult in the Soviet intelligence network, Guy Burgess and Donald Maclean continued to collect intelligence during the flurry of communications between Great Britain, France and Germany during 1938. Donald Maclean was the only spy who was able to maintain consistent contact with Moscow Centre, once he reached Paris. He saw nearly every official communique which passed through the British Embassy, and he maintained his usual industrious pace, sharing volumes of documents with Kitty during their romantic trysts at her apartment.

Donald Maclean was, and would remain, the most productive London agent for Soviet intelligence. It was a lonely life, though, and not without consequences. While on the train in Paris, Maclean was recognised by his old friend, James Klugmann, who was working for the French Comintern. Maclean, who had known Klugmann since their schoolboy days at Gresham's, became immersed in his newspaper and refused to converse with the friend who had led him to communism in the first place. Given Klugmann's role in the recruitment of John Cairncross, it is not clear whether or not Klugmann knew of Maclean's espionage work. It is clear, however, that Maclean was worried enough about his own exposure that he felt he could not engage with one of his oldest friends.

In the absence of a consistent Soviet handler, Burgess took it upon himself to recruit more agents. He set his sights on his old friend, Goronwy Rees, now editor of *The Spectator*, as well as a fellow at All Souls College, Oxford. Rees had written a book review for *The Spectator* in which he expressed sympathy for the Welsh, who were suffering from mass unemployment. Rees expressed an understanding for those who might turn to communism under such dire circumstances. Reading the article, Guy's ears perked up. He saw an opportunity to bring in Rees as an agent, preferably a talent spotter, like Anthony Blunt. Perhaps Rees could help to build a secret spy ring at Oxford, much like the one that Deutsch had cultivated at Cambridge.

Burgess began, over a bottle of whiskey at Rees' flat, by praising his article for getting straight to the point. Burgess then solemnly confessed that he had been working as a secret agent since leaving Cambridge. Rees claimed, for the rest of his life, that he had never agreed to work for the Soviets. However, it was revealed in 1999 by author, Christopher Andrew, and former KGB archivist, Vasili Mitrokhin that Rees had, in fact, been taken on as an agent. A file on Rees was kept in the KGB archives. He was issued two code names, FLEET and GROSS. Though the Centre held high hopes for a potential Oxford spy ring, evidence of such a cell at Oxford has not yet materialised.[1]

Due to his French connections, Guy Burgess was used as a back channel for communications leading up to the 1938 Munich Summit. Unfortunately, he, like Cairncross, was cut off from Moscow due to the liquidation of the London Rezidentura. While on holiday with Anthony Blunt in France, Burgess tried, unsuccessfully, to make contact with the Centre through the Paris Rezidentura. He eventually crossed into Spain and transmitted his messages through the Spanish Rezident, Leonid Eitingon.

Guy Burgess, as part of his job at the BBC, had the opportunity to meet Winston Churchill during this period. He drove to Churchill's home to persuade him not to cancel his scheduled radio appearance in an upcoming series on the Mediterranean. The two men talked for hours, bonding over their common opposition to Chamberlain's appeasement policy toward Germany. The October afternoon was a personal highlight in Guy's career.[2]

As Germany initiated low-level hostilities in Czechoslovakia in mid-September, Hungary aggressively moved troops to its own border with Czechoslovakia, as did Poland. As tensions heated up, the Soviet Union publicly declared its willingness to defend Czechoslovakia against Germany. In response to the crisis, an emergency summit between Great Britain, France, Germany and Italy was convened in Munich. The Soviet Union was not invited; nor, curiously, was Czechoslovakia. Instead of demanding that Germany pull its troops out of Czechoslovakia, France and Britain formally asked Czechoslovakia to cede the Sudeten territory to Germany.

Under pressure from the main European powers, Czechoslovakia acquiesced, and relinquished the mountainous Sudetenland, which had provided protection for hundreds of years, to Germany. Upon his return to London, Neville Chamberlain spoke triumphantly outside of 10 Downing Street:

> *My good friends, for the second time in history, a British Prime Minister has returned from Germany bringing peace with honour. I believe it is peace for our time.*[3]

Subsequently, in November, Czechoslovakia was forced to give up even more of its borderland territories to Poland and Hungary. Having occupied the Sudeten Mountains, which had served as its main obstacle, Germany effortlessly invaded Czechoslovakia in March 1939. Great Britain, in response to Germany's deceit, pledged to defend Poland in the event of a German invasion. The alliance was formalised on 6 April 1939.

Hitler's violation of the Munich agreement preceded a rapid deterioration of conditions in Europe. As German troops marched into Prague, Franco's forces overtook Madrid, effectively ending the Spanish Civil War. The following month, Italy invaded Albania. Great Britain, France, and the Soviet Union scrambled for ideas on how to contain the Nazi threat. Formal negotiations were scheduled to begin in June.

As the fascist powers overtook Europe, the espionage career of Guy Burgess rapidly advanced. In a stunning turn of events, Burgess was offered a full time posting with section D of MI6 in January 1939.

Created in 1938, Section D (for 'Destruction') was the sabotage wing of the Intelligence Service. Burgess was sought out for its propaganda operations, owing to his broadcasting experience with the BBC. He was instrumental in establishing the Joint Broadcasting Committee (JBC), which was created to play subversive messaging over the airwaves in Germany. In this capacity, Burgess acted as a liaison between Section D and the Ministry of Information, which gave him broad access to sensitive intelligence.

Meanwhile, Europe's major powers were failing to reach an agreement on the handling of Nazi Germany. Great Britain was reluctant to guarantee support for a two-pronged attack on Germany, as the Soviets wanted, and Poland refused to allow Soviet troops to march through their country to reach Germany.

As mutual distrust caused negotiations to break down, dashing hopes for an Anglo-Franco-Soviet alliance against Germany, the Soviets entered into secret talks with Germany. Both nations had been devastated by the Great War, and both needed to open trade with one another to advance their ambitions. On 19 August 1939, while ostensibly still participating in tripartite negotiations with France and Great Britain, the Soviets signed an economic agreement with Germany. Negotiations with the western powers were officially ended two days later. On 22 August, German Foreign Minister, Joachim von Ribbentrop, flew into Moscow to meet with Soviet Foreign Minister, Vyacheslav Molotov. The following day, an agreement was finalised. On 23 August, Molotov and Ribbentrop shocked the world by signing a ten year non-aggression pact between the Soviet Union and Germany.

For the non-communist fellow travellers on the left, the non-aggression pact was a deal breaker. They were not committed Marxists, they had simply joined forces with the communists in the fight against fascism. Now that the Soviets and the Nazis were on the same team, it made little sense to support them. The Molotov-Ribbentrop Pact, as it came to be known, destroyed the United Front.

As for members in the Communist Party, the decision was not so easy. Some, like Arthur Koestler, left the party in anger. Many more communists stayed, as they struggled to rationalise Stalin's volte-face. As the terror of the Great Purge was winding down, the alliance with Nazi Germany forced loyal communists to accept and explain another appalling Stalinist policy. The Cambridge spies were no exception.

When news of the pact reached Guy Burgess, he was on holiday in Cannes with Anthony Blunt. Anthony's first book, *Artistic Theory in Italy*, had recently been submitted for publication. Burgess was ordered by Section D to report to the London office immediately, cutting their trip short. Blunt and Burgess rushed to board the first ship back to London, leaving Guy's car behind at the dock. Burgess spent much of the trip rationalising the pact and blaming the British for negotiating in bad faith. Blunt followed his lead, agreeing with Burgess, as he always did.

Back in London, Burgess rushed to meet with his close friend, Goronwy Rees. Just as Guy had feared, Rees was horrified by the Nazi-Soviet pact, and eager to end his brief tenure as a Soviet agent. Rees told Burgess, in no uncertain terms, that he was done with communism, and he was done with Burgess, as well. Fearing that Rees would turn him in, Burgess attempted to reassure him. Carefully, Burgess urged Rees to forget the whole matter, and they wouldn't speak of it again. Rees was led to believe that Guy, also, was through with communism, and through with espionage.[4]

Nothing could be further from the truth.

From the embassy in Paris, Donald Maclean thought, like Burgess, that the Soviet Union was only protecting itself. He had seen most of the cables sent during the negotiations, and concluded that Britain and France had no serious intention to ally with the Soviets against Germany. This did not mean that Maclean was necessarily at peace with the Russo-German alliance. He was not at liberty to share his Soviet-approved position with his colleagues, but was also unable to express his real doubts about the pact to his lover and handler, Kitty. Maclean, so accustomed to living his double life, now watched helplessly as his divided loyalties split themselves once more. He coped as he always did; he threw himself into his work, then threw himself into drinking.

Meanwhile, Kim Philby was on a visit home to London. He was still working for *The Times* as a correspondent in Spain, and was planning to return, to report on the post-war reconstruction. When news broke of the pact, his employer immediately changed course. Kim was placed on standby to be sent to France instead. He would be a special correspondent to the British Expeditionary Forces, in the case of a possible war with Germany. Unlike Burgess, Philby was not ready to accept the new reality of a Russo-German alliance. He had begun his secret work to aid in the mission to defeat fascism, and now the Soviets were on the same team with them. When Philby met with his new handler, Anatoly Gorsky, he expressed his dismay and confusion over the non-aggression pact. He stopped short of breaking with the KGB completely, knowing full well the long reach of Stalin's henchmen. He instead packed up, waited for word on his new assignment, and skipped his next meeting with Gorsky.

John Cairncross suffered the deepest crisis of conscience. His singular motivation for spying was to thwart Hitler's ambitions. He was not an ideological Marxist, and harboured no illusions about a proletariat revolution in Great Britain. He had loudly and repeatedly protested the British appeasement of Hitler, at great cost to his career. Furthermore, he had placed himself at considerable risk by meeting with Deutsch. He now felt that his sacrifice was wasted, as the Soviet Union joined forces with their sworn enemy.

On 1 September 1939, Germany invaded Poland, setting the wheels in motion for the war that France and Great Britain had tried so hard to prevent. Making good on their promise to Poland, Great Britain declared war on Germany two days later, on 3 September. The Second World War had begun.

Another smaller, fateful event took place the same day. Kim Philby met an old friend, Flora Solomon, for tea. Solomon, a Zionist and activist, had spent the latter 1930s assisting refugee children from Central Europe. She had also been hired to improve working conditions for employees at Marks and Spencer, a major retailer. Philby so trusted Flora that he had attempted to recruit her for secret Comintern work in 1937, but she had refused.

When she met with Kim that September afternoon, Solomon brought with her a friend and co-worker, Aileen Furse, a floor detective from Marks and Spencer. Philby took an immediate liking to the slender blonde, and found her friendly and kind. She came from a good family, and though not well read, was smart in practical ways. She was not ideological, nor even politically astute, but she was open, loyal, and a good listener. Aileen appeared to be a nice match for the young journalist hoping to enter the intelligence service. Kim turned on the charm, and Aileen matched his energy with a ready smile. In a world of uncertainty, Kim and Aileen wasted no time in their pursuit of romance. Before long, they had moved into a flat together.

What Kim did not yet know was that Aileen, like he, had a few secrets. She was a deeply troubled soul, and was prone to serious bouts of depression. She had a history of self-harm and sometimes made herself sick in her desperate cries for help. Not much is known about her home life, except that her father was killed in the Great War when she was still a small child. On the recommendation of her doctor, she had recently moved out of her family home and applied for the job at Marks and Spencer. Her newfound independence, in her late twenties, seemed to lift her spirits quite a bit, but her struggles with mental illness were never far below the surface.

A month after meeting Aileen, Kim headed to France. He was sent by *The Times* on assignment to report on the British Expeditionary Force as they prepared for battle with the Germans. When Kim arrived at British Headquarters in Arras, in the north of France, he discovered that there wasn't much to report. Behind the scenes, the British and French were arming and preparing, but for the 158,000 British troops gathered at the Belgian border, it looked like a game of 'hurry up and wait'. With the Germans busy fighting Poland on the eastern front, the period of inactivity became known as the 'Bore War', the 'Sitzkreig', and, officially, the Phony War. It was a particularly challenging period for correspondents like Kim Philby. Even when there was something to report, the story was likely to be censored by the commanding officers.

Anthony Blunt, who had been inactive in the spy ring since leaving Cambridge, applied for a position with British Military Intelligence in September 1939. The War Office, overwhelmed with applications, sent not one, but two letters in response. One letter rejected his application, the other accepted him, asking him to report for training in Hampshire. His acceptance to Field Intelligence owed largely to his language skills, which were desperately in need. His rejection letter, which he ignored, was likely related to his communist associations. His avoidance backfired ten days into his training, when he was summoned to London for a meeting with

Brigadier Kevin Martin. Martin questioned Blunt extensively about his communist past at Cambridge, about his visit to Moscow, and about the many Marxist-themed articles he had written for *The Spectator*.[5]

Guy Burgess quickly intervened. Burgess sent his friend, Dennis Proctor, to visit Brigadier Martin the following day. Proctor, the Permanent Secretary of the Ministry of Power, knew Martin personally. He vouched for the integrity of Anthony Blunt, and dismissed his communist past as youthful dabbling in Marxism. Proctor, who had no idea of Blunt's (nor Burgess') clandestine activities, was nonetheless shamelessly deployed to advance them. The matter of Blunt's loyalty was put to rest and he returned to his intelligence training in Hampshire.

Anthony Blunt dutifully took detailed notes in his classes, which he then gave to Burgess, to pass on to the Centre. In December, Blunt was sent to Boulogne, France, to oversee Port Security for the British Expeditionary Forces. Most of his duties involved searching soldiers departing on leave, to make sure they were not carrying letters revealing strategic information. The work was not only tedious, it offered no useful intelligence that he could give to the Soviets. It appears that his commanding officers were still wary of him.

Meanwhile, in Paris, Donald Maclean, like Kim Philby, had found love.

When he wasn't attending the boring, protocol-ridden dinners associated with the embassy, Maclean enjoyed the Parisian cafes that were haunted by artists and writers. He liked to explore that now-buried side of his personality, which once wrote poetry and indulged in the sexual freedom of a glamorous counter culture. The bohemian atmosphere offered a release from the pressure of Maclean's two stressful jobs; working in the diplomacy wing of a nation at war, and transmitting staggering volumes of documents to their enemy.

On a cold December night in the last weeks of 1939, he spotted an attractive American woman in a dark café. Her name was Melinda Marling and she was studying French literature at the Sorbonne. She and her sister, Harriet, had rented a room at the Hotel Montana next door to the café. When war broke out in September, the embassy had advised Americans to return home, which Melinda's sister did. Melinda, revealing her hidden appetite for danger, did not. Their attraction was immediate, though they were perhaps unable to articulate why. Melinda admired Donald's intellect, but did not share his passion for politics. She was certainly drawn to his risky double life, though she could not have known about it when they met. Melinda had a somewhat rocky childhood, which had taught her strength and resilience. She represented a stability that Donald badly needed, having lived on the edge for some time now. Though Donald needed to have a secret life, he wasn't immune to the weight of his choices. The burden of keeping so many secrets wore on him and he needed someone with whom to share it. In yet another violation of KGB rules, Donald told Melinda about his clandestine work on behalf of the Soviet Union.

Donald's spy handler, Kitty Harris, realised that things were getting serious with Melinda when she spotted a woman's nightgown in Donald's apartment. Stung as she was by his rejection, Kitty continued to participate in their espionage work together, accepting that their love affair was over.

As 1939 came to a close, the New Year ushered in a resurgence of paranoia in London's Soviet Rezidentura, as the shock waves from the Great Purge continued to reverberate.

In 1937, an illegal KGB agent named Walter Krivitsky had defected after the assassination of his friend and fellow illegal, Ignace Reiss. Krivitsky fled his post in The Hague, taking refuge in France. In 1938, he moved to the United States, where he wrote a book about his career in Soviet intelligence, and the extent of Stalin's global spy network.

In January 1940, Krivitsky reluctantly travelled to London to be interviewed by MI5. Fearing his own assassination by the KGB, he refused a saccharine tablet for his tea, suspecting that it might be poison. Under questioning by agent Jane Archer, Krivitsky reported that the Soviets had a mole in Spain. Krivitsky did not know his name, but described him as a young British journalist reporting on the movements of Franco. He also claimed that an employee of the Foreign Office was working as a Soviet agent. Archer was unable to pin down the alleged turncoat, mainly because Krivitsky seems to have unintentionally conflated the biographical details of two, or possibly three, different individuals. The profile given from his faulty memory reads like a composite of Donald Maclean and John Cairncross, possibly with Guy Burgess sprinkled in. Krivitsky described a Scotsman of good family who had been educated at Eton and Oxford, an idealist who worked without pay. The mystery agent allegedly hung around artistic types, and occasionally wore a cape. Cairncross was a Scotsman working in the Foreign Office, though not from a prominent family. Maclean was a diplomat of Scottish descent, and did come from a notable family. Neither man attended Eton, though Guy Burgess had. None of the five had attended Oxford; perhaps Krivitsky had confused it with Cambridge, the other prestigious English University. None of the spies accepted direct payment for their services, though Burgess sometimes accepted reimbursement for expenses. Maclean enjoyed 'slumming' in the artist communities, but it had been a while since he had donned a cape.[6]

The lead was not pursued, because MI5 officers were busy following up with another spy on Krivitsky's list. He implicated a Foreign Office cipher clerk named John Herbert King, who confessed after interrogation. King was part of an entirely different spy ring, although he also had reported to Theodore Maly.

Lavrenty Beria, the newly installed head of the KGB, promptly shut down the London Rezidentura. Soviet intelligence had once again cut off contact with their top British agents, except for Donald Maclean, who was still in Paris. Kim Philby later claimed that he had stopped work during this period out of disgust for the non-aggression pact, but the records reflect that he attempted to re-establish connection later that year, through Donald Maclean.

As the Krivitsky drama played out in London, and Kim Philby waited for a shooting war to report on, Guy Burgess headed to France to set up a radio station for the purpose of broadcasting propaganda over the airwaves into Germany. While working for Section D of MI6, he continued to supply intelligence to MI5 on a freelance basis. On top of his already full schedule, Burgess maintained contact with Blunt, Philby, and Cairncross in the absence of a functioning Rezident. Cairncross, who had tried to break from Gorsky in the wake of the non-aggression pact, was contacted by Burgess. Burgess said he had friends in the German resistance who could use some information. Though Cairncross was now working in the Treasury, Burgess asked if Cairncross might invite some of his old Foreign Office colleagues to lunch and pick their brains a bit. If Cairncross did not realise, as he later claimed, that this information was really for the Soviets, he would have been very naïve, indeed.[7] John's handwritten notes about the meeting would later come back to incriminate him, when they were found in the apartment of Guy Burgess.

Meanwhile, seismic global events continued to move along at a rapid clip. Unbeknownst to the rest of the world, the Nazi-Soviet agreement included a secret provision, like an imperial relic of wars past. In exchange for an economic and military alliance, the Germans and Soviets negotiated agreed upon spheres of influence. In other words, the two dominant nations bargained for possession of the smaller nations of Eastern Europe and Scandinavia, in order to exploit their badly needed resources.

Two weeks after Germany invaded Poland from the west, the Soviet Red Army invaded from the east. Poland was divided between the two powers at the Curzon Line, as per the secret agreement. In November, the Soviets invaded Finland.

In the spring of 1940, the British and French discussed possibly intervening on behalf of Finland. They also began planning for operations in the caucuses, specifically with an eye toward Baku, the oil rich capital of Soviet Azerbaijan. It is widely believed, though never proven, that Donald Maclean, catching wind of the allied plan, notified the Soviets through Kitty.[8] Hoping to head off a confrontation over Baku, the Soviets pulled out of Finland in April. Later that same month, Nazi Germany invaded and occupied Denmark and Norway.

In a strange alignment of the fates, all five of the Cambridge spies were somehow led to France in May 1940, the most consequential month of the war thus far. Donald Maclean was at the embassy in Paris, still churning out reams of documents for Soviet intelligence; Kim Philby drank and caroused with the British soldiers at Arras; Guy Burgess was producing propaganda radio programs; and Anthony Blunt was checking passports in Boulogne. John Cairncross was on holiday in the south of France. Their old friend, James Klugmann, was also there, organising students for work in the Comintern.

At 4:35 am on the morning of 10 May 1940, three German Panzer tank divisions crossed the border at Luxembourg. At the same time in the Netherlands and in Belgium, the citizens were awakened by the plane engines of the German Luftwaffe, followed by the bombardment of major airfields. Allied forces were thus lured into Belgium to fight the Germans, while the Luftwaffe began the most aggressive bombing campaign to date in the Sedan region of France, and Panzer tanks made an unexpected push through the Ardennes. French and British forces in the north were now encircled by the Germans. By month's end, French forces were overwhelmed, and the British Expeditionary Forces were forced to retreat.

John Cairncross, his vacation interrupted by the Battle of France, rushed to the British Embassy in Paris to obtain a ferry ticket back to London. Upon his arrival, Cairncross found an embassy in disarray as the staff prepared to evacuate. He encountered his old colleague, Donald Maclean, who asked Cairncross to help him destroy documents in a fire in the courtyard.

Maclean also heard from Kim Philby during the chaotic retreat. Cut off from Moscow Centre, Philby reported to Maclean that he had important information to pass along. He was hoping Maclean could help him to reconnect with the London Rezidentura. Maclean spoke with Kitty Harris about Kim's request, which she then forwarded to the Centre. A full week later, Maclean received approval to give Philby a location and a password. Days later, Philby sailed back to London with the rest of the delegation of reporters from *The Times*. On his way out, Philby met Anthony Blunt at his post in Boulogne, which was overrun with British refugees fleeing the country.

In the final weeks before the surrender of France, Donald Maclean had desperately pleaded with Melinda to marry him. Melinda, though she adored Donald, wasn't sure. Though Donald's espionage was surely enough reason to give her pause, she was also concerned about his drinking. Her own father's alcoholism had led to the divorce of her parents, and Donald's frequent binges were hard to ignore, even at this early stage of their relationship. She saw for herself the toxic effect of Philip Toynbee, who had come to Paris on his honeymoon. To his new wife's annoyance, Philip spent much of the trip drinking with Donald. Melinda told Donald that she wanted to go home to America, to think about it, and talk it over with her family. Donald reminded her that if she left Europe now, as the war was starting, she might not be able to come back for a very long time. As the Germans marched closer to Paris, Melinda's decision was made for her; she discovered that she was pregnant.

On 10 June, when Donald should have been at the embassy ensuring a safe passage home for British subjects, he instead went to city hall to marry Melinda. They spent their first days as a married couple fleeing south to Bordeaux, where they boarded the HMS *Berkeley*, a naval destroyer, bound for the British Isles. Their whirlwind courtship, the dramatic first weeks of their marriage, and the shared secret of Donald's espionage forged a seemingly unbreakable bond between them.

Maclean's former lover and handler, Kitty Harris, took the rejection in her stride. She remained professional to the end, submitting a glowing report upon her return to Moscow. Donald Maclean had, since 1935, submitted enough stolen documents to fill 45 boxes containing 300 pages each.[9]

It was only the beginning.

Above left: Kim Philby gives a press conference, 1955. (Published in the United States; author unknown)

Above right: Donald Maclean, year unknown. (Published in 1968 by United Press International; public domain)

Guy Burgess, year unknown. (Published in 1968 by United Press International; public domain)

Above: John Cairncross, year and author unknown.

Left: Anthony Blunt, author and date unknown. (Courtesy of Bridgeman Images)

Trinity College, at Cambridge University. (Photo by Suicasmo – Own work, CC BY-SA 4.0, Wikimedia Commons, public domain)

Regent's Park, London, where Kim Philby, and later John Cairncross, were recruited as Soviet agents. (Malc McDonald, CC BY-SA 2.0, Wikimedia Commons, public domain)

St John Philby, Kim's father. Unknown author. Image from *The Heart of Arabia: A Record of Travel and Exploration* (London: Constable and Company, 1922) by H. St. J. B. Philby. (Public domain)

Britannia Royal Naval College (also known as Dartmouth), where young Guy Burgess attended school. (Photo by David Hawgood, CC BY-SA 2.0, Wikimedia Commons, public domain)

Eton College, where Guy Burgess attended school as a teenager. (Alwye – Own work, CC BY-SA 4.0, Wikimedia Commons, public domain)

KGB Headquarters in Moscow. (Rudolf Simon – Own work, CC BY-SA 3.0, Wikimedia Commons, public domain)

Left: General Francisco Franco, who became the leader of Spain at the end of the Spanish Civil War, *c.*1930. Author unknown. (Virtual Library of Defence)

Below left: Flora Solomon (nee Benenson), close friend of Kim Philby. Precise year unknown. Author unknown. Original image from *Baku to Baker Street: The memoirs of Flora Solomon* by Flora Solomon, 1984. (Public domain)

Below right: Clarissa Churchill (later Eden), *c.*1960. Close friend and possible fiancée of Guy Burgess. (Keystone Pictures USA – Keystone Press Agency, public domain)

Above left: Minister of Parliament Harold Nicolson, *c.*1939. Nicolson was a close friend, mentor, and probable lover of Guy Burgess. (Bassano Ltd., public domain)

Above right: Maurice Hankey, politician, former secretary of the War Cabinet, *c.*1934. John Cairncross served as his personal secretary from 1940–1942. (Bassano Ltd., public domain)

Wormwood Scrubs Prison, which was taken over by the war department during the Second World War. The prisoners were relocated, and MI5 was housed there from 1939 to 1940. Anthony Blunt worked there briefly. (Chmee2 – Own work, CC BY-SA 3.0, Wikimedia Commons, public domain)

Left: Illegal Soviet agent-turned-defector Walter Krivitsky, *c*.1930. Krivitsky's testimony revealed the first clues pointing to Donald Maclean. By unknown author. Image from *Book De GPOe op de Overtoom. Spionnen voor Moskou 1920–1940* (Amsterdam, 1989) by Igor Cornelissen. (Public domain)

Below: Bletchley Park, home to the Government Code and Cipher School (GC&S), where John Cairncross worked as a translator for the Allied code breaking project, ULTRA. (Outwivcamera – Own work, CC BY-SA 4.0, Wikimedia Commons, public domain)

The Broadway Buildings, former home of the British Secret Intelligence Service. (Dormskirk – Own work, CC BY-SA 3.0, Wikimedia Commons, public domain)

Stewart Menzies, right, shown here with his brother Keith, *c*.1914. Menzies later became head of the Secret Intelligence Service, where both Kim Philby and John Cairncross served under him. Author unknown. Image from *The Secret Life of Sir Stewart Graham Menzies* (Macmillan Publishing Co, New York, 1987) by Anthony Cave Brown, pp.338–9. (Public domain)

Above: Victor Rothschild, *c*.1973. Rothschild was deeply connected to the Cambridge spies, but was not an agent himself. (The Letcombe Laboratory Agricultural Research Council (1974), defunct since 1985. Letcombe Laboratory Annual Report for 1973. ISBN 0 9022 83 5; the photograph was released into the public domain in 1975)

Left: Portrait of Lavrentiy Beria, head of the KGB. Date Unknown. Author unknown, presumed official. (*Izvestia* (Известия), 29 March 1949, public domain)

Above left: British Embassy in Washington, DC, USA, *c*.1945. Donald Maclean was stationed here, as later were Kim Philby and Guy Burgess. (Gottscho-Schleisner Collection, Library of Congress; public domain)

Above right: James Jesus Angleton, date and author unknown. From the records of The US National Counterintelligence Centre. (Public domain)

Above left: German Abwehr officer and defector Erich Vermehren, date and author unknown. Commemorative plaque. *Vaterstädtische Blätter*, (1914/15) no.50, 12 September 1915, pp.202–204. (Public domain)

Above right: Author and journalist Graham Greene. Greene worked for Kim Philby at SIS during the Second World War where he also met John Cairncross, with whom he remained lifelong friends. Image from *S-F Magazine*, January 1963. (Public domain)

Arlington Hall, Virginia, home to American top secret Venona Project, 1940s. Author unknown. (Public domain)

Above left: Meredith Gardner, a principal codebreaker on the Venona Project. Date unknown. From the US National Security Agency. (Public domain)

Above right: Robert Lamphere, FBI agent working with Venona. Date and author unknown. From the US National Security Agency. (Public domain)

69 Dean St, the former home of the Gargoyle Club. (SpeedyCheetah66 – Own work, CC BY-SA 4.0, Wikimedia Commons, public domain)

Left: Wanted poster circulated after the disappearance of Guy Burgess and Donald Maclean. By the US Federal Bureau of Investigation. (Public domain)

Below: Burgess and Maclean's first Russian apartment in Kuybyshev (now Samara). (Apetrov09703 — Own work, CC BY-SA 4.0, Wikimedia Commons, public domain)

Right: Queen Elizabeth II, who employed Anthony Blunt as Surveyor of the Queen's Pictures, *c*.1953. (Associated Press, public domain)

Below: St George Hotel, Beirut, *c*.1950. Notorious hangout of journalists, spies, and Kim Philby. (Willem van de Poll, Wikimedia Commons, public domain)

Soviet defector Vladimir Petrov, 1954. Australian Security Intelligence Organisation. (Public domain)

Philby stamp.

Chapter Nine

The Unholy Alliance
Alone in the War, Surviving the Blitz

Once the stagnation of the Phony War was shattered by the German lightning attack on France, Great Britain suddenly found itself in a full-blown shooting war. Making matters worse, they were now fighting without their ally, France, now seeking armistice with the Germans. Anticipating a German invasion of England, newly elected prime minister, Winston Churchill, imposed a state of siege. He stood before parliament, giving perhaps the most stirring speech of his career. He laid out the stakes for the coming fight, encouraging his people to stand fast against the Nazi threat:

> *Hitler knows that he will have to break us in this Island, or lose the war. If we can stand up to him, all Europe may be free and the life of the world may move forward into broad, sunlit uplands. But if we fail, then the whole world, including the United States, including all that we have known and cared for will sink into the abyss of a new Dark Age, made more sinister, and perhaps more protracted, by the lights of perverted science. Let us therefore brace ourselves to our duties, and so bear ourselves that, if the British Empire and its Commonwealth last for a thousand years, men will still say, 'This was their finest hour'.*[1]

The Soviet Union was still allied with Germany, and was therefore, if not the enemy, at least a hostile neutral. There was no way of knowing how many British secrets, gleaned from the London spy network, might be passed from the Soviets to the Nazis. The Cambridge Five were now, undeniably, in a state of treason.

Their secret lives did not stop them from gaining access to classified material. Employment security screenings, historically lax, became practically non-existent when the war started. British Intelligence Services, rapidly expanding to meet wartime demands, were in urgent need of competent personnel. Guy Burgess, already employed by Section D of MI6, was perfectly situated to help his fellow spies enter the world of British intelligence.

Victor Rothschild, Guy's old friend from Cambridge, had been working for MI5 for about six months when he recommended Anthony Blunt to Guy Liddell, the new head of MI5's B Division. It is not known whether Rothschild was prompted by Burgess, but Blunt likely was. He rarely made such career moves without Guy's encouragement. In any case, when the meeting was set up, Liddell was impressed enough with Blunt to offer him a position in D Division, which handled military security.

At the same time, Guy Burgess was working on a job for Kim Philby. Burgess set up an interview with a veteran MI6 recruiter named Marjorie Maxse. After her first meeting with Philby, she ran his name through the Security Index, a database of people with criminal or otherwise problematic backgrounds. Philby's report came back marked with the letters 'NRA – nothing recorded against'. Whatever his previous communist, and later fascist, associations had been, he was not flagged as a security risk by any authority.[2]

This episode reveals the limitations of the Security Index, and indeed, the SIS hiring process itself. Like the Foreign Office, applicants were largely accepted on the basis of their references. It was sufficient for a few trusted people, known to MI6, to vouch for an applicant (in Philby's case, one of those 'trusted people' happened to be the Soviet agent Guy Burgess). The process of positive vetting was unheard of at the time. Interviews with former employers, classmates, friends, and professors would surely have revealed Kim's communist associations. A perusal of his published articles during the Spanish Civil War would have left the impression that Kim had fascist sympathies, as would his membership in the Anglo-German Fellowship. A look at the stamps on his passport would have reflected his time spent in Austria during their civil war. At the very least, a cursory check of public records would have revealed that, although he listed Aileen as his wife on his application, and Aileen had changed her last name to Philby, Kim was still legally married to the communist Litzi Friedmann.

Having been cleared for classified work, Maxse invited Philby for a second interview. This time, Burgess tagged along. With his good friend and fellow Soviet agent across the table from him, Philby answered Maxse's questions with confidence. He was offered the position with Section D and was ordered to report for duty to Guy Burgess.

Burgess was teaching at a seventeenth-century mansion called Brickendonbury Manor, located twenty miles north of London. The mansion was taken over by the War Office in order to house a training facility where foreigners could learn how to organise resistance groups and saboteur cells in their home countries. The school had actually been Guy's idea; one solid concept amid many half-baked schemes he had concocted.[3]

As Kim sailed through his security screening, his father, St John Philby, was busy failing his.[4] When the British declared war on Germany in September 1939, St John learned that he was being considered for appointment as Chief of British Counterespionage in the Middle East, due to his extensive experience and connections in the region. By November, the offer was withdrawn without explanation. The position was offered instead to Colonel Gerard de Gaury, his nearest professional rival. St John, insulted, departed for Saudi Arabia to visit his old friend, King Ibn Saud. He was alarmed to find de Gaury already there, laughing and sharing conspiratorial winks with the king. A bitter jealousy welled up in his stomach, and from that moment forward, St John engaged in a petulant vendetta, not only against de Gaury, but the British government that had rejected his services. He publicly told King Saud that the outlook for British victory looked bleak, and told him privately that he had turned down the counterintelligence job because Great Britain had refused to grant full independence to the Arabs. He spoke disparagingly of Great Britain in the king's palace, complaining that the current war was unnecessary and unwinnable, and that the British would never deliver on their promises made to the Arabs during the previous war. When a French diplomat overheard St John comparing Adolph Hitler, favourably, to Christ and Mohammed, it wasn't long before word reached Lord Halifax, the British Foreign Secretary.

Under new British wartime regulations, false or disloyal statements made by a British subject about their country or its government while abroad were prohibited. More immediately, St John's defeatist rhetoric in the ear of the Saudi king could jeopardise British access to Saudi oil, just when it was needed the most.

St John left Saudi Arabia for India in the summer of 1940 and was promptly arrested in Karachi as a security risk. Kim had only been working for MI6 for one month.

Shortly after Kim started his new job, Section D was absorbed into a new department, the Special Operations Executive (SOE). Prior to the outbreak of war, there existed three separate organisations doing similar work. Department EH, created by the Foreign Office after Hitler annexed Austria, handled propaganda operations. The War Office created a special unit called MI(R) to study sabotage and guerrilla warfare. MI6 created Section D in 1938, which specialised in both areas. In the summer of 1940, all three organisations were combined. Gladwyn Jebb, a civil servant from the Foreign Office, was appointed to direct the SOE. Jebb took the opportunity of the reorganisation to fire Guy Burgess, who had recently been arrested for driving drunk in a Foreign Office vehicle.[5]

Burgess, undaunted, went back to work for the BBC, where the Talks Department secured a military deferment for him.

Between his father and Guy Burgess, Kim Philby had some problematic associations that could have cost him his new position. Fortunately for Kim, he was uniquely qualified for the irregular mission of the SOE. In addition to propaganda and sabotage, an important SOE strategy involved the organising of underground resistance movements against the Nazis in European countries. These resistance movements would necessarily include leftist, and indeed communist, elements. Philby had experience and connections in these communities that were badly needed by the SOE. Furthermore, his journalistic work for the Anglo-German Alliance gave him some insight into the structure of the German government.

Philby was soon approached by Brigadier Colin Gubbins, the Chief of Operations for the SOE. Gubbins, a forward-thinking Scotsman of profound courage and creativity, personified the stated goals of the SOE. He had received the Military Cross for his rescue of the wounded in the Great War before surviving a gunshot wound to the neck, mustard gas, and trench fever. Afterward, Gubbins fought against the Bolsheviks in the Russian Civil War, and fought against the Irish Republican Army (IRA) in the Irish War of Independence. He developed a fascination with guerrilla warfare during these conflicts, which he then taught to the Czechs and Poles after their respective invasions by Germany.

Brigadier Gubbins summoned Philby to his Baker Street headquarters and asked him to write a paper outlining his proposed objectives for the SOE, specifically in the area of propaganda and subversion. In his brief proposal, Philby boldly asserted that the mission of SOE was incompatible with the goals of the Foreign Office, which, he claimed, wanted a return to the imperial status quo. The SOE should connect with revolutionaries and seek common cause against fascism. Once the fascist regimes were overthrown, Kim argued, there was no returning to the old European order.

Gubbins undoubtedly recognised the radical language and tone of Philby's essay, given his experience in the Soviet Union. Though he had seen things in the North Russia Campaign that had sown in him an unbending hostility to communism, Gubbins, like every good military officer, was a pragmatist. His priority was to undermine the Nazis by unconventional means. Labour unions, radicals and communists were the natural enemies of the fascists; it only made sense for the SOE to recruit them to rise up against their common enemy.

Gubbins not only approved the paper, he chose Philby to teach the principles of revolutionary warfare to SOE agents in training. Philby was given permission to visit Woburn Abbey, home to an ensemble of high level experts in the art of political warfare and deception. He received briefings from such legendary figures as Robert Bruce Lockhart, the former British envoy to Russia, who had been tried and convicted in absentia for plotting to kill Vladimir Lenin in 1918 (a charge that Lockhart denied). Lockhart would later go on to become Director-General of a new wartime agency, the Political Warfare Executive, where he maintained contact with Kim Philby.

Once he had received his high level training in propaganda, Philby was ready to educate the SOE's first generation of clandestine saboteurs. He was sent to Beaulieu, a charming village in Hampshire. Philby was placed at the German School, where he taught agents about the internal culture and organisational structure of agencies like the Gestapo. He also taught about the underground resistance movements in Germany, as well as techniques of whisper campaigns and disinformation.

As Kim Philby's career was finally gaining traction, Donald Maclean's was entering its first slump.

After escaping France just ahead of the invading Germans, Donald Maclean walked into to a Foreign Office crowded with displaced staffers returning from the Continent. Most of his colleagues from the Paris Embassy were reassigned to the French Department, newly created to manage Charles de Gaulle and the French government-in-exile. Due to his abandonment of the Paris Embassy during the evacuation, Maclean was excluded from participation in the French Department. He instead was assigned to the General Department, which was mainly concerned with obtaining supplies for the war effort, and with denying those materials to the Germans. Though the work was important, it could not compete with the drama he had left behind in Paris. He also became disengaged and depressed, because, like the other spies, he was now cut off from Moscow Centre. Maclean no longer had his secret work to look forward to; no smuggling of documents at the end of the day, no surreptitious meetings with mysterious foreigners, no smug satisfaction of a secret held close.

Meanwhile, the Battle of Britain had begun. The German Luftwaffe, which started off bombing supply ships in the English Channel as early as June, engaged in full-scale dogfighting with the Royal Air Force (RAF) by 10 July. In the world's first military battle conducted entirely by air forces, the Battle of Britain marked a milestone in warfare technology. The RAF mounted a strong defence against the Luftwaffe, and the German objective to destroy the RAF was a failure.

As the RAF fighter planes were battling the Luftwaffe, the RAF bomber command had been conducting small, sporadic raids on Germany since the invasion of France in May. In the late summer of 1940, they escalated their attacks. On 25 August, eighty-one bombers were sent on a large-scale air raid to strike industrial targets in Berlin. In the early days of strategic bombing, the accuracy was terrible. The jet stream, a wind current which carried falling bombs far from where they were dropped, was still an unknown factor. Compounding the problem, British air raids were conducted only at night, to avoid German anti-aircraft defences. On top of all this, a cloud cover over Berlin on the night of the 25th obscured what little visibility the pilots may have had. Residential areas were inevitably hit, and civilian casualties were suffered. In retaliation for the RAF bombing raids against Berlin, Hitler authorised air raids on British cities. A massive series of air raids on London, which became known as The Blitz, began on 7 September 1940.

Donald and Melinda Maclean were living in a room in the Mount Royal Hotel in London when the air raids started. The Mount Royal Hotel sustained sufficient structural damage in an early strike that it had to be evacuated. The Macleans then moved into a flat in Mecklenburgh Square near King's Cross, which also was soon bombed as residents took cover in a nearby shelter. After being forced out of their lodgings for a second time, both Donald and Melinda realised that the peril was real. For her own safety, and that of her unborn child, Melinda sailed home to New York.

Donald stayed behind. He spent his days on the important but tedious work in the War Office, and spent his nights on fire watch, standing on the roof of the Foreign Office to extinguish the fires from incendiary bombs. Without his wife, demoted to a junior position in the Foreign Office, and out of contact with Moscow, Donald Maclean was cut adrift from all that he held dear in the final months of 1940. When word reached him in December that his and Melinda's baby boy had arrived stillborn, he wept inconsolably. Despondent, Donald wrote to Moscow Centre, begging to be reinstated as an espionage agent.

After a brief stint in Moscow, Anatoly Gorsky returned to London to begin the process of reopening the Rezidentura and reactivating the scattered London spy network. He discovered, to his surprise, a spy ring that was largely running itself. He was amazed to find out that Guy Burgess had been doing much of the legwork in his absence, helping the other spies to secure employment in critical places, collecting their intelligence, and generally maintaining the network. Furthermore, he learned that Kim Philby, a full six years after his recruitment by Arnold Deutsch, had finally entered MI6, and Anthony Blunt, previously inactive, was now working for MI5.

Gorsky contacted John Cairncross, who, like Donald Maclean, had suffered a difficult year in 1940. John's older brother, Bill, died in June from wounds suffered in the devastating Battle of Dunkirk. John had to break the tragic news to his closest brother, Alec, before returning to Scotland for Bill's funeral. Soon after returning to London, John's new apartment in Dolphin Square was destroyed in the Blitz, forcing him to move in with Alec.

A lucky break, for both Cairncross and the KGB, emerged in December. John Cairncross was offered a position as private secretary to Lord Maurice Hankey, a minister without portfolio in Churchill's Cabinet. Lord Hankey, now in the twilight of his career, boasted a long and distinguished tenure in the government. He became Secretary of the Committee of Imperial Defence in 1912, a posting he held for twenty-six years. He simultaneously served as secretary of Great Britain's first War Council beginning in 1914, and continued serving through the War Cabinet's many incarnations until his retirement in 1938. His reprieve from public service was brief; Neville Chamberlain tapped him to sit on his newly organised War Cabinet in 1939. When Winston Churchill became prime minister in May 1940, Lord Hankey was removed from the War Cabinet, but stayed on in the General Cabinet. Though they often disagreed politically, Churchill had a great deal of respect for Hankey's experience, and Hankey remained influential in Churchill's decisions.

John Cairncross, despite his disagreement with Lord Hankey's prior support of Chamberlain's appeasement policy, liked Hankey as a person and enjoyed working in his office. Gorsky, of course, liked his access. As one of the more respected and influential cabinet ministers, Hankey was consulted on many issues, particularly those concerning the ongoing war. As his private secretary, Cairncross was able to listen in on phone calls and meetings, and to read all of Hankey's mail. Of prime importance to the KGB was Hankey's position as Chair of the Scientific Advisory Committee (SAC). The SAC, among other things, was tasked with exploring the possibility of atomic weapons.[6]

After connecting with John Cairncross, Anatoly Gorsky approached Anthony Blunt, which marked his first contact from the Rezidentura in three years. When Gorski caught up with Blunt at the end of 1940, he learned that he was now working for MI5 and had access to Military Intelligence files. Blunt offered to search for information on the Red Army. In January 1941, Blunt turned up with his biggest intelligence coup so far: a copy of the transcript from the debriefing of Walter Krivitsky, the Soviet defector whose testimony had triggered the closure of the London Rezidentura. On the strength of this gesture, trust was restored between Moscow and the Cambridge spies. Burgess, Philby, and Maclean were officially reinstated to their prolific espionage work for the KGB.

Personally and professionally, the Blitz had been as eventful for Anthony Blunt as it had for the rest of the Cambridge spies. Wormwood Scrubs, the prison commandeered for use by MI5, sustained a direct hit in September 1940. Half of the displaced staff were sent to Oxfordshire, and the rest, including Blunt, resettled at 58 St James Street.

Soon after the relocation, Tess Mayor, who worked with Victor Rothschild, returned home to find her flat destroyed by bombing. Rothschild offered Tess and her roommate, Patricia Rawdon-Smith, a lease on his property at 5 Bentinck Street. Patricia, who dated Anthony at Cambridge, and was the only woman that Anthony Blunt had ever slept with, invited Anthony to move into the lower rooms. Guy Burgess visited often, and eventually moved in, as well.

The house on Bentinck Street became something of a hot spot during the Blitz, due to its convenient location and its basement bomb shelter. The scene was often described as a nonstop party, interrupted only by air raid sirens, when everyone would pick up their cocktails and move down to the basement. The diverse ensemble of guests included politicians and society notables, as well as soldiers, sailors, artists, and journalists. Kim and Aileen Philby sometimes stopped by when Kim was in town. Donald Maclean, backsliding into his old bachelor ways in the absence of his wife, spent a few evenings at the house on Bentinck Street, drinking his sorrows away.[7] Goronwy Rees, Louis MacNeice, Malcolm Muggeridge, and John Strachey were frequent fixtures. Even John Cairncross once made an appearance, according to Jack Hewit.[8] Hewit had moved into the lower floor with Burgess, but was often displaced by Guy's *other* long term boyfriend, Peter Pollock. Burgess and Pollock had been in an on-again, off-again relationship since they met in 1936. When they were 'off', Hewit shared a room with Burgess. When Burgess and Pollock were 'on', Hewit simply moved across the hall to be with Anthony Blunt. Blunt and Hewit's affair continued until the end of the war, albeit sporadically. Burgess, while juggling two partners, somehow found time for a series of one-night stands.

Guy Burgess was keeping an impossible schedule. Between his espionage activities, his numerous boyfriends, his social life, and his drinking, something had to give. Problems began to surface right where one might expect – at his workplace, the BBC.

When Burgess was fired from MI6, management at the BBC agreed to request a military deferment on his behalf, based on the strength of his earlier work for them. The BBC's W. R. Baker, in his letter to the Ministry of Information, argued that radio programming was necessary to maintain the morale of the British people during wartime, and that the contribution by Burgess was essential to that effort.

Guy began on the production team for *Can I Help You?*, a program designed to guide listeners through the new issues arising during the ongoing war – food rationing, war gardens and the like. He invited Aileen Philby, now pregnant with Kim's first child, to speak on the air about community kitchens. He was also tasked with running a religious show called *Three Men and a Parson*.

Though Burgess was a talented producer, he was becoming increasingly difficult to work with. Unhappy with his salary, Burgess postponed the signing of his contract several times. First presented in January 1941, the contract wasn't finalised until April. His co-workers noticed that he was often intoxicated at work, and his supervisors were nonplussed with his increasingly defiant remarks. In late May 1941, after his secretary had accidentally taken home the key to his office, an inebriated Burgess made a terrible racket outside of the locked door. He yelled and pounded on the door, finally hitting it with a fire extinguisher in an attempt to break in. BBC security was summoned to investigate, and Burgess was later forced to apologise for his outburst, and for the damage inflicted upon his office door, the spent fire extinguisher, and the soaked hallway carpet.

Because the incident was his first offence of this kind, Burgess was not terminated from his employment at the BBC. On the contrary, he was soon promoted to European Liaison Officer.

Meanwhile, Kim Philby was pleased to be allowed back into his work for the Rezidentura. He now wanted desperately to get out of the SOE and back into the SIS, where he would once again have access to intelligence. In spite of his aptitude for teaching the dark arts of propaganda, his true calling was espionage. As Kim was trying to get himself out of Beaulieu and back to London, Kim's father, St John, was trying to get out of his own predicament.

After his arrest in India, St John Philby was shipped back to Liverpool and eventually detained in a camp for dissidents in Ascot. In February 1941, St John petitioned the government to release him from incarceration. His wife, Dora, and many of his friends in high places wrote letters of support. He appeared before a panel, where he rambled on about his disagreements with the British policies in the Middle East. They were persuaded less by his arguments than by his passion. The panel concluded that St John was intense, but harmless, and recommended his release. They did, however, confiscate his passport, which confined his verbal mischief to the British Isles.

Upon St John's release, he was contacted by Valentine Vivian, a long-time friend who had lobbied for his release. Vivian was now commanding the counterespionage unit of the SIS. He invited both St John and Kim to meet him for lunch at the East India Club. According to notes kept by Colonel Vivian, he was trying to assess Kim's suitability for the counterespionage unit. Based on his experience in the Spanish Civil War, Kim was recommended for the position by his friend, Tomás Harris, an art dealer whom Philby had met in Spain. Harris, now an agent with MI5, told his supervisor, Dick Brooman-White, that Philby would be a good fit in the new MI6 Iberian section. Brooman-White mentioned it to his boss, Dick White (no relation), who then mentioned Philby's name to Felix Cowgill, Head of Section V.

When Kim left to use the restroom, Vivian asked St John about Kim's communist associations at Cambridge. St John scoffed, waving off his concern. He assured Vivian that Kim had outgrown his radicalism long ago.

Having known St John since their days working together in India, Colonel Vivian felt that he could trust the judgement of an old family friend. There was more to the story than even St John knew, though. The head of SIS, Stewart Menzies, was interested in Kim Philby *because* of his communist past, not in spite of it. A Soviet representative from the KGB, General I. A. Chichayev was on his way to London. Menzies wanted to use Philby as a secret liaison to the Soviet Secret Service. Menzies hoped to use Philby to feed disinformation to the Soviets. Colonel Vivian, an expert in communism, was asked by Menzies to assess Philby for the position. The plan was so guarded, not even Felix Cowgill, Kim's future supervisor, would know.[9]

Valentine Vivian later gave Kim Philby his unqualified endorsement for employment in Section V of MI6. For the moment, however, Kim's appointment was shelved, as one of the most bizarre events in history unfolded.

On 10 May 1941, the third highest ranking officer of the Nazi Party piloted a Messerschmitt Bf 110 fighter plane into British airspace. Rudolf Hess, on an unauthorised diplomatic mission, flew in spirals over Scotland before ejecting and deploying his parachute. The plane, now unmanned, crashed a few miles away. Unbeknownst to Adolf Hitler, Hess was seeking a meeting with the Duke of Hamilton. Concerned about the two-front war that would result from the upcoming German invasion of the Soviet Union, Hess hoped to negotiate a peace treaty between Germany and Great Britain. Through Duke Douglas-Hamilton, Hess planned to speak with King George

VI. When Hitler learned of Hess' grandiose plans, he became enraged. As for Rudolf Hess, he was captured and detained as a prisoner of war. In 1945, he was convicted of war crimes at Nuremberg and spent the remainder of his life at Berlin's Spandau Prison.

Kim Philby learned of the Hess incident from his friend, Tom Dupree, deputy chief of the Foreign Office Press Department. Philby immediately notified the Rezidentura, which cabled Moscow Centre on 14 May.

Donald Maclean, relieved to be back in the spy game, also had pressing information to share. Though he wasn't at the centre of the action anymore, Maclean still saw the weekly intelligence briefings at the Foreign Office, as well as many of the individual communiques. In particular, he had seen a cable referring to a conversation between Adolf Hitler and Prince Regent Paul of Yugoslavia. In March 1941, while Hitler was trying to persuade Yugoslavia to join the Axis, he revealed to Prince Paul his plans to invade the Soviet Union. The tip was backed up with an intelligence report from MI6 on German military plans. Maclean was anxious to warn Moscow of the impending invasion.[10] Still near the height of his paranoia, Joseph Stalin refused to heed the warning.

Stalin also ignored the same information from other sources. Due to the breaking of coded German cables, the British government had knowledge of German plans as early as August 1940, and had actually passed that information to the Soviet Union. Stalin dismissed the reports as British disinformation. Soviet agent Richard Sorge, working in Japan, gave Stalin the planned date of the invasion. Mao Zedong passed along news from one of his own spies, who had attended a dinner where a German military attaché described plans for the operation. American intelligence, too, warned of a German attack.[11] Stalin remained unconcerned.

It wasn't that he trusted Hitler. To the contrary, Stalin expected an eventual attack by Germany. Tensions were already rising over their agreed upon spheres of influence. Stalin simply didn't believe that Hitler would be foolish enough to open a second front in the east, while still fighting the British in the west.

In the early morning of 22 June 1941, the Luftwaffe began bombing major cities in the Soviet zone of Poland, before moving on to Kronstadt, near Leningrad. The entire front of the Red Army defence was assaulted by artillery units, as German Wehrmacht troops crossed the border into the Soviet Union, flanked by Finnish and Romanian platoons. Foreign Minister

Joachim von Ribbentrop announced the German declaration of war against the Soviet Union. At noon, Soviet Foreign Minister, Vyacheslav Molotov, took to the airwaves to denounce the surprise attack and to rally the Soviets to the Great Patriotic War against Nazi Germany and the Axis powers.

On 12 July 1941, Vyacheslav Molotov met with the British Ambassador to the Soviet Union, Stafford Cripps. They signed the Anglo-Soviet Agreement, forming a military alliance against Germany and the Axis powers.

For the Cambridge Five, the alliance between Great Britain and the Soviet Union made their work, and their ideology, much less complicated.

Chapter Ten

The Great Patriotic War
Fighting the Common Enemy

For Kim Philby, the dramatic collapse of the Nazi-Soviet pact brought his work for the KGB back in line with his own ideology. He could once again be both a communist and an anti-fascist. As an added bonus, the alliance between Great Britain and the Soviet Union transformed his treasonous leaks to the enemy into helpful information for an ally – at least, in the mind of Kim Philby.

More good news arrived in the autumn of 1941. Philby was hired on to Section V of the SIS, which was responsible for counterintelligence. He arrived at War Station XB, where he signed the Official Secrets Act. Like many wartime agencies, Section V had been relocated to a country estate outside of London, mainly to protect it from destruction during the Blitz. War Station XB was set up in a mansion called Glenalmond, located in St Albans, about thirty miles from London.

Philby reported to Felix Cowgill, Head of section V. Cowgill came to MI6 from the Indian Imperial Police, where he had extensive experience with intelligence work, as well as counterterrorism. Later in life, Kim spoke of Cowgill with a sneering condescension,[1] but while he was at War Station XB, Philby worked hard to win his friendship and trust. He became an important deputy to Cowgill, who grew to depend on him. Kim and Aileen would often get together socially with Felix and his wife, Mary, during their time at St Albans, and the couples enjoyed each other's company.

One responsibility of Section V was to analyse a trove of decrypted German cables, collectively referred to as ULTRA. In January 1940, the Government Code and Cypher School (GC and CS) at Bletchley Park made the first break in the supposedly unbreakable German Enigma code. They began decoding communications from the Luftwaffe, before moving on to the German Navy, then the Wehrmacht, and finally the Abwehr, Germany's military intelligence service.

The German cables decoded at Bletchley made possible the celebrated counterespionage project, Operation Double Cross, or XX, run by MI5. In a poorly planned espionage endeavour, the Abwehr sent about two dozen agents into Great Britain to gather intelligence and commit sabotage. Unlike the elite cadre of Soviet agents in London, the spies sent by Germany had little training and spoke poor English. They weren't even German; most of the agents came from Eastern Europe, and thus lacked any national or ideological commitment to their German masters. Through intelligence gathered at Bletchley, every single German agent was identified, and all were captured except one, who committed suicide. Some were imprisoned or executed, but most, with no real loyalty to Germany, were amenable to a compromise. When offered a deal to work for British Intelligence, they took it. These spies were turned as double agents, and were used to pass disinformation back to the Germans.

Despite the unprecedented success of Double Cross, there existed a cultural divide between MI5 and MI6. The staff of MI5, a domestic security service, was largely made up of former police officers. MI6, on the other hand, was overwhelmingly dominated by graduates of Cambridge and Oxford. The law enforcement background of MI5's workforce often clashed with the exclusive clique at MI6. An environment of distrust and competition led to secrecy, and breakdowns in communication between the two agencies were common. Felix Cowgill, especially, had doubts about the security of MI5, and their ability to protect sensitive intelligence. He controlled the flow of information from Bletchley, and passed the intelligence to MI5 only on a 'need to know' basis. Cowgill, of course, decided which information MI5 needed to know.

Based on his experience with Spain and his knowledge of its politics, Philby was appointed head of the new Subsection VD, which administered the Iberian Peninsula. Geopolitical events had necessitated the creation of a new team to manage the growing espionage industry flourishing in the region. Franco's Nationalist forces had won power in the Spanish Civil War, but Spain was now devastated. Unable to risk a British invasion in the current war, Franco chose to declare neutrality, rather than form an alliance with Germany. Though officially neutral, Franco was very accommodating to his fascist patrons, Germany and Italy, who had helped him to win his civil war. Franco allowed the German military intelligence service, the Abwehr, to operate freely in Spain. Conversely, Spain's neighbour, Portugal, also neutral, maintained friendly relations with Great Britain. As in all wars, neutral states served as fertile ground for spies to do the dirty work of clandestine operations. The Iberian Peninsula, naturally, became a hotbed of espionage.

Philby's old schoolmate from Westminster, Tim Milne, was now working for him in Subsection VD. Milne's job was to analyse handwritten code, decrypted by Bletchley Park under a special section led by cryptologist Oliver Strachey. The handwritten messages were known collectively as ISOS (Intelligence Services Oliver Strachey). Milne's work on ISOS proved a tremendous help in understanding the Abwehr's operations in Spain. He also supervised author Graham Greene and journalist Malcolm Muggeridge. Nearly everyone described Philby as hardworking, dedicated, and affable.

In late 1941, Felix Cowgill was sent by Stewart Menzies to New York to set up an office at British Security Coordination (BSC), a liaison to facilitate communications between America's FBI and the British SIS, and to coordinate pro-British propaganda in the United States. Located on the 35th and 36th floors of the International Building in Rockefeller Centre, the BSC was listed on the marquee as the British Passport Office. In his absence, Cowgill left Kim Philby in charge at Section V.

Part of Cowgill's mission in the United States was to use intelligence gleaned from the ISOS decryptions to help persuade the United States to join in the war against Germany. Fortuitously (for Great Britain, anyway), Cowgill arrived on 7 December 1941 – the day Japan stunned Americans with a surprise attack on Pearl Harbour. The United States declared war on Japan, and days later, bound by the Tripartite Pact, Germany and Italy declared war on the United States.

Cowgill, most of his work now done for him, set about introducing Americans to the ISOS program, and to the information that it yielded. The need for an American intelligence service now made obvious, President Roosevelt asked William Donovan to set up an organisation modelled on the British SOE.

William J. 'Wild Bill' Donovan was a larger-than-life character with an unusual resume. After graduating from Columbia School of Law in the same class as President Roosevelt, Donovan went into private law practice, formed and led a Cavalry troop of the New York National Guard, fought against Pancho Villa at the US-Mexico border, received the Croix de Guerre and the Distinguished Service Cross during the Great War, served as US Attorney for Western New York, and spent his spare time travelling the world and studying the art of secret intelligence. His swashbuckling history and attitude dovetailed seamlessly with the 'anything goes' philosophy of the British SOE. Donovan envisioned an American version, which would combine the unorthodox methods of the SOE with the technology of the SIS. Working with British Intelligence Officer William Stephenson, Donovan proposed the Office of Strategic Services (OSS), which came into being on 13 June 1942. The first OSS agents arrived in London for training with the SOE later that month.

While Cowgill was in Washington, Kim Philby used the opportunity of his absence to access the Central Registry of the Secret Intelligence Service. The Central Registry was filled with source books, carefully researched binders of detailed information on places, history and people; in particular, agents and suspects. The Central Registry was located next door to Glenalmond, in another mansion called Prae Wood. Philby walked over to Prae Wood and chatted up the head of the registry, a gentleman named William Woodfield. They soon began meeting for drinks at the local pub to exchange office gossip or to talk politics. Philby perused the source books on agents in the Iberian Section, which was relevant to his work, but it was the source books on the Soviet Union that really caught his eye. Wanting to know about British operations in the Soviet Union, he checked out the two volumes and pored through them before returning them to the registry. A wave of panic rushed through Philby when Woodfield rang him a few days later. Woodfield was searching for the second volume of the source book on the Soviet Union, which had gone missing. He was calling because Kim had been the last to check it out. The proper procedure was for Woodfield to immediately notify SIS Chief Stuart Menzies, but Philby was able to stall him for a few days. The missing volume would have resulted in an investigation of Philby, which could easily have led to his exposure as a Soviet agent. Kim was saved when Woodfield's secretary remembered that she had recently consolidated the two volumes into one, in order to save space on the shelf.[2]

When Cowgill returned to his posting at St Albans in February 1942, Philby went back to the Iberian Section, where he had an important project in the works. The German Abwehr, from the shores in Spain, had been watching and counting British ships passing through the Strait of Gibraltar since the war began. They were there with Franco's permission, and the British knew about their activity. To keep Abwehr knowledge to a minimum, ships were advised to travel at night, or during daytime periods of low visibility, whenever possible. In September 1941, ISOS intelligence revealed an Abwehr plan called Operation Bodden. The Abwehr was building installations in Spain and Morocco with infrared equipment, in order to watch the ships at night. Now, they would be able to keep an accurate count of British ships entering and leaving the Mediterranean Sea.

Upon learning of Operation Bodden, Philby notified Menzies immediately, who then notified the Admiralty and the Foreign Office. John Godfrey, Head of Naval Intelligence, wanted the installations destroyed. Menzies disagreed. He feared that a provocation of Franco would lead to the expulsion of British nationals from Spain, depriving the British of a wealth of valuable intelligence. Philby submitted a paper to Cowgill outlining an alternative plan. He suggested that they embarrass Franco by exposing the Bodden Operation, revealing that Spain was not so neutral after all.[3] He also recommended implying they found out from some traitor in the Abwehr, to avoid the exposure of ISOS.

Cowgill was impressed by Philby's proposal and showed it to Menzies, who, in turn, presented the idea to the Foreign Office. In July, the British ambassador to Spain, Samuel Hoare, was sent to visit General Franco personally. He presented the evidence of what the Abwehr was doing, and protested loudly that Franco's accommodation of Nazi Germany on Spanish soil was a violation of international law.

The plan worked as intended. Franco rebuked Admiral Canaris, the head of the Abwehr. Canaris subsequently pulled the plug on Operation Bodden, and Philby won a great deal of recognition for his role in its disruption. It helped to clear the way for November's Operation Torch, a joint Anglo-American invasion of North Africa, which could not have been executed with German surveillance up and down the Strait of Gibraltar.

As his family grew (his daughter Josephine was born in late 1940, son John in 1941, followed by Dudley in 1942), Kim Philby continued to advance his career in the SIS. His responsibilities were expanded to include Italy, Sardinia, and the west and central Mediterranean islands. His team at Section VD was scoring major accomplishments. Through Tim Milne's work on ISOS, they had helped MI5 to identify and turn 130 German agents in Spain.

Philby's career as a spy was progressing nicely, too. As Menzie's secret liaison to the Soviets, Philby had an excuse to openly visit the Rezidentura in London, where he took the opportunity to divulge everything he knew.

Meanwhile, Guy Burgess was trying to wiggle his way into MI5. Anthony Blunt, now working as personal assistant to Guy Liddell, was in a position to help. Liddell was the head of MI5's B Division, the counterespionage unit. Blunt suggested to Liddell that Burgess be hired as an officer in the Security Service. Liddell was at first receptive to the idea, but a colleague named Jack Curry nixed the plan on account of Guy's well-known erratic behaviour. Burgess was, however, used by MI5 on a freelance basis. He was managed by his good friend, roommate, and fellow Soviet agent, Anthony Blunt. He was also supervised by Kemball Johnston, another Trinity alumnus. Just as Burgess had run Soviet agents during the closure of the London Rezidentura, he now ran two agents for the British Security Services.

The first was Eric Kessler, a press attaché for the Swiss Embassy. He provided valuable insight on the Germans from the vantage of neutral Switzerland. Burgess had known Kessler since 1938, when he was the London correspondent for the Swiss newspaper, *Neue Zurcher Zeutung*. As one of Guy's numerous boyfriends, Kessler had actually worked for him previously on behalf of the Soviets.[4] Now, Kessler's intelligence went to MI5, as well.

Burgess also recruited a Hungarian exile and former boyfriend named Andrew Revai. Revai was a London correspondent for the Hungarian newspaper *Pester Lloyd* and an activist within the Hungarian exile community. Burgess met him while working at the Ministry of Information, and had also previously used him as a source for the KGB.[5]

Meanwhile, Burgess tried his best to keep his steady boyfriends out of combat. He enlisted Peter Pollock to infiltrate the Hungarian exile community to watch for German agents, for which he drew a small fee from MI5. Despite Guy's best efforts, Pollock was eventually called up for military service, and was captured as a prisoner of war in March 1944.

Jack Hewit took on a more active role with MI5, working for Anthony Blunt on a project called Triplex, or XXX. Triplex involved the pilfering of material from inside the diplomatic pouches from neutral countries. Hewit's role was to seduce couriers on the train, and temporarily separate them from their diplomatic pouches.

In October 1942, the Rezidentura floated the idea of recruiting Dennis Proctor as a Soviet agent. Burgess had known Proctor since his time at Cambridge, where Proctor had been a fellow Apostle. Proctor had been a good friend to Burgess over the years; he had written a letter of reference for Guy when he first applied for a position at the BBC. When Anthony Blunt's communist past had surfaced in 1939, jeopardising his admission to Military Intelligence, it was Dennis Proctor, at Guy's request, who had vouched for Blunt's integrity. Proctor remained close to Burgess, and was a regular guest at the house on Bentinck Street. Proctor, who was now working at the Treasury, had trustingly given Burgess more information than he should have. Proctor never claimed to have been recruited by Burgess, but admitted he shared too much with him. It appears that recruitment was unnecessary; Proctor was already giving enough.

As Guy Burgess ran Anthony Blunt's casual agents for MI5, Blunt focused on cultivating British informants inside the foreign embassies of London. Using a local employment service as cover, he sent agents into the embassies to work as housekeepers and janitorial staff.

In 1942, Anthony Blunt's stuffy, by-the-book handler, Anatoly Gorsky, was replaced by the genial Boris Kreshin. Anthony got along much better with Kreshin than he had with Gorsky. Blunt, the once-reluctant talent spotter, had spent the past two years slowly wading deeper into full blown espionage, but the assignment of Kreshin as his new handler took his work to another level. Over the following two years, Blunt delivered documents at a rate he had never produced before. He stayed behind at lunch to rifle through his co-worker's desks, he searched the office files, and he listened in on every possible conversation between Dick White and Guy Liddell. Blunt took bi-weekly meetings with Leo Long, whom he himself had recruited at Cambridge. Long was now working at MI14, where he analysed decoded Enigma cables about German battle strategy. Blunt met with Kreshin once a week, around nine in the evening, with a stack of paperwork. Kreshin would take the pages to be photographed, and met with Anthony early the following morning to return them.

After he was stopped by a policeman one night while carrying some ISOS material, Blunt quit removing documents from the office. Though the patrolman could not have known what exactly the ISOS messages were, Blunt took the incident as a wake-up call. He began memorising documents, and staying up late at night writing reports on what he saw. In a major intelligence coup, Anthony revealed to the Soviets the top secret Operation Double Cross.

In January 1942, John Cairncross was called up for military service. His boss, Lord Hankey, intervened on his behalf to postpone his entering active duty until spring, when Hankey was scheduled to leave the government and would no longer need his services. In the meantime, Cairncross arranged a lunch with Colonel Freddie Nichols, Head of MI8, which was in charge of military communications and intercepts. From his work for Hankey, John had learned about a top secret program called the Government Code and Cypher School (GC & CS). Over lunch at the Traveller's Club, John made his case to Nichols that his skill set, particularly his command of the German language, would better serve the war effort in codebreaking, rather than in regular infantry. Nichols was convinced, and by August, Cairncross arrived at Bletchley Park with the rank of captain.

Due to the highly sensitive nature of the work, security at Bletchley Park was paramount. If the Germans found out that the British had cracked the Enigma code, they would change it, and the intelligence source would dry up forever. Or worse still, the Germans might begin sending cables with disinformation to misdirect the British. The workers were compartmentalised to limit the amount of intelligence any one person knew. They worked in small, prefabricated huts on the property of an old country mansion. Cairncross, a translator, was assigned to Hut Three. Raw decryptions in German were brought over from Hut Six, then John and his team would translate and edit the transcripts.

Upon his arrival, John was told that the Soviets had not been informed of the British breakthrough of the Enigma code. This was not the case; Churchill had authorised the sharing of information from Bletchley with the Soviets to help them fight the Germans on the eastern front. Cairncross first gave Gorsky a training manual on Enigma, and a guide for deciphering cables. He then began passing along German plans for military manoeuvres.

Cairncross enjoyed the work itself. It reminded him of the time he had spent at Cambridge, translating French and German literature. He worked alongside highly educated academics like himself, and was proud to be part of an intellectually challenging project. Unfortunately, there wasn't much opportunity for John to socialise with his new colleagues. The urgency of the project meant that the work was conducted at an intense pace. The translators were split up into three eight-hour shifts, which further isolated him from his co-workers inside of his own hut, after already being separated from personnel in the other huts.

Bletchley Park itself was not very picturesque, consisting of an ugly mansion surrounded by huts, and contained by fences and guards. It was located sixty miles north of London, and Cairncross usually took the train home to his London flat on his days off. During these breaks, he met with Gorsky and handed over raw decryptions in German, and occasionally, fully translated texts. During his work at Hut Three, the decryptions from Hut Six would be discarded on the floor after being translated. They were then gathered at the end of the shift to be burned, so they would not end up in the wrong hands. Cairncross found it easy to pick them up off the floor and stuff them into his trousers. He walked out with the documents and was never searched.

In May 1943, John Cairncross was informed by a delighted Anatoly Gorsky that some of the intelligence he provided led to a major success in an air strike, in which the Soviets had destroyed 600 German airplanes. This action led to decreased air support for German ground operations in the upcoming Battle of Kursk, the last major German offensive on the eastern front. The Battle of Kursk ended in victory for the Soviets, and Cairncross was later awarded the Red Army's Order of the Red Banner for his work at Bletchley Park.[6]

In spite of knowing that his work helped both the Soviets and the British in the war against Germany, John Cairncross was ready for a change. After barely a year at Bletchley, the erratic schedule and loneliness had taken its toll. The irregular shifts disrupted sleep and eye strain had begun to catch up to him. On his days off, John would sometimes sleep for twelve hours or more. He was encouraged by Gorsky to apply for a transfer to Bletchley's Diplomatic Section in London. Due to the importance of the decoding and translating work that he was doing, his request was denied.

As luck would have it, John Cairncross met Frederick Green, a former professor from Cambridge University, who was now employed as the liaison between Bletchley Park and Section V of MI6. Exploiting not only the Cambridge connection, but also the Scottish one (Green was a fellow Scotsman), Cairncross convinced Green of the necessity of a transfer based on health reasons. John's machinations riled not only the leadership at Bletchley, but also Gorsky, who offered to pay him £100 to stay on with the unit. The ULTRA decrypts were as important to the KGB as they were to the British military. Not to mention, they already had a very effective mole in Section V, Kim Philby.

Unfortunately for Gorsky and his superiors, Cairncross' attempts to get himself out of Bletchley resulted in his detachment from the unit, leaving him in a state of limbo for several weeks while he waited to learn of his next assignment. He couldn't return to Bletchley if he wanted to.

Fortunately for Cairncross, his Cambridge connection, Frederick Green, managed to secure a position for him at Section V of the SIS. He was assigned to the German Section, again due to his linguistic skills. He worked at St Albans under David Footman, the MI6 officer who had recruited Guy Burgess back in 1938. He rose at six every morning to take the train from London. The regular work hours and pleasant environment agreed with his health and temperament, though his espionage output was significantly reduced.

The type of work performed by Cairncross in the German Section was similar to the translation and analysis he had done at Bletchley Park, but was less urgent, and less consequential. It involved reading and translating intercepted cables from the Abwehr, as well the Gestapo and the SS. These cables contained important details on the names and locations of German spies working in Great Britain, but Cairncross didn't see these. The names of German agents were already removed from the messages by the decoders at Bletchley Park and passed on to MI5 for use in Operation Double Cross (the Soviets received most of this information from Anthony Blunt). Cairncross was left to interpret and record the general policies of the German Intelligence Agency, which was much less exciting. One of his extraneous office duties was to dispose of the documents when his team finished their work, which gave him the opportunity to smuggle them out of the office.

Cairncross met for lunch with Kim Philby only twice during his tenure at Section V, and they were once joined by Victor Rothschild. As it was in the Foreign Office when he worked with Donald Maclean, John didn't know that Philby was a Soviet agent, but Kim knew that John was. In an amusing episode in 1944, Cairncross gave his Soviet handler a letter addressed to the Foreign Office, written by Philby.[7]

Soon after arriving at Section V, John made friends with Philby's subordinate, Graham Greene. Greene and Cairncross were both riding the train to St Albans, and Greene, recognising him from the office, asked John about the book he was reading. Cairncross was actually reading one of Greene's own novels, *England Made Me*, published in 1935. Not realising who his fellow passenger was, John told Greene how much he was enjoying the book, to Greene's flattery and amusement. Cairncross went on to tell him that the author had written an even better book, *The Power and The Glory*. Greene agreed with John's assessment. Cairncross asked his new friend if he knew Graham Greene, at which point Greene confessed his identity, to John's surprise and delight. Thus began a friendship which lasted until Greene died, almost fifty years later.

In his personal memoir, John Cairncross described his move from Bletchley to MI6 as his attempt to escape his espionage work for the Soviets; indeed, he said that of every career transition during this period. However, he continued to meet with Gorsky, and later with his successor, Boris Kreshin, handing over intelligence week after week, and he was glad to have helped the Soviets with their victory in the Battle of Kursk.

As John Cairncross quietly basked in the triumph of his secret Soviet award, Anthony Blunt descended to one of the lowest points in his life. Whether due to exhaustion, heavy drinking, or simply the anxiety induced by keeping so many secrets, Anthony became very sick at the end of 1943. Already slender, Blunt soon lost enough weight to alarm his friends and colleagues. By spring of 1944, he was admitted to a Welsh nursing home to rest and recover.

Like John Cairncross, Kim Philby was about to make a new friend, too. In January 1944, an American OSS agent arrived in London to assist Norman Holmes Pearson in the X-2 counterespionage branch of the OSS. His name was James Jesus Angleton.

After failing his exams at Harvard Law, Angleton joined the US Army and became a specialist in military government. He was stationed in Michigan when he was first interviewed by a representative from the OSS, who claimed to see in him an aptitude for their special wartime work. In reality, James Jesus Angleton was recommended by his father, James Hugh Angleton, who was already serving with the OSS. As with St John and Kim Philby, it was the father who was more famous than the son (at first, anyway).

When Angleton arrived, MI6 and SOE had moved back to London, into the old Broadway Building on Ryder Street. Pearson's office was just down the hall from the office of Kim Philby. When the young Angleton met and got to know Philby, his reaction can best be described as hero worship. He was impressed with Philby's knowledge and experience, and sought to learn all that he could from his new mentor. He attended lectures given by Philby, and learned from him the organisational structure of the Intelligence Services. Angleton, along with his fellow apprentices, was given access to the ULTRA decryptions at Bletchley Park, as well as the Double Cross program, in which Philby was deeply involved. The 26-year-old James Angleton had previously felt aimless, unsure what he wanted to do with his life. His first exposure to the clandestine work of the SOE and MI6 immediately captured his imagination. Once he entered the world of secret intelligence, he never looked back. James Angleton had found his calling.[8]

It is difficult to know Philby's true feelings toward his American protégé. Whether Philby took a genuine liking to Angleton, or simply saw the potential to use the rising star for his own nefarious means, is hard to say. All that is known for certain is that the seeds of treachery were planted as their friendship began in 1944.

As James Angleton was training with the SOE, Kim Philby was trying to manage a developing situation of international intrigue. Erich Vermehren, a German Abwehr officer, and his wife, Elisabeth, had defected to Great Britain. The couple, long disaffected with the Nazi regime, saw their opportunity to escape when Erich was transferred to the Abwehr's Istanbul office. Erich approached Philby's friend and MI6 colleague, Nicholas Elliott, who was in charge of the SIS station in Istanbul. In a daring ruse, the Vermehrens, with Elliott's help, staged their own kidnapping while attending a party at the Spanish Embassy. They were spirited away to London via Algiers, then Morocco. German officials were not fooled for long, and the defection resulted in the arrests of the Vermehrens' family members. The Abwehr station in Istanbul was investigated and purged of disloyal officers. Adolf Hitler, already suspicious of the German intelligence organisation, ordered the entire Abwehr disbanded. The absence of a functioning intelligence service left Germany vulnerable, and was later blamed for the failure of German defences against the D-Day invasion later that year.

When the Vermehrens arrived in London in February 1944, they were debriefed in Kim Philby's apartment. In order to secure asylum in the United Kingdom, Erich Vermehren gave the British inside information about the growing opposition to Hitler within the Abwehr, up to and including its chief, Admiral Wilhelm Canaris.

The Vermehrens also gave MI6 information about the anti-Nazi movement within the bureaucracy of the German government. The Vermehrens were converts to Catholicism, and were part of a Catholic resistance movement in Germany, which hoped to build a new democratic government after the defeat of Adolph Hitler. The Vermehrens gave MI6 a list of the members of this Catholic underground, who were ready and willing to take part in the post-war reconstruction.

Kim Philby, who always considered himself an anti-fascist, proved himself to be a communist first. The Catholic resistance movement was not just anti-Nazi, it was also anti-communist. Communism itself was opposed to any religion, but particularly Christianity. Among Christians, the feeling was mutual. Additionally, the Soviet Union was fundamentally opposed to a democratic government in post-war Germany. Joseph Stalin had a reconstruction plan of his own. He hoped to implement a communist puppet regime under his control in a conquered Germany, and Christian democrats would have no place in his imagined Soviet satellite.

Though unclear on the precise details of Stalin's post war ambitions, MI6 knew enough to be wary. It was decided that the Vermehrens' list of Catholic resistance members would not be shared with the Soviets. Kim Philby, present for the interrogations, had other plans. Philby handed over every name to his Soviet handlers. The following year, when the British sought out these people, they were all found to be either missing or dead.[9]

As Kim Philby was sealing the fate of the Vermehrens' friends and family, he moved quickly to protect the safety of his own. Through intercepted ISOS messages, Philby learned of Germany's deadly new weapon: the V-2 rocket. As the world's first guided long-range missile, the V-2 threatened to repeat the carnage of the Blitz, without risking the loss of Luftwaffe planes, or their pilots. When Philby learned that the Germans were staging V-2 missiles in France, he worried for the safety of his young family. In violation of the National Secrets Act, he warned Aileen and his mother, Dora, of the danger, and sent his wife and three children to stay with St John in his mountain cottage in Wales.

By this time, Guy Burgess was wrapping up his career with the BBC. Following his usual behavioural pattern, Burgess had spent the previous year alternating between dazzling achievements and alcohol induced crashes. In addition to producing two shows aimed at assisting the audience with wartime difficulties, *Signpost* and *Can I Help You?*, he took over a third program, *The Week In Westminster*, a political talk show which featured journalists and politicians discussing current events and the agenda in parliament. Though he had received favourable performance reviews and a raise in salary, Burgess had a number of personality quirks that could irritate management and colleagues alike. He arrived hours late to the office, had terrible grooming habits, and often stunk of garlic. He insisted on engaging in petty disputes with management over things like expense reports and reimbursements for meals and taxi cabs. His alcoholism was never far below the surface. Still, his skilful handling of technical and editorial matters, as well as his legendary networking abilities, made his downside worth the trouble, as far as the BBC was concerned.

Burgess became so confident that he began to feature guests on his programs who preached very pro-Soviet messaging. These included not only Russophile politicians like MP Willie Gallagher and Ambassador Archibald Kerr, but also, incredibly, a Soviet Illegal named Ernst Henri, who was operating as an agent in London under journalistic cover. Burgess was attempting to expand his mission from intelligence gathering to influencing public opinion.

By January 1944, Burgess was ready for a change. With the help of his old friend, Harold Nicolson, Guy was able to arrange an interview with William Ridsdale at the news department of the Foreign Office. Now that the war had turned in the Allies' direction, Ridsdale was interested in formulating propaganda for the post-war period. With his extensive experience at the BBC, Section D of MI6, and the JBC, Guy was well qualified to take part. He was offered a posting at the News Department, and gave notice of his resignation from the BBC on 4 March 1944.

Donald Maclean was about to make a big career move, too. In April 1944, Maclean was appointed Second Secretary to the Embassy in the United States. He and Melinda, now pregnant again, sailed for Washington at the end of the month.

As the Cambridge spies managed their own career transitions, the ongoing war entered its turning point. Planning for a major allied offensive was underway. Code named Operation Overlord (later called D-Day), the Allies had a classified plan for the surprise invasion of German occupied France. The plan was so secret that even Joseph Stalin, who had been pushing the Allies for months to open a second front in the west, was not informed. In order to surprise the Germans, an elaborate system of deception was constructed in the lead up to the invasion, collectively known as Operation Bodyguard. Under the umbrella of Bodyguard, numerous deception plans were created, including Operation Fortitude. Like any secret military operation, MI5 and MI6 played an intrinsic role.

Anthony Blunt, upon returning to work after his illness, was moved from his job of analysing ULTRA decrypts to a less demanding assignment. He joined the planning group for Operation Fortitude. Blunt dutifully informed his handler, Boris Kreshin, of the planned Allied invasion a full two weeks before the landings at Normandy.

Kim Philby had a role in the success of Operation Fortitude, as well. With MI6 unaware of his backstabbing of the Vermehrens, Philby shared in the credit for the fallout from their defection. With Admiral Canaris under house arrest and the Abwehr dissolved, Germany had no functioning intelligence agency at the moment when one was most needed. Subsequently, British Intelligence was free to execute some of history's most audacious deceptions. A fake radio campaign suggested an impending attack on Norway, while dummy landing crafts were staged at Kent, just across the Strait of Dover from Calais, France. The Germans were led to believe that the Allies were preparing to strike at Calais, the location closest to the British Isles. The real invasion point was Normandy, over 200 miles away. Disinformation was leaked to the Germans insinuating that the invasion of France was planned for July, when in fact in would happen in June.

One of these agents, Juan Pujol Garcia, pulled off one of the most daring deception schemes of the war. Pujol Garcia, code named GARBO, had already been operating as a German double agent in Spain for several years. Working with MI5's Tomás Harris, a good friend of Kim Philby, agent GARBO had taken payment from the Germans to run a phantom spy ring in London, then gave false intelligence reports on the work of German agents who never actually existed. Having spent years establishing trust with the Germans, GARBO transmitted over 500 radio messages in the days leading up to Overlord, convincing the Germans that the impending invasion would strike at Calais, in early July.[10]

Because of his access to ISOS, Philby was able to monitor the GARBO operation, among others, in real time. More importantly, he could monitor the German reaction to them, in case adjustments to the plan were needed.

On 6 June 1944, under the command of US Army General Dwight D. Eisenhower, the first wave of allied divisions set off for France from twenty different departure points. One thousand bombers took flight before sunrise to assail German coastal defences, and by 6:30 am, the first 133,000 infantryman began storming the beaches at Normandy, a number that would grow to 850,000 by 30 June, nearly 1.5 million by the end of July, and 2 million by the end of August. Though the first day's objectives were not achieved, allied forces quickly recovered. A second invasion from the Mediterranean followed on 15 August, and Paris was liberated by the 25th. When German forces were forced to retreat across the Seine River five days later, the momentum had shifted in the Allies' favour, and Germany never recovered.

The summer of 1944 marked a turning point for the Cambridge Five, also.

Since their recruitment, the five spies had never been fully trusted by the KGB. They all began their espionage careers during the Great Purge, and had worked closely with controllers who were subsequently liquidated. The defection and devastating testimony of Walter Krivitsky forced the temporary closure of the London Rezidentura, and cast suspicion on all its agents. The Nazi-Soviet alliance tested the loyalty of every communist. Any spies who didn't get on board immediately, like Philby and Cairncross, were flagged as a problem.

In an ironic twist, the Cambridge spies were victims of their own success. No foreign agents had ever produced as much as they did, especially Donald Maclean. The more material the Cambridge spies handed over, the more suspicious the Centre became.

The naiveté, and sometimes incompetence, of the British Secret Intelligence Services fed the Centre's doubts. The case officers in Moscow found it unconscionable that the British intelligence agencies would hire anyone with a communist past. They were also incredulous with the sheer volume of documents being smuggled out of the offices. They simply could not believe the lack of security practised by the Foreign Office and the Intelligence Services.

Kim Philby, in particular, was doubted. During the war years, as Philby was transmitting important German military intelligence, the Centre was instead focused on finding penetration agents within the KGB. When Operation Double Cross came to light (thanks to Anthony Blunt), officers in Moscow became convinced that some of their own British agents were probably caught and turned for use as double agents against the Soviet

Union, just like the German spies had been. When Philby checked out the SIS Russian source book at Prae Wood, he was searching for double agents at the behest of his Soviet handlers. When he found nothing, the KGB took this as evidence that he, Kim Philby, must be the double agent.

In 1943, an employee of the Information Services of the Soviet Intelligence Directorate named Elena Modrzhinskaya[11] was ordered to investigate. Modrzhinskaya was a dedicated officer, committed to rooting out traitors within the ranks of the KGB. Like her superiors, she was alarmed by the number of documents submitted by the Cambridge spies. She also could not fathom that Kim Philby, with his communist past, not to mention his communist wife, would be hired by British Intelligence. She found it inconceivable that he, and his friends, could leave the office unnoticed with briefcases full of classified documents. Could their colleagues and supervisors be so foolish?

Instead of realising that yes, they were, Modrzhinskaya came to a more sinister conclusion. She was convinced that Philby, Burgess, Blunt, and Cairncross were all double agents planted by the SIS, and Donald Maclean was their unwitting patsy. In a novel theory, she posited that Kim's father and Guy's stepfather both had backgrounds in military intelligence, and therefore, their sons must have been planted *at Cambridge* to lie in wait for their recruitment by Arnold Deutsch. She asserted that all of their thousands of submitted documents must be disinformation from the treacherous British.

In a bureau where no employee was above suspicion, and alleged spies lurked around every corner, none of Modrzhinskaya's colleagues felt safe enough to challenge her theories. She was very certain of her conclusions, and had a rather forceful personality. The purge was still fresh in the minds of Soviet bureaucrats, and no one dared speak up to defend a suspected traitor, lest he cast suspicion on himself.

Her supervisors, likewise, were in a difficult position. They did not wish to be branded as spies, either. They wanted access to the wealth of intelligence provided by the Cambridge Five, but could not be fully certain of their loyalty. In a masterful strategy, the directorate went along with her hypothesis, but folded in their own brand of KGB doublethink. They concluded that, though there may be false information among the reams of documents submitted by the Cambridge spies, *some* of the intelligence turned over was probably true. Indeed, much of it had already proven reliable. The Cambridge spies would therefore be kept as agents, even if they were believed to be double agents, and would simply be monitored more closely.

By 1944, however, the Cambridge Five had finally established credibility, and proven themselves worthy of trust by the KGB. Anthony Blunt had told the Soviets about the planned D-Day invasion, many of the related deception schemes, and most of the agents involved. John Cairncross had contributed intelligence that was instrumental in the Red Army's victory in the Battle of Kursk. Guy Burgess, as challenging for the KGB as he was for the BBC, had nonetheless taken responsibility for running agents while the Rezidentura was closed. Kim Philby submitted documents about the limited cooperation between the British and Soviet Intelligence Services, which the Centre was able to independently corroborate. Most importantly, the ever-vigilant Elena Modrzhinskaya had finally retired from her job in Soviet intelligence.

In recognition of their service, the KGB offered lifetime pensions to their five best agents in London. None of the Cambridge spies accepted the generous offer of £1000 per year. It had nothing to do with principle; it would simply be impossible to hide that much money. Philby did accept a bonus of £100, and Cairncross graciously accepted £250. In light of their extensive work for the Soviet Union, the Centre stopped referring to them as 'interns', and began calling them 'athletes'. Unofficially, they became known in Moscow as 'The Magnificent Five'.

As the war headed toward an ever more certain victory for the Allies, the Cambridge Five prepared for their next moves.

Chapter Eleven

A Shift in Focus
New Horizons for the Magnificent Five

With a new mission and a new code name, HOMER, Donald Maclean set sail for America just before D-Day. When Donald and his pregnant wife Melinda arrived, it was nearly impossible to find family housing in Washington, DC. Luckily, his American wife had family in New York. Melinda stayed first with her mother and stepfather in their Park Avenue apartment. Donald, while working in Washington, stayed with friendly staffers from the embassy. He took the train to New York on weekends to be with Melinda. The arrangement, while inconvenient for a young couple starting a family, perfectly suited Donald's other purpose: spying for the Soviets. Anatoly Gorsky was scheduled to follow Maclean to America, leaving the London Rezidentura in the capable hands of Boris Kreshin. Gorsky's arrival was delayed, and he had as much trouble as Maclean did setting up housing in Washington. Donald was instructed to make contact with the existing handler in New York, Vladimir Pravdin. While ostensibly traveling to New York to spend time with his wife, and soon their new baby, Maclean was also meeting with his Soviet handler. His first meeting with Pravdin was on 25 June 1944. The Macleans welcomed their son, Fergus, in September 1944. Gorsky arrived in New York the same month.

By January, Maclean had managed to lease a home in Washington, and Melinda and little Fergus were finally able to join him. In April 1945, Maclean was promoted to First Secretary of the embassy, making him a rising star in the Foreign Office as well as in the KGB.

Back in London, Guy Burgess was making a fresh start, too. He began work at the Foreign Office in June 1944. The press office was an intimate environment, with only ten people led by William Ridsdale. One of his co-workers was Alan Maclean, the younger brother of fellow Cambridge spy, Donald Maclean. The role of the press office was to communicate the news of the day for the diplomatic world, and to issue statements of opinion on behalf of the Foreign Office. Ridsdale held several briefings a day for reporters from the major news services. Guy's job was to be a liaison to the foreign press, issuing statements and explaining official policies. He occasionally led a press conference, when no one else was available. Every morning the press office staff was briefed about the day's events, and about the Foreign Office's position regarding them. Burgess was able to see nearly every document and telegram passing through the Foreign Office.

Guy's colleagues described him as very intelligent, funny, and capable, but also dishevelled, malodourous, tardy in the morning, and drunk after lunch.[1] His deteriorating condition didn't slow down his real mission: spying for the Soviets. Burgess was eager to hustle, volunteering to work late, and to come in on Saturdays, when he could work alone. Grateful for the extra help, Ridsdale allowed Burgess to take documents home to work on them. With access to so much information, and the freedom to exploit it, he impressed the Centre with the volume and quality of information that he delivered. Burgess received a bonus of £250 for his productivity and for the value of what he brought forth.

Like his colleagues in the press office, Guy's handler, Boris Kreshin, noticed his increasing alcoholism and deteriorating condition. During one of their meetings at a local pub, Guy's briefcase popped open and a stack of documents and telegrams scattered on the floor, forcing him to scramble to gather them up.[2]

After D-Day, the threat of an ascendant Nazi Germany began to subside. As the staff at Section V was gradually downsized, John Cairncross was transferred to Section I of MI6, the political division. John was able to continue giving intelligence to the Soviets about the Germans, which included plans by Heinrich Himmler to create a secret Nazi resistance group against Hitler.[3]

Meanwhile, back at Section V, Kim Philby was engineering a coup of his own. As the danger of Nazi Germany began to ebb, the old fears of a Soviet threat bubbled once more to the surface. Section IX, a small department managing records on communism, had been largely dormant since the Anglo-Soviet alliance began in 1941. It would soon be reactivated and its agenda expanded. Section IX became the anti-Soviet counterintelligence unit, and John Curry, a retired MI5 officer, came over to MI6 temporarily to get it started. Once things were up and running at Section IX, it was only natural that Felix Cowgill, who had been hired on to MI6 in 1939 as an expert on communism, would take over its leadership. Philby, of course, was interested in heading Section IX. So was Moscow. The only thing standing in the way was Felix Cowgill.

In every workplace, there are petty rivalries and personality conflicts. Kim was clever enough to exploit the drama at SIS. After all, he couldn't count on such an important promotion if he pushed out Cowgill himself. Someone else would have to do it. Cowgill had enemies of his own, who were more than happy to participate in his downfall, however unwittingly. Valentine Vivian was one of them. In his memoir, Kim outlined a devious scheme to topple his own supervisor and friend.

Philby, on the pretext of post war intelligence planning, allegedly spoke with Colonel Vivian about improving relations between MI5 and MI6. Kim recommended a meeting with the sister agency, and suggested SIS staff officer Christopher Arnold-Foster. Vivian set up the meeting between Arnold-Foster and Guy Liddell, where Liddell complained repeatedly about Section V, and Felix Cowgill's lack of cooperation with MI5 (these complaints were no doubt encouraged by Anthony Blunt, Liddell's personal assistant). Arnold-Foster was left with the impression that Cowgill's leadership of Section IX, with his petty territorial disputes, might create a real problem in dealing with Soviet counterintelligence. Arnold-Foster, conveniently, occupied an office across the hall from Stewart Menzies, Head of SIS. He naturally shared the insights gained from his little talk with Liddell.[4]

Like many other stories told by Kim Philby, his own role was exaggerated. Liddell had been vexed with Cowgill's lack of cooperation for years, and Menzies had already fielded many complaints from inside the department. Though he was an intelligent man with good organisational skills, his personality sometimes made him hard to work with. It was easy for Menzies to compare Cowgill unfavourably with his deputy, Kim Philby, who was careful to maintain friendly relations with MI5, as well as with his colleagues in Section V. This isn't to say that Philby wasn't working to exacerbate these tensions. His friend, Graham Greene, noticed a change in Philby during this period, finding him a little too ambitious, and engaging in too much office intrigue.[5] Philby was certainly involved in a whisper campaign against Cowgill, it just wasn't as masterfully orchestrated as

Philby described, nor as consequential. Cowgill had been a thorn in the side of MI6 for quite a while, and was often his own worst enemy.

When Cowgill was informed by Vivian that Kim Philby had been promoted to head of Section IX, Cowgill was disappointed at being passed over in favour of his young lieutenant and, so he thought, his good friend. Stung by the betrayal, Cowgill soon tendered his resignation.

Kim's old friend, Tim Milne, was promoted to Cowgill's old job, Head of Section V. Graham Greene was offered Kim's former job, head of the Iberian Section. Now wary of Kim's intentions, Greene demurred. He left the SIS shortly thereafter.

Philby could not be more pleased with the promotion, nor could his Soviet controllers in the KGB. As head of the anti-Soviet unit, Kim went from simply sharing intelligence to actively sabotaging operations. Even better, Philby was appointed to a new committee, which was made up of the top five officers in the SIS, and was charged with reorganising the agency for peacetime. He now wielded considerable influence within MI6.

In the final months of the Second World War, another period of seismic realignments was on the horizon. Allied leaders met both publicly and privately to remake the world. As the British Empire graciously receded from her place as the dominant global superpower, a new, bipolar world order began to take shape. The United States, an ocean away and relatively untouched by the war's carnage, emerged as the world's economic and industrial powerhouse, and soon, as the world's first new superpower. The Soviet Union was determined to be the second.

Re-enacting an imperial ritual from a bygone age, Churchill and Stalin met, without Roosevelt, to divide the lesser powers in Europe into 'spheres of influence', spoils to be awarded to the victors. Stalin laid claim to Bulgaria, Churchill to Greece. In February 1945, President Roosevelt, Winston Churchill and Joseph Stalin travelled to the Crimean Peninsula to meet in a resort town called Yalta. Roosevelt and Churchill offered Stalin a portion of Manchuria in exchange for the Red Army's entry into the Pacific theatre. In a euphemistic phrasing, the nations of Eastern Europe, already occupied by the Red Army, would be 'friendly' to the Soviet Union when the war was over. In reality, the Soviet occupation would remain, long after the fall of Berlin. Included in these puppet states would be Poland, for whose sovereignty the British had entered the war in the first place.

Since 1932, Adolf Hitler had dodged no fewer than forty-two assassination attempts. On 30 April 1945, he finally died by his own hand, having shot himself in his underground bunker as the Red Army approached Berlin. Two days later, Berlin fell, and on 8 May, the Instrument of Surrender was signed by Field Marshall Wilhelm Keitel on behalf of the Third Reich. Germany was immediately subject to the de facto occupation by the Allies, and the Nazi German Empire ceased to exist.

As Europe began to dig out from the wreckage, Winston Churchill secretly commissioned a feasibility study called *Operation Unthinkable*, a contingency plan for a possible offensive war against the Soviet Union. The planners concluded that a British victory was not possible without help from the Americans, and the plan was shelved. Nonetheless, Guy Burgess somehow got wind of the project, and promptly told his handler, Boris Kreshin, all about it.[6]

On 17 July, the three world powers met again, this time in Potsdam, Germany, just outside of Berlin. President Roosevelt had died in April, and a new president, Harry S. Truman, now represented the United States. The occupation of Germany by the three major powers plus France, as well as the fateful four-way division of Berlin, was decided at the conference. President Truman, still naïve about some of the global dynamics, bragged to Stalin about a new and terrible weapon that would soon be used against Japan. He was referring to the atomic bomb, which was, up until now, still a secret.

On 6 August, the atomic bomb was dropped on Hiroshima. Four days later, Nagasaki was hit by a second atomic weapon, forcing Emperor Hirohito to announce Japan's surrender in a radio broadcast on 15 August. A formal instrument of unconditional surrender was signed by Hirohito on 2 September 1945.

John Cairncross and Anthony Blunt, the least enthusiastic of the Cambridge spies, began to pull away from their espionage work as the war came to a close. Anthony Blunt was demobilised from the army, and subsequently from MI5, in April 1945. He was offered the prestigious job of Surveyor of the King's Pictures. Blunt finally moved out of Guy Burgess' flat, and into a room at the Courtauld Institute of Art, a college of the University of London. Anthony, now Deputy Director of the Courtauld, had given lectures there since 1933.

Cairncross was asked to stay on with MI6, but declined the offer. He suspected that a long term career with the agency would lead eventually to a foreign posting, and a promotion would involve running agents. John was interested in neither, and so returned to work at the Treasury. He was tired of secret intelligence, both British and Soviet. It appeared that, for Blunt and Cairncross, their spying days were behind them.

In August 1945, Anthony Blunt embarked on a secret mission of a different kind. He was sent by King George VI to Friedrichshof Castle in Germany. The Allied forces had seized the opportunity to pillage Germany's treasures in its post-war wreckage. England's royal family hoped to recover some family treasures left behind by the deposed Kaiser Wilhelm and the rest of Queen Victoria's German descendants. The heirlooms would be held safe from the looters and returned when things were more stable, many years later. The expeditions were to be kept secret, lest the world think the royal family was simply joining in on the free-for-all.

On his first confidential trip, Blunt was tasked with finding the archive of the late German Empress Victoria, the mother of Kaiser Wilhelm and eldest daughter of Queen Victoria of England. Anthony was specifically seeking 4000 letters written by Queen Victoria to her daughter, which were now in the possession of Princess Margaret of Hesse, the youngest sister of Kaiser Wilhelm. Blunt succeeded in convincing Princess Margaret to allow the archive to be brought to Windsor Castle for safekeeping (the letters were returned in 1951).[7]

Anthony Blunt embarked on three subsequent missions over the following two years. He went to Westphalia that December, and with the help of his old spy recruit, Leo Long, he returned with the diamond crown of Queen Charlotte, the wife of King George III (it was not returned until 1963). A second trip was made to Westphalia in March 1946. In August 1947, Blunt visited the final home of Kaiser Wilhelm in the Netherlands, where he had been exiled after the First World War. The few objects recovered included a portrait of the Duke of Clarence and three diamond Garter Badges.

Meanwhile, Anthony Blunt was attempting to break away from the KGB. His double life, coupled with his responsibilities to the royal family and to the Courtauld Institute, were taking a toll on his health. Anthony had been hospitalised for exhaustion twice in 1945, and was hoping to pull away from at least one of his jobs.

To reassure the KGB of his loyalty, Blunt offered information concerning his old friend, James Klugmann. Klugmann had been assigned to the SOE station in Yugoslavia during the war, despite his openly communist past (his MI5 records were destroyed in the bombing of Wormwood Scrubs). Though Klugmann previously disdained espionage, he operated as a KGB talent spotter while working for the SOE in Yugoslavia. Blunt informed the London Rezidentura that Klugmann had somehow been exposed, and MI5 knew all about his work on behalf of the Soviets.[8] Anthony was granted a one year hiatus from espionage.

Anthony Blunt wasn't given a vacation due to the benevolence of the KGB. The autumn of 1945 forced all of the Cambridge spies into temporary exile. In the first week of September, just days after the surrender of Japan, two Soviet defectors came forward, from separate corners of the world, with potentially devastating information. The first emerged in Turkey.

On 4 September, the Soviet Vice Consul in Istanbul, Konstantin Volkov, walked into the British Consulate with his wife, asking to meet with his counterpart, British Vice Consul Chantry Hamilton Page. Through an interpreter, Volkov revealed that he was a KGB officer and wanted to defect. Volkov offered to expose 314 Soviet agents in Turkey, as well as 250 agents in the United Kingdom. Specifically, he offered to reveal the real names of two agents working in the British Foreign Office, and one agent working as the head of a British intelligence organisation. In return, Volkov requested £27,500 and asylum in Cyprus. He requested an answer within three weeks, or he would seek asylum elsewhere. Volkov insisted that his request not be sent by cable, which he claimed had been compromised. His plea for asylum was sent via diplomatic courier to London.

Stewart Menzies, Head of SIS, received word a few days later and promptly informed his head of Soviet counterespionage, Kim Philby. With great alarm, Philby immediately recognised the two employees of the Foreign Office as Guy Burgess and Donald Maclean. Even worse, he realised that the agent named as head of an intelligence service was, in fact, himself.[9]

Philby made haste to inform Boris Kreshin, his Soviet handler, of the crisis. Next, he interfered with Menzies' plan to send Douglas Roberts, head of security in the Middle East, to Istanbul to handle the particulars of Volkov's defection. Philby insisted on travelling to Istanbul himself, reminding Menzies of Roberts' fear of flying. Travel by ship, Philby helpfully noted, would eat up valuable time in this urgent situation. Philby had a meeting scheduled in Cairo, after which he could fly immediately into Istanbul. When Kim finally boarded his flight, a storm forced an unscheduled landing in Malta, which caused him to miss both his meeting and his flight from Cairo. The three week deadline, already tightened by the use of diplomatic courier instead of cable, rapidly raced to a close.[10]

By the time Philby arrived in Istanbul on 26 September, the exact expiration date of Volkov's three week deadline, Volkov was nowhere to be found. The British Vice Consul made a phone call to the Soviet Consulate, asking to speak with Volkov. He was informed that Volkov had gone home to Moscow.

It was later revealed that two KGB assassins, posing as diplomatic couriers, were issued visas from the Turkish Consulate the week prior. Volkov and his wife, Zoya, did indeed board a flight bound for Moscow. The sedated couple were loaded, on stretchers, onto a Soviet transporter plane, and were never heard from again.

While Philby's actions may have saved his cover for the moment, he was now on the radar of MI6. His bumbling incompetence was not only reason enough for discipline, it was wildly out of character for the overachieving intelligence officer. He was investigated for his failure in the botched defection, which likely cost the Volkovs their lives. Philby was able to demonstrate enough plausible deniability to clear him of discipline, but not enough to erase suspicion in the minds of his colleagues.

Meanwhile, on the other side of the world, a second defection was underway. On 5 September, just one day after Volkov first entered the British Consulate, an employee of the Soviet Embassy in Canada named Igor Gouzenko walked into the office of the *Ottawa Journal*, seeking asylum. Unlike Volkov, Gouzenko was not a high level diplomat, nor was he a KGB officer. He was simply a cipher clerk in the Soviet Rezidentura, fearful of his impending recall to Moscow. He had access to all of the coded cables sent to Canada from Moscow, and had been smuggling documents out of his office for months in preparation for his defection.

The night staff at the *Ottawa Journal* were unable to understand Gouzenko's English through his heavy Russian accent, and Gouzenko was forced to return home, frustrated. The following day, he brought his pregnant wife and toddler son to the Department of Justice, then to the office of the Minister of Justice, followed by the Canadian Crown Attorney's office, before finally securing a meeting with a police detective the following morning. That night, four Soviet Embassy security officers ransacked Gouzenko's apartment as the family cowered, terrified, in their neighbour's apartment across the hall. The police were summoned, and the Soviet home invaders were dispersed without triggering an international incident.

When Canadian officials finally decided to take Gouzenko seriously, they discovered that he had smuggled out evidence of a large Soviet spy ring operating in Canada, as well as a separate spy ring in the United States. William Stephenson, chief of the British Secret Service in the Americas, met with Gouzenko, who put forth two astonishing revelations. A British physicist named Alan Nunn May, code named ALEK, was a Soviet agent and had worked on the Manhattan project. Secondly, a Soviet agent code named ELLI was chief of counterespionage in London. Once again, Philby recognised himself.

Luckily for Philby, MI5 and MI6 were so preoccupied with the British physicist turned atomic spy, they didn't make the ELLI/Philby connection. To the contrary, Philby was actively involved in the investigation of Alan Nunn May (another Cambridge alumnus, though not recruited as a spy until 1940). Gouzenko's documents revealed an impending meeting between Nunn May and his Soviet contact in London, where British Intelligence hoped to catch him red-handed in the act of atomic espionage. Philby warned his own handler of the planned sting operation, and the meeting was cancelled.[11] Nonetheless, Alan Nunn May was eventually arrested and made a partial confession. He was later prosecuted and sentenced to ten years as the first convicted atomic spy.

Once again, Philby had narrowly eluded exposure.

In November 1945, Kim Philby notified his handler, Boris Kreshin, of yet another bombshell. Gouzenko's revelations about a spy ring in the United States had been corroborated by Elizabeth Bentley, an American spy runner under the control of Anatoly Gorsky. Bentley had decided to break with the KGB, and revealed to the FBI the names of 150 Soviet agents in the United States, including 37 employees of the federal government. Her list overlapped that of Gouzenko, as well as that of Whittaker Chambers, a member of the communist underground who had approached the government in 1939, inspired by the defection of Walter Krivitsky.

The Volkov and Gouzenko defections, as well as the Bentley testimony, sent shockwaves through the KGB, and all operations in London were ceased for one year. In order to protect Donald Maclean, their most valuable asset, all meetings with Anatoly Gorsky were cancelled. Gorsky, who noticed that he was being followed by FBI agents after meeting with Bentley, was recalled to Moscow.[12] Maclean, reading all of the cable traffic coming through the embassy, began to realise the danger that he was in.

Unbeknownst to the five Cambridge spies, they were in greater peril still. The wheels of their downfall had been set in motion, and it was already too late to pump the breaks.

The US Army Signals Intelligence Unit had been collecting Soviet cable traffic since 1939. Unfortunately, the messages were all encrypted. In 1943, Army intelligence officer Colonel Carter Clark enlisted the help of Gene Grabeel, a cryptanalyst with Signals Intelligence, to create a special department for the decoding of the Soviet cables. On 1 February 1943, the top secret project, code named Venona, was established at Arlington Hall, a former school for girls in Virginia.

The Soviets had double encoded their messages; first, with a general codebook, and again, using something called a one-time pad. Each letter in a message was substituted with a number, or a different letter. The recipient had to decode the message with a key, a page of characters with their substitute alphabet letter. Only two copies of the key existed: one for the sender, and one for the recipient. After decoding the message, the key was burned. Each key was used only once. The small number of encoded words, robbing code breakers of comparative material, made the codes virtually unbreakable.

After the surprise invasion by the Germans, the demand for messages increased sharply, and the supply of one-time pads was quickly used up. In the ensuing urgency, a printing press replicated 35,000 one-time pads. An opening was thus created for their possible decryption. The mistake was discovered at Arlington Hall in 1943, and the Venona team began breaking codes. The first decoded messages related to mundane issues of trade and supply. When the war ended in 1945, Venona continued.

In 1946, a gifted linguist named Meredith Gardner was hired on to the project. He taught himself Russian and got to work, separating the messages written in Russian from the messages written in English. Gardner was able to make the distinction by isolating the word 'the', an article which does not exist in the Russian language. On 31 July 1946, Gardner cracked the first KGB cable. It was sent from the Soviet Rezidentura in New York to KGB headquarters in Moscow in 1944 and concerned activity in Mexico.

A more shocking breakthrough came on 13 December 1946. The message, originally dated 2 December 1944, contained a list of scientists working on the top secret Manhattan Project.

As the team broke more cables, and Gardner began studying the code names given to places and people, it became clear that the Soviets were operating an extensive espionage operation in the United States. The FBI was brought in on the project.

Donald Maclean, the most important Soviet agent working at the British Embassy in Washington, was mentioned in several cables, naturally. Even worse, he had sent a few cables to Moscow himself. Once the Venona team began breaking the codes, Maclean was vulnerable to discovery. It was only a matter of time.

Chapter Twelve

A Precipitous Decline
The Magnificent Five Begin to Show Weakness

While their Soviet handlers reeled from the shock of Gouzenko's revelations, the Cambridge Five focused on their own lives and careers.

In September 1946, Kim Philby finally divorced his first wife, Litzi. With the war now over, she was safe from deportation to Nazi occupied Austria, and no longer needed the protection of her marriage to a British subject. A few days later, Kim married Aileen, who was now pregnant with their fourth child.

In January 1947, Kim was appointed Head of Station in Istanbul, and the Philbys packed up the children, including their new baby, Miranda, and moved to Turkey. They rented a Turkish villa on the shore outside of the city, overlooking the Bosporus Strait.

Donald and Melinda Maclean also welcomed another child into their family. Little Donald, nicknamed 'Beany', was born via caesarean section in July 1946. As his family grew, so did Donald Maclean's access in Washington. He was selected to assist Sir Roger Makins, Assistant Under-Secretary, in his role at the Combined Policy Committee (CPC). The CPC was established in 1943 to coordinate British and American atomic research and policy. Roger Makins was the Joint Secretary of the committee, and he enlisted Maclean to help him in this capacity in 1947.

In November 1947, Maclean was issued a permanent pass to the headquarters of the Atomic Energy Committee (AEC), due to his work on the CPC, which held its meetings there. This unprecedented access allowed Maclean to enter the building without an escort, which he often did after business hours. Alone in the quiet building, he dove into the files, searching for anything the Soviets might want to see in the critical area of atomic policy. He discovered that the United States had fewer atomic bombs than anyone thought (twelve, by 1948), and only twenty-seven specially modified B-29 bombers capable of their delivery. He also learned that the Soviet Union was not expected to develop their own atomic weapon before the early 1950s.[1]

In 1948, Maclean's position enabled him to attend classified Anglo-American talks concerning the development of the North Atlantic Treaty, which would eventually result in the creation of NATO, the North Atlantic Treaty Organisation, an alliance meant to protect Western Europe from Soviet aggression.

Back in London, Guy Burgess also made a career advancement. He was appointed private secretary to Hector McNeil, Minister of State at the Foreign Office. In his role as the de facto deputy to Foreign Secretary Ernest Bevin, McNeil presented Burgess with unfettered access to foreign policy intelligence. In the autumn of 1947, contact with the Soviet Rezidentura in London was re-established, and Burgess met with his new handler, Yuri Modin.

Anthony Blunt, now entirely free from MI5, became president of the Courtauld Institute, while maintaining his position as Surveyor of the King's Pictures. His espionage work for the Centre was downgraded to courier, and he mainly transported documents for Guy Burgess.

John Cairncross sought to finally pursue his dream of an academic career. He became an occasional contributor at the BBC, and continued his research into the original writings of Molière. He also began a collaboration with his brother, Alec, on a book about William Shakespeare's outlook on business and money (the book was never completed). John began spending more time with his friend, Graham Greene, who had become a mentor to him, supporting him in his academic ambitions.

Cairncross also began a relationship with Gabrielle Oppenheim, an elegant, cultured woman who had left Germany with her family as Jewish refugees in 1934. After obtaining British citizenship, she worked for the Jewish Refugee Committee. She was intelligent and sophisticated, and shared John's love of literature, as well as his aptitude for learning languages. John had met Gabrielle through mutual friends during the war, and the two stayed in touch through letters when, after the war, she moved to California. Though he had dated other women, Gabrielle was his first serious relationship.

In 1948, Cairncross submitted his resignation to his supervisor at the Treasury, but then withdrew it, for unknown reasons.[2] He was instead transferred to the Defence Personnel section. Cairncross' failure to leave the Civil Service may have had something to do with the London Rezidentura, which re-established contact with him in 1948 through a new handler, Yuri Modin. The value of his contributions would never again reach the level of his wartime work at Bletchley Park, but he continued to smuggle documents from the office, and to meet with Modin.[3]

Modin grew impatient with John's long established habit of tardiness. To remedy this, Modin secured the approval of funding by the Centre to buy Cairncross a car. Unfortunately, John had no driver's licence and no actual experience behind the wheel. After passing his driving test, John purchased a vehicle, but struggled to operate it. In a terrifying, yet hilarious, episode, Cairncross, with Modin in the passenger seat, stalled the car in the middle of traffic. A policeman approached to help as John struggled to restart it. The policeman climbed into the driver's seat beside a petrified Yuri Modin. Modin refused to speak, fearful that his Russian accent would lead to a search of the vehicle. The car was started without incident, and the policeman patiently explained to Cairncross the necessity of pushing in the choke.[4]

Though all five spies appeared to be getting their lives in order, the facades were beginning to crack.

During Donald Maclean's time in Washington, his casual dislike of America mushroomed into a bitter hatred. From his office at the embassy, he witnessed first-hand the hardening of relations with the Soviet Union. He watched helplessly as irreversible events, one after another, unfolded across the world stage.

In 1946, Winston Churchill gave an address in Fulton, Missouri, lamenting what he called the Soviet 'Iron Curtain', erected by Stalin to imprison Eastern Europeans in oppressive Stalinist puppet states. In March 1947, US President Harry Truman established the Truman Doctrine, vowing to protect democratic nations from Soviet rule. In June 1947, the Marshall Plan was enacted, a massive American foreign aid project meant to dissuade struggling European nations from resorting to Soviet communism. In June 1948, tensions culminated in the Soviet blockade of all roads and waterways into West Berlin.

West Berlin had been a constant irritation for Joseph Stalin, almost since the end of the Second World War. When Nazi Germany was defeated, the Allies divided Germany into four occupation zones to be individually administered by the United States, Great Britain, France, and the Soviet Union. Germany's capital, Berlin, was likewise split into four occupation zones. When the Western Allies combined their zones to facilitate easier trade and commerce, Stalin held fast to the Soviet Zone. He was staunchly opposed to the reunification of Germany, which had invaded Russia twice in the previous thirty years. The Western Allies, in turn, refused to forfeit their occupation zones in Berlin, which was located deep inside the Soviet zone.

With his 1948 blockade of roads, rails, and waterways, Stalin attempted to starve West Berliners and force the Western Allies out of their Berlin occupation zones. The Western Allies responded with a massive airlift of food and supplies to West Berlin, and refused to abandon the small German outpost of democracy in Soviet territory.

Donald Maclean had a front row seat to the rising global tensions. Bound by his many lies and conflicting interests, he slid ever deeper into his well-established alcoholism. Maclean's binge drinking was already a problem when he first arrived in Washington, and it only became more public.

In his first few weeks in America, Maclean befriended Isaiah Berlin, a special attaché at the British Embassy. Berlin invited Maclean to a dinner party hosted by Katherine Graham, heiress to *The Washington Post*. He attended without Melinda, who was still living in New York. Late in the evening, an inebriated Donald Maclean verbally berated his new friend, Isaiah Berlin, for sharing an amusing anecdote involving Alice Longworth, Teddy Roosevelt's daughter. Maclean then called Longworth stupid, reactionary, right-wing, and fascist. When Berlin verbally defended himself, Maclean grabbed him by the collar.[5] The other guests were shocked at his behaviour, and though Maclean later apologised to Berlin, their friendship never recovered.

After the war, Maclean's drinking became even worse, and Melinda took on the unwelcome role of Donald's babysitter at the frequent Washington parties they were obliged to attend. She was able to intervene when Donald began to speak out of turn and could persuade him to retire early with her, when necessary. Occasionally, though, Melinda would be away visiting family and Donald would inevitably embarrass himself again. He attended a party hosted by Stuart Alsop, columnist for the *Herald Tribune,* where, engaged in a conversation about the Iranian Crisis, Maclean went on a tirade. He first complained about the Iranian Shah, then about the American policy in Iran, and finally began to slander the new Secretary of State, James

Byrnes. Alsop, a close friend of Byrnes, protested, but Maclean continued his rant until he was asked by his host to leave.[6]

Melinda grew weary of keeping up Donald's facade, and his constant criticism of her country. Though he was widely respected for his tireless dedication and professionalism, Donald was a different person after hours. Due to the impeccable quality of his work, the diplomatic community accepted his drinking problem, treating it as an open secret in Washington. When, in 1948, Donald was offered a promotion to Head of Chancery at the British Embassy in Cairo, Egypt, both he and Melinda were anxious for a change, though perhaps for different reasons.

Guy Burgess, curiously, was on a similar track as Maclean; as his diplomatic career, and his esteem with the KGB, sailed ever higher, his mental and physical health deteriorated at an equally rapid pace. His work for Hector McNeil brought him ever closer to world-changing policies, decisions and events. Burgess delighted Modin with over 300 documents smuggled from the Council of Foreign Ministers meeting, which he attended with McNeil in late 1947. He provided updates on the British and American positions concerning the Berlin blockade, so that Soviet Foreign Minister Molotov would be prepared going into negotiations.[7]

The Centre provided money for Burgess to buy a vehicle, and he purchased a used Rolls Royce, which he drove like a maniac. He offered to take Modin for a ride, which he accepted. Modin immediately regretted his decision, fearing for his safety as Burgess sped, ran stop lights, and wove in and out of traffic.[8]

Guy's friends and colleagues noticed a self-destructive element that had begun to overtake his usual *joie de vivre*. He kept a flask of whiskey in his desk, from which he sipped throughout the day. He took sedatives to calm his anxiety, followed later by stimulants to keep him awake. His moods shifted violently between depression and mania, as he self-medicated by drinking and popping pills.[9] He exhibited stranger behaviour still, expressing to friends his desire to get married and settle down. His homosexuality notwithstanding, Burgess had previously indulged in occasional affairs with women, many of whom found him quite attractive. He claimed to have slept with Patricia Rawdon-Smith, his old roommate at Bentinck Street. He had talked about marriage with Peter Pollock's sister, Gale. Rumours began to circulate that he was going to propose to his close friend, Clarissa Churchill, Winston Churchill's niece.[10]

At McNeil's urging, Guy took a position with the newly established Information Research Department (IRD), which was created to address and combat anti-western Soviet propaganda. With his wartime experience in propaganda, Burgess seemed like a good fit. In spite of his knowledge of the Soviet Union and communist ideology, his behavioural quirks ensured his termination from the new department. The department head, Christopher Mayhew, fired him after only a few weeks, describing him as 'dirty, drunk, and idle'.[11]

Burgess returned to his posting at McNeil's office in March 1948. Soon afterward, he accompanied McNeil to Belgium for the signing of the Treaty of Brussels, a precursor to the North Atlantic Treaty. Burgess picked up right where he had left off, pilfering over 2000 documents over the next six months, and handing them over to the Soviets.[12]

In August that same year, Burgess travelled to Istanbul on holiday to visit his good friend, Kim Philby. He arrived, likely unannounced, allegedly on government business. Philby's old friend, Tim Milne, was already staying with the Philbys when Guy arrived. Milne had recently been posted to Tehran, and his pregnant wife, Marie, was planning to have their baby in Istanbul. Tehran was still somewhat primitive in those days, and Kim Philby had invited her to stay with his family in Istanbul, a more advanced city with better doctors and hospitals.

Milne enjoyed Guy's presence, for the most part. He was funny, free spirited, and open. Milne's favourite memory was of driving around the Turkish countryside with Kim in an open topped jeep, as Burgess sang at the top of his lungs from the backseat.[13]

Milne also saw Guy's down side. Burgess stayed out all night, then spent the whole day lazing about the house in his dressing gown. He was messy, leaving dishes in the sink, and cigarette butts behind the sofa pillows. Once, Kim and Guy, joined by two young women, spent an evening at the Moda Yacht Club where the four of them drank fifty-two brandies. Burgess once dove from the second floor balcony into the Bosporus and injured his back. He frightened Philby by disappearing one night, only to return the following day with no explanation. Though he could be great fun, Burgess was a bad influence on Kim, and a terrible houseguest for Aileen.

When a telegram from the Foreign Office arrived at the house, informing Burgess that he was not needed back to work right away, Philby attempted to hide it from Burgess. Alas, Guy found the message, and was pleased to stay for a third week.

Kim Philby's personal life was taking some hits as well. Though now Head of Station in a city that was emerging as an important geopolitical location in the Cold War, his marriage was beginning to falter. He had begun an affair with his secretary, Esther Whitfield. Aileen, likely aware of his dalliance, possibly aware of his espionage, and challenged by the stress of managing four children alone while her husband went out drinking with Burgess, began to regress into her childhood pattern of hurting herself for attention. Though nobody could understand why, her mental illness might today be diagnosed as Munchausen Syndrome.

The order of events differs in the many accounts of Aileen's troubling episode, but the principal details are generally agreed upon. Aileen turned up one afternoon, bruised and bleeding, claiming to have been violently attacked by a local Turk. The police were summoned, and suspects were questioned. No evidence was found to corroborate Aileen's story beyond her cuts and bruises, which appeared to be self-inflicted. She may have re-infected her own wounds while in the hospital. In desperation, Kim asked his friend, Nicholas Elliott, if he knew of a specialist. Elliott found a suitable psychiatrist in Switzerland, where he was serving as Head of Station. Kim and Aileen flew to Switzerland, where Aileen was checked into a clinic for observation. Aileen proceeded to set her room on fire and doctors suspected that she had injected herself with urine, causing painful boils to rise on her skin. Though the psychiatrist was unable to 'cure' Aileen, she eventually was stabilised and was allowed to return home.[14]

Thoroughly frustrated with Aileen by this point, Kim Philby was relieved and excited to accept a major promotion. He was going to be Chief of British Intelligence in the Americas, and would soon be moving with his family to Washington, DC.

As the Philbys were preparing to move to America, the Macleans were packing up to leave. Donald's term as First Secretary was coming to a close, having spent an extended period at his posting. In spite of his numerous drunken outbursts, his diligent service had earned him an impressive promotion. He was to become Head of Chancery at the Cairo Embassy, making him the youngest counsellor in the Foreign Service, at 35 years old. The promotion skipped the traditional step of serving as First Secretary of a second embassy, which signalled a possible ambassadorship in his future.

Furthermore, Cairo was one of five 'Grade A' embassies, increasingly important in the Cold War era.

The prestigious new posting presented a mixed blessing for Maclean. As much as he despised America, particularly during the rising tide of anti-communism in the late 1940s, he had access to the most valuable intelligence available. Washington was now the locus of power in the west, and he had been at the centre of everything. Cairo would not offer Maclean the same level of prestige, in the eyes of the KGB.

After a brief holiday in London, the Maclean family set out for Egypt. They were provided with a three-story house in the suburb of Gezireh, with large, shuttered windows, exotic rugs, and a colourful garden. With Donald's raise in salary, they were able to employ housekeepers and an English nanny. Melinda, already anxious for a fresh start after her difficult tenure in Washington, was now liberated from housework and could pursue her own interests and friendships. Donald stayed busy swimming and playing tennis at the local club. His drinking stayed within reason (at first), which freed her from having to mind him at parties. She went to coffee with local women outside of diplomatic circles and found that they respected and admired her; her experience living in Paris and Washington bestowed on her a certain sophistication in the eyes of the local women. With help from her domestic servants, Melinda was finally able to host proper diplomatic parties, as well. The bachelor ambassador, Sir Ronald Campbell, was so impressed with Melinda that he asked her to host parties for him, too. Away from the more rigid British protocol and the judgement of her American relatives, Melinda came out her shell and thrived in Egypt.[15]

Donald, on the other hand, did not. Though poised on the precipice of a dazzling career, he soon embarked on a mission of self-sabotage. His duplicity gnawed away at him, as he took a front row seat to the injustice of wealth inequality, and he witnessed first-hand the poverty of local Egyptians under British occupation. He lived with his diminished importance to the Soviets after his move from America, juxtaposed against his rising status in the British Foreign office. Accustomed to being the centre of attention, Donald began to resent Melinda's newfound confidence and popularity. He began to make passive-aggressive comments denigrating her lack of culture, or her lack of concern for important political issues. His disdain for society parties only increased, and his introverted nature led him, inevitably, back to the social lubricant of alcohol.

Donald and Melinda began leading somewhat separate lives and it wasn't long before rumours began to circulate about Donald passing out in gardens and sleeping on doorsteps. His true feelings began, once more, to slip out after a few drinks. During the investigation of Alger Hiss by the House Un-American Activities Committee, Maclean casually remarked to the wife of the Dutch Ambassador, 'If Alger Hiss felt as he did about communism, he was quite right to betray his country'.[16]

Reports of Maclean's inebriated wanderings (he once was found walking confusedly through traffic, carrying his shoes) eventually were reported to Ambassador Campbell, who quickly swatted down any criticism of the esteemed counsellor. His high regard for the Macleans, particularly Melinda, hampered his objectivity.

Back in London, Guy Burgess continued along on his own downward slide. He had taken a job in the Far East Department at the Foreign Office, having been passed over for the General Department, the American Department, and the Northern Department. Though not a prestigious transfer, his new posting allowed him access to information about the final phase of the Chinese Civil War, and the impending crisis in Korea. His knowledge about Marxism impressed his colleagues, and his insight was sought after during policy formulation. Both conflicts were directly related to the spread of communism. Burgess was able to report to the Soviets on British policy towards China and Korea, which differed significantly from American policy. While the United States saw the emergent communist China as just another Soviet satellite to oppose, the British advocated diplomatic relations.

In spite of things going relatively well for Burgess in the Foreign Office, his drinking and drug use were spiralling out of control. In February 1949, he had engaged in a heated argument with his colleague and friend, Fred Warner, at a club in the West End. The dispute, reportedly over Spain, escalated into fisticuffs, and Burgess was sent tumbling down two flights of stone stairs. Warner, still drunk but now mortified, picked him up and pushed him into a taxi. Rather than call an ambulance, or at least take the taxi to a hospital, the two men rode together to Guy's apartment. Warner phoned numerous doctors, none of whom picked up in the middle of the night. He finally reached Jack Hewit, who managed to get Guy, his head still bleeding, into a hospital the next morning. A series of X-rays revealed a skull fracture, a broken elbow and three dislocated ribs.[17]

After ten days in the hospital, the doctors recommended a long rest, and above all, sobriety. Guy went on holiday to Ireland with his mother. He was arrested in Dublin on 4 March and charged with drunk driving after a car accident. He called his old lawyer friend, Dermot McGillycuddy, who was able to convince the Justice to dismiss the charges.

Making matters worse for Burgess, he began taking a dangerous combination of drugs to help with the headaches and insomnia resulting from his head injury. Peter Pollock's sister, Sheila, was a veterinarian, and was persuaded to give Burgess the barbiturate Nembutal to help him sleep, and the inhaled amphetamine Benzedrine, to wake him back up the next morning. The Benzedrine likely contributed to his insomnia, and the Nembutal, mixed with Guy's normal alcohol intake, could have resulted in cardiac arrest. Guy's friend, Goronwy Rees, described the formerly brilliant conversationalist as 'rambling and incoherent' during this period.[18]

By June, Burgess had pulled himself together well enough to attend the annual Cambridge Apostles dinner. Also attending was Anthony Blunt and, visiting from America, former Soviet spy Michael Straight. Whether or not Burgess realised it, there was a sense of apprehension in the air. In January, Anthony Blunt, while meeting with Yuri Modin, was stopped in the street by a policeman. He was carrying a briefcase full of papers from Guy Burgess to give to Modin.[19] The policeman had no idea what kind of confidential documents he had, but Anthony was given quite a scare, nonetheless.

Michael Straight, meanwhile, had outgrown his earlier communism. Thought he had passed information to a Soviet handler while working as a speechwriter for President Roosevelt during the 1930s, he had since become disenchanted with Marxism. Straight had become a new type of American Cold War liberal, one who zealously opposed communism. As owner and editor of the Washington-based *New Republic* magazine, he now posed a real threat to his old Cambridge friends. After Straight engaged in a heated discussion with communist Eric Hobsbawm, Blunt and Burgess nervously approached their old friend and fellow spy out of earshot from the rest of the crowd. They were reassured that Straight was still loyal to his old friends, if not to their cause. Their secret was safe, for the moment.[20]

During the same month that Blunt and Burgess dined with their old college chums, Donald and Melinda Maclean were hosting their own dinner party in Cairo. The plan was simple enough. The Macleans and six guests were to board two *feluccas* (traditional wooden sailboats) at seven o'clock, and sail fifteen miles up the Nile River with dinner and cocktails. They were to land in Helouan at the home of British businessman, Eric Tyrell-Martin, where they would join his dinner party, already in progress. They planned to have coffee and games before driving back to Cairo. Among the passengers were Melinda's visiting sister, Harriet Marling, Donald's friend from the embassy, Lees Mayall, and his wife, Mary.

The adventure seemed doomed from the beginning, when the Maclean party arrived an hour late to the dock. Only one *felucca* was still waiting for them at eight o'clock, so all eight passengers boarded the small boat. Now heavy with extra passengers plus the three man crew, the sluggish vessel struggled upstream on the windless evening. With plenty of alcohol on board, Donald became increasingly intoxicated. After hours of slow progress in the moonless night, they went ashore to determine their location. Donald, embarrassed and frustrated with the botched plan, took out his anger on Melinda. He wrapped his hands around her neck to choke her, to the horror of his guests. Lees Mayall, with the help of another man, managed to pull him away. They boarded the *felucca* again, with Donald pouting alone at the end of the boat, and Melinda putting on a happy face to reassure her guests.

They believed the worst was behind them.

The unhappy group arrived at Helouan in the wee hours of the morning. Lees Mayall, John Brinton, and a military colonel disembarked to find the home of their host. They spotted a local peasant lurking in the trees. The colonel forcibly grabbed and detained the man, demanding to know where Tyrell-Martin's house was. The terrified peasant guided the party to Tyrell-Martin's house, where he was released and generously tipped.

The house was now dark, and their knocks at the door were met with silence.

When their drunk and belligerent host finally threw open the front door, he startled the equally intoxicated John Brinton, who fell backward down the porch steps, knocking himself out and cutting his head. Tyrell-Martin, furious that the party had not arrived while his own guests were still there, reluctantly allowed the men to carry Brinton inside. Tyrell-Martin had sent their cars back to Cairo after they failed to show, so now the party was stranded.

Mayall and the colonel went back to the *felucca* to get the rest of the guests, where they found Maclean arguing with the boat skipper over the fee. A local armed patrolman approached. As it turned out, the boat skipper was his cousin, and he joined in the argument on his cousin's side. Maclean, enraged, grabbed the guard's rifle and began to beat him with it. A small crowd of locals had gathered to watch the developing scene. The colonel urged Mayall to knock Maclean out. Fearing an international incident, but unwilling to inflict the second head injury of the evening, Mayall chose instead to tackle Maclean. He flung himself at Donald's 6 feet tall, 220 pound frame, which collapsed on top of Mayall, breaking his ankle and shin. Mayall was helped back to Tyrell-Martin's house, where the beleaguered party guests tried to sleep on couches and floors. Maclean, still inebriated, but now remorseful, helped Mayall into a taxi at sunrise. None of the traumatised guests reported the incident to Ambassador Campbell. Adding insult to injury, Lees Mayall, approaching the end of his term in Cairo, was soon heading back to London to work in the Far East Department with Guy Burgess.[21]

On 29 August 1949, the Soviet Union stunned the world by testing its first atomic weapon. Most experts predicted this development around 1952, some as late as 1954. As recently as July 1949, the CIA had estimated that the Soviets could not produce an atomic bomb until at least 1950. The intelligence community in the United States wondered how the Soviet scientists had been able to accelerate their timeline so dramatically.

The cryptanalysts from Venona knew how. In September 1949, mere days after the Soviet atomic test, Meredith Gardner deciphered a cable referring to a spy, code named CHARLES, sent from New York to Moscow in June 1944. The message said that CHARLES had been working on Project ENORMOUZ (the KGB code name for the Manhattan Project), and that he might be returning to London soon. A numbered report from the British Embassy was referenced in the cable. Very few British scientists were in New York that summer, and through the process of elimination, a physicist named Klaus Fuchs was unmasked as CHARLES.

Klaus Fuchs was a communist refugee from Germany who had settled in London in the 1930s. A brilliant young physicist, he obscured his communist past to become a British subject in 1942, and to get hired on to the British Tube Alloys Project. Already working as a spy for the Soviets, he was sent to Columbia University to conduct research for the Manhattan Project in 1943. He went on to Los Alamos to work on the theoretical physics department in August 1944.

In the wake of these revelations, Kim Philby prepared for his new posting in Washington, DC, as head of British Intelligence in the United States. Because he would be acting as the liaison between US and British intelligence, Philby was briefed on the Venona project before leaving London. As Americans reeled from news of the Soviet nuclear test, Philby was stunned by the possible exposure presented by Venona. The fallout could be catastrophic for himself and his fellow Cambridge spies. The best that he could do was to inform the Soviets of the compromised cables, so they could shut off the spigot of information now flowing freely to the Americans. There was no possibility of supressing anything that had already been sent. Philby, and his Soviet controllers, could only brace themselves as they waited to see what Arlington Hall was able to uncover.

Philby had to get the news to Modin. He told Guy Burgess to inform Modin about Venona, especially the unmasking of Klaus Fuchs, who was now back in England working for the Atomic Energy Research Establishment at Harwell. Fuchs needed to be exfiltrated immediately. It was only a matter of time before he would be apprehended.

Guy Burgess simply forgot to pass this information on to Yuri Modin, and by February 1950, Fuchs was arrested.[22]

Of more immediate interest to Kim Philby was a Venona breakthrough regarding Donald Maclean. For years, the cryptanalysts at Arlington Hall, with the assistance of FBI agent Robert Lamphere, had been searching for a Soviet mole working in the British Embassy in Washington. They had been confused by a Russian linguistic quirk; the letter 'H' does not exist in the Cyrillic alphabet. Meredith Gardner and Robert Lamphere had been searching for an agent with the code name of 'GOMER.' He had also been referred to simply as 'G', or 'MATERIAL G', leading the codebreakers to believe they were dealing with three separate agents. Finally, they figured out that GOMER was actually HOMER, as were G and MATERIAL G. A total of six messages out of Washington involving HOMER were deciphered.

Due to the double encryption of the cables and the use of the one-time pad, the Soviets had believed their codes to be unbreakable. This led to occasional sloppiness; agents' real names were occasionally used instead of code names, for example. In the case of Donald Maclean, a Soviet cipher clerk in New York had encrypted a stolen telegram to be sent back to Moscow, and had made the mistake of including an internal serial number used by the British Foreign Office. The telegram was from 1945, and there was no doubt that it came from the British Embassy in Washington. The FBI now had a code name, HOMER, and they knew he was from the British Foreign Service.

The FBI immediately informed MI5. The clock was ticking.

Chapter Thirteen

The Unravelling
A Series of Spectacular Disasters

In spite of the chill brought on by the Venona revelations, Kim Philby did his best to settle in with his family in their new home on Nebraska Avenue in Washington. Aileen soon gave birth to their fifth child in America, a son named Harry George.

Officially, Kim's new title was First Secretary at the British Embassy. This was just a cover; MI6 still did not officially exist. Philby's real job was to represent the British Secret Service in the United States. He acted as a liaison between MI6 and the CIA, its new American counterpart. He was also expected to maintain good relationships with the National Security Agency (NSA) and the FBI, as well as the Canadian security service. His new posting was a prized promotion, and colleagues began to whisper that he was on track to one day become head of SIS.

The new posting was also an impressive achievement for Philby's *other* career with the KGB. By the time he reported for duty in the autumn of 1949, there was no doubt that the new world order now centred on the silent battle between the two emergent superpowers: the United States and the Soviet Union. From Washington, Kim Philby had his finger on the pulse of every new development in the world of foreign intelligence.

Unfortunately, due to the panic ignited by the testimony of Elizabeth Bentley, Philby was left without a Soviet handler in Washington. Anatoly Gorsky, who had worked with Donald Maclean, had been evacuated from Washington after being photographed with Elizabeth Bentley. In any case, clandestine meetings with Philby were too risky during a time when everyone was looking for spies. Kim was forced to send intelligence to the London Rezidentura through the sometimes unreliable Guy Burgess.[1]

Upon his arrival in Washington, Philby was reunited with his old American friend from the OSS, James Angleton. Angleton had grown up quite a bit since their days at War Station XB. His skinny frame now looked tall and lanky in his Brooks Brothers suits, and his thick rimmed glasses, which once looked too large for his face, now rested comfortably on his high cheekbones. He had a few years of experience under his belt and was now working in the CIA's Office of Special Operations. Angleton would be Philby's point man; his main contact with US foreign intelligence.

Angleton had served as head of X-2 in Italy during the Second World War, then continued working in Italy after the war ended. Once the SOS had been disbanded, it was eventually replaced by the CIA. Angleton became one of the CIA's founding officers.

Angleton had been deeply involved in one of the CIA's first foreign interventions. The parliamentary election for the First Italian Republic in April 1948 was an exciting historical event for the fledgling Italian democracy. However, the communist coup of Czechoslovakia in February left the Western Allies worried. They feared that the Popular Democratic Front, a coalition of communists and socialists, would win a majority of seats in the new Italian government, giving the Soviets another foothold to expand their control in Europe. At a time when the United States placed a priority on the containment of Soviet expansion, a drastic step was taken. The CIA stepped in, giving monetary support to the Christian Democratic Party, and spreading anti-communist propaganda in Italy. The communist faction was defeated. James Angleton played a leading role in the unprecedented American intervention. He looked forward to orchestrating more covert foreign interventions in the future.

Kim Philby turned on the charm for Angleton, as he always did. Both men had young families, and they would often get together on weekends. Angleton introduced Philby to fly fishing, and shared with him his techniques for growing orchids. The two agents met weekly for lunch at Harvey's, an upscale seafood restaurant adjacent to the Mayflower Hotel. The alcohol flowed freely as Philby and Angleton ate their weight in oysters, as they indulged in lengthy discussions on current events, politics, and, of course, foreign intelligence.

As Philby spent time ingratiating himself with Washington's inner circle, he tried to come up with a plan to deal with the ticking time bomb that was Venona. He decided to revisit the old case of Walter Krivitsky, the Soviet defector who had spoken of a journalist working in Franco's Spain, and of a diplomat in the Foreign Office, both spying for the Soviets. In a bold manoeuvre, Kim wrote a memo to the head of embassy security, Robert Mackenzie, about Krivitsky's revelations, so that Mackenzie could be on the lookout for this mystery man, HOMER. In the memo, Philby carefully excluded some of the more specific details pointing to Maclean, such as the fact that he ran in artistic circles and sometimes wore a cape. He included only the vaguest of Krivitsky's descriptions – the spy was young, idealistic, and came from a good family.[2]

Philby of course left out any mention of Spain, or of any journalist. He couldn't be too careful. The team at Arlington Hall had recovered a cable mentioning a spy code named STANLEY, whom Kim immediately recognised as himself. Though no identifying details were mentioned, Philby thought it best to deflect any and all attention away from himself, and onto HOMER. By appearing to contribute to the investigation, Kim was able to stay in the loop, and be notified of ongoing developments.

As hard as the cryptanalysts at Arlington Hall were working to bring down HOMER, it seemed that Maclean himself might do the job for them. After the disastrous picnic party on the Nile, Maclean was coming to the realisation that he could no longer tolerate living with so many secrets. He wrote to Moscow Centre in December 1949, hinting that he would like to work in Russia, where he could better take up the struggle against the West. The letter was ignored, for reasons unknown. It could be that the KGB was reluctant to give up its most valuable agent. Conversely, reports of his destructive behaviour may have reached Moscow, and the Centre may have concluded that he was already burned up and not worth the effort. Still another possibility remained – his handler may have interpreted his small cry for help as evidence that he had finally been turned and now sought to work as a double agent for the British. Maclean wrote again in April 1950, begging to be exfiltrated to Moscow. Again, he received no response.[3]

Guy Burgess continued apace in his own downward spiral, mirroring that of Donald Maclean. In November 1949, Burgess went on holiday with his mother to Gibraltar and Tangier. He engaged in his usual heavy drinking, but this time, instead of indulging in brawls or drunk driving, he became careless with his words.

Wherever Burgess went, it seemed like he ran into someone that he knew. The Rock Hotel in Gibraltar was no exception, nor were the bars of Tangier. He was introduced to two British intelligence officers stationed in Gibraltar named Teddy Dunlop and Kenneth Mills, and the three of them had a few drinks. As Guy drank, his tongue was loosened, and he began sharing all of his opinions, his *real* opinions, on British Foreign policy, on the intelligence services, on China, and on Russia. His praise of Marxism surprised everyone around him.

Burgess first got off on the wrong foot with Dunlop and Mills by starting an argument over Franco, whom they had supported during the Spanish Civil War. Guy went on to extoll praise for Mao Zedong and to express his disdain for American foreign policy. As he ingested more alcohol, Burgess moved on from political discussions and let slip that British Intelligence had smuggled classified documents out of Switzerland in diplomatic pouches. He even revealed the names of a few agents. Alarmed, Dunlop lodged a complaint with the Foreign Office. Kenneth Mills filed one with MI5.[4]

Upon his return to London, Burgess was summoned to the personnel office. The episode in Gibraltar was not his first slip; he had recently compromised an MI6 agent named Alexander Halpern and had leaked classified information to an American journalist, Freddie Kuh. The Foreign Office, as well as the intelligence services, had tolerated Guy's erratic behaviour for many years. What they could not tolerate was indiscretion. Guy Liddell, deputy director of MI5 and good friend of Guy Burgess, refused to believe that Burgess would intentionally compromise information. He did, however, acknowledge Guy's drinking problem, and the fact that intoxication might lead him to become chatty about confidential matters. Liddell recommended a stern reprimand from the Foreign Office.

A full investigation by a disciplinary board of the Foreign Office cleared Burgess of the complaint issued by MI6, largely influenced by the recommendation of Guy Liddell. Burgess was given a warning and allowed to return to work. George Cary-Foster, the head of security in the Foreign Office, strongly disagreed with the board's findings; he wanted Burgess fired.

As Burgess was being investigated, Donald Maclean's attempt at sobriety was sabotaged by the arrival of his old friend, Philip Toynbee, to Egypt. Toynbee, who Maclean had not seen much of since their wartime days in Paris, was a dangerous enabler of Maclean's worst impulses. Toynbee was going through a bitter divorce and had taken on work as a correspondent for *The Observer*. He was sent to Cairo to write a series on the issues in the Middle East and asked Maclean if he could stay with him. Donald welcomed his old friend with open arms.

Not everyone was happy with the arrangement. Toynbee's communist past created visa issues for him, which were resolved by Maclean vouching for his old friend. He assured the Foreign Office that Toynbee's communist days were behind him, which was true. William Ridsdale, chief of the Foreign Office Press Department, knew of Toynbee's drinking problems, as well as his recent divorce, and politely suggested to Maclean that Philip stay in a hotel. Maclean insisted that he could watch over his old chum and help him to stay clean. Melinda knew better, having watched Donald and Philip in action in Paris. She shuddered at the idea of Toynbee's influence on the already fragile Donald, but was unable to thwart the impending tsunami of chaos.

Philip Toynbee was as miserable in Cairo as Donald was. He was compelled to attend dinners with the British press corps, all of whom were racist, according to Toynbee. The dislike was mutual; they found him lazy, combative, and usually drunk.[5]

Within two weeks, Philip, depressed over his separation and unhappy with his work, and Donald, despondent over Moscow's failure to respond to his pleas for help, teamed up for an epic drinking binge. Melinda, probably needing a break from the two troublemakers, was out of town sightseeing for the week with her sister, Harriet.

Now free from Melinda's stabilising influence, Donald and Philip went to a party and proceeded to get hammered together. Philip returned to the Maclean residence around midnight, but Donald stayed at the party. He broke glasses against the wall, and punched his friend, Eddy Gathorne-Hardy. Philip woke up the next morning to find Donald passed out on the floor in a pool of urine. Toynbee helped clean him up, and Maclean impressed him by reporting to work that day. It was then that Philip created names for Donald's alter-egos: 'Sir Donald', the sober, accomplished diplomat, and 'Gordon', the out-of-control drunk.[6] Maclean, still unwilling to accept the complexities of his own character, embraced the compartmentalisation. Toynbee's observation was more astute than he realised. It harkened back to Maclean's college days, when Donald himself had given names to his three personalities.

Toynbee was awakened by Donald, or 'Gordon', at two o'clock the next morning. He was forced to listen as Maclean went on a tirade, angrily deriding Melinda. He alarmed Philip by wishing for Melinda's death. Philip was left to conclude that Donald both loved and hated Melinda, in equal measure.

Melinda's return home did not put a stop to Donald's intoxicated rampage. The next few days were filled with Donald's attempts to provoke Melinda and Harriet, his sojourns away from home in the middle of the night, and his failure to return home until the next day. One morning, he tearfully confessed to Philip that, the previous night, he had insulted Harriet and struck Melinda, who was pregnant.[7]

In a final devastating performance, the Macleans began the evening by attending a cocktail party with Harriet and Philip. Melinda, Philip, and Harriet eventually tired and went home, but not Donald. After drinking his way through a second party, Donald finally returned home around two in the morning and awakened Philip.[8] The pair snuck out of the house like two juvenile delinquents.

Donald and Philip turned up at the home of John Wardle-Smith, a colleague of Donald's from the embassy. Not wanting a confrontation with the intoxicated men, he placed the two on his balcony, where he served them bottle after bottle of gin, hoping they would eventually just pass out. He then headed to the office.

Maclean and Toynbee did not pass out. They instead wandered the neighbourhood, searching for more alcohol. They walked to the home of Eunice Taylor, secretary to the US Ambassador to Egypt, Jefferson Caffrey. Thankfully, she wasn't home to witness what was about to happen. Maclean and Toynbee pushed past the servants to enter the apartment. When they didn't find any liquor, they proceeded to vandalise the home. They broke dishes, pulled out drawers, and flushed underwear down the toilet. In a climactic finish, Donald lifted a mirror over his head and smashed it into the bathtub.[9]

Maclean and Toynbee returned to Wardle-Smith's house, crying in remorse. They both passed out, finally, on his bed, Donald inexplicably clutching a leg of lamb.

Melinda, after a series of frantic phone calls, located her husband and his partner in crime. With the help of Harriet and a servant, Donald and Philip were dragged from the house and pushed into the car. Philip was summarily banished from the home by Melinda, but Donald was a more serious matter. Humiliated, Melinda went to speak to Ambassador Campbell, alone. Without going into detail, she told Campbell that Donald was having a nervous breakdown, and must return to London to rest and to see a doctor. Campbell, ever protective of Melinda, acted quickly. He sent a discreet telegram to the Foreign Office in London, mentioning nothing of the previous day's vandalism and debauchery (probably because he didn't yet know).

It was the American Embassy that brought the incident to Campbell's attention. Ambassador Campbell begged Ambassador Caffrey to keep the matter quiet, because Maclean clearly had a problem and was now going into treatment. Caffrey graciously agreed. Melinda and Harriet paid a visit to Eunice Taylor, apologising and offering to pay for the damage to her apartment. They explained that Donald was having a breakdown, and was returning to London for medical attention.

Maclean's team of enablers, led by Melinda, had successfully covered for him.

On 11 May 1950, Donald Maclean boarded a flight to London, where he planned to stay with his mother and see a psychiatrist. Melinda stayed in Cairo, unsure whether she and the children should join Donald in London, or wait for his eventual return. Melinda's mother, Mrs Dunbar, arrived to help sort things out. It was finally decided that Melinda and the children would join her mother on holiday in Spain, far away from the gossip of Cairo and soon, the gossip in London. Melinda never returned to Egypt.

As Donald Maclean was making his humiliating return to London, Guy Burgess was preparing to leave. Not only had he narrowly escaped termination of his employment at the Foreign Office, he was also in a bit of hot water with his Soviet handlers. He had forgotten to pass along Kim Philby's urgent message the previous September, warning the London Rezidentura that Fuchs had been unmasked by Venona. Had Burgess done his job, Fuchs may have been exfiltrated to Moscow in plenty of time. Having not received the message, Moscow Centre could do nothing, and Fuchs was arrested in February. After a confession, Fuchs was sentenced to fourteen years in prison on 1 March 1950. The Rezidentura cut off contact with all agents for six weeks after the arrest, as a security measure.

In May, Burgess was informed that he would be transferred to the United States, becoming Second Secretary of the embassy. It was a puzzling decision by the Foreign Office. Guy Liddell and his associates in MI5 were opposed to the move, given Guy's recent indiscretions.[10] The embassy in Washington was an important one, and Burgess would have access to even more confidential information than he did in London. The staff at the Washington Embassy didn't want him there either, protesting that his issues with alcohol, along with his growing anti-Americanism, should have disqualified him. Furthermore, his chaotic lifestyle was likely to disrupt the important work that needed to be done. His superiors at the Foreign Office considered the American posting a last chance for Burgess. Some thought that it might actually be easier to control him, or perhaps for him to blend in at such a large office.

For his part, Burgess did not want to go to Washington. He wanted to stay in London with all of his friends. He considered resigning from the Foreign Office, but was in significant financial debt for the first time in his life. He also was likely under pressure from his Soviet handlers, who could always use more information on the Americans. With the matter settled, Burgess sailed to the United States on 28 July 1950.

Over Aileen's objections, Kim Philby allowed Burgess to move in with them, until Guy could find his own apartment.

Meanwhile, Kim Philby was busy at work, preparing his most deadly sabotage yet. During a three day meeting between Gladwyn Jebb, George Jellicoe, and the CIA's Frank Wiesner, Philby learned of the joint Anglo-American plans for a covert foreign operation. Specifically, the plans fell under the CIA's Office of Policy Coordination (OPC). The benign-sounding department was working on a radical and dangerous idea. Breaking a long tradition of American isolationism, the OPC was planning to overthrow the communist governments of Eastern European nations, by stoking resistance movements among their citizens.

The CIA itself was something of a clandestine and extra-constitutional government agency, which was secretly funded and had a classified budget with no congressional oversight. The OPC, within the CIA, had even less accountability. Many of the OPC's operations were kept secret even from other departments within the CIA. Additionally, some of their operations were likely illegal under US law.

Despite the successful allied Berlin Airlift and the subsequent withdrawal of Stalin's blockade, the Western Allies were still desperate to push back on the spread of Soviet communism. The first Soviet nuclear weapons test emboldened Stalin, and alarmed NATO Allies. China had recently fallen to Mao Zedong's communist revolutionaries, and communist North Korea had invaded the democratic south in June 1950, triggering the Korean War.

Not wanting to enter a shooting war with a nuclear Soviet Union, British and American intelligence sought an alternative strategy. Though the Soviets controlled the nations of Eastern Europe, many of their people wanted to be governed by western-style democracies. If they were funded and supported by the United States and Great Britain, perhaps the citizens could be empowered to rise up and overthrow their Stalinist dictators.

The British Foreign Office recommended Albania as a good testing ground for their disruption plan. The British SOE had worked with Albanian resistance fighters during the war, while Albania was under Italian occupation. They continued to maintain contact with some of these fighters, now living in exile. Albania was also in a favourable location. To the south was Greece, whose communist faction was losing their civil war. Across the northern border was Yugoslavia, whose communist leader, Marshall Tito, was now engaged in a nasty feud with Joseph Stalin. The western border of Albania was entirely coastline on the Adriatic Sea, conveniently located just fifty-five miles from Italy. Most importantly, the CIA estimated that the overwhelming majority of Albanians were opposed to the regime of their communist leader, Enver Hoxha.[11] Of all the Soviet satellites, Albania was quickly becoming the most isolated and the most oppressive. Albania seemed ripe for revolution.

British Special Forces established a training camp for Albanian exiles on the island of Malta. These Albanian commandos were small in stature, likely due to years of malnutrition. For this reason, the British soldiers called them 'pixies'. The plan was simple – small groups of pixies were to row ashore on the Albanian coast under cover of night. They would then make their way to their home villages and rally their people to the cause of resistance.

The first group of pixies boarded a small vessel called the *Stormie Seas*. At about nine o'clock at night, British soldiers rowed two dinghies ashore, dropping off nine men equipped with radios, leaflets, food, medical supplies, cash, guns, and ammunition. They split into two groups and headed inland. Despite travelling at night, they were soon tracked down and ambushed by the Albanian secret police. Of the nine pixies, only four survived by crossing the border into Greece.

Though the second group of eleven pixies fared a little better (most of them escaped into Greece), the mission was still a failure. The British continued to ferry groups of pixies to the Albanian shores, but they kept getting gunned down or captured by the secret police. Those that survived failed to create resistance groups in the villages, due to the fears of the residents. One pixie left a radio with his cousin; the cousin was subsequently arrested and tortured. The family members of another pixie were all arrested when the police learned of his escape into Yugoslavia.

While the British launched one failed mission after another by sea, the Americans were training commandos in Germany for parachute drops. Using exiled Polish pilots flying below radar, resistance fighters were dropped into Albania, where they, too, were captured and killed.

It was later revealed that Kim Philby had given details of the plans to Guy Burgess, who acted as his courier.[12] Burgess made frequent visits to New York, where he stayed with Donald Maclean's brother, Alan, whom he had worked with in the Foreign Office Press Department.[13] Alan had moved to New York to begin his new job working for Gladwyn Jebb, the British Representative to the United Nations. While visiting his friend, Burgess met with Soviet handler Valeri Makayev. Burgess gave Makayev the dates, times, and locations of every arrival of pixies into Albania. The Soviets then informed Albanian dictator, Enver Hoxha, who sent his secret police to wait for them. The operation was doomed from the start. Over the course of the operation, an estimated 300 operatives and civilians were executed in connection with the attempted subversion, and many of their family members were imprisoned in gulags.

All the while, Kim Philby continued to laugh with his friend, James Angleton, over martinis and oysters at their weekly lunch at Harvey's. Angleton suspected nothing of Philby's betrayal.

Back in London, Donald Maclean was trying to put himself back together after the debacle in Egypt. He began seeing a psychiatrist, but of course, could not reveal the true cause of his troubles. Unless Donald could be open about the deep secrets, the pressure, and the double life he was leading, healing could not begin. Donald's brother, Alan Maclean, saw Donald before he left for New York. Alan was shocked to see how much Donald's condition had deteriorated by the summer of 1950.

Maclean moved out of his mother's house and into a hotel, where he was largely cut off from any forces of accountability. Melinda was still in Spain with the children, Donald was on sick leave from work, and was out of contact with the Soviet Rezidentura for the first time in years. Within the vacuum left by the absence of his normal responsibilities, Donald began to backslide again. He often missed his appointments with the psychiatrist, and began crawling the pubs, notwithstanding the wreckage already inflicted by his drinking. Instead of going to the usual upscale clubs, where he might encounter staffers from the Foreign Office, Maclean instead joined the Gargoyle Club, a gathering place for artists and writers. He found himself trapped in the cycle of addiction; his remorse over the impact of his drinking inflicted a pain that could only be numbed by more drinking. Friends reported seeing Maclean, once so smooth and put-together, now trembling and swaying. He often became violent while intoxicated, and repeated his old tricks from Cairo, climbing garden walls and sleeping in flower beds. He became increasingly paranoid, convinced he was being followed.

At last, in September, Donald wrote a desperate letter to Melinda. His self-pitying complaints that he could never be a good husband or father, and his insistence that the family was better off without him, hinted at suicide. Melinda was sufficiently alarmed that she came immediately to London, leaving the children with her mother in Paris.

Melinda, who had recently lost the baby she had carried in Cairo, was pressured to return to the marriage by Donald's mother, his psychiatrist, and his superiors at the Foreign Office. It seemed that everyone, even Donald, recognised the stability that Melinda provided. In spite of all that he had put her through, she still loved him, and they were connected by a powerful bond of loneliness and secrecy. Donald and Melinda reunited at last, and Melinda was soon pregnant again. Donald returned to work at the Foreign Office in London on 1 November, where he became head of the American Department. In December, the couple bought their first home together in the village of Tatsfield, an hour's drive from London. By all appearances, the Macleans were getting back on track.

In reality, it was the beginning of the end. The New Year brought new trouble for the Cambridge spies, right out of the gate.

In early January 1951, Kim Philby was told by Dick White to be on the lookout for a mole in the Foreign Office. Knowing full well that the real spy was Donald Maclean, Philby worried that MI5 was finally catching on to the FBI's lead. The Foreign Office, as well as MI6, had first received the news of Venona's scoop on the HOMER spy a little too casually. It appeared that MI5, at least, was now taking the matter seriously.

On 19 January, Kim and Aileen hosted a formal dinner party at their home on Nebraska Avenue. The guest list read like a roster of the most important figures in Washington's intelligence community. Their guests included CIA counterintelligence officer William Harvey and his wife, Libby, as well as British Embassy Head of Security Robert Mackenzie with his date, Geraldine Dack. Also present was physicist Wilfred Mann, who had advised Donald Maclean on the technical aspects of nuclear policy. Mann brought his wife, Miriam. FBI agent Robert Lamphere, who was working on the Venona cables, attended with his wife, Martha. And of course, Philby would never leave out his good friend, CIA foreign liaison officer James Angleton and his wife, Cicely.[14]

The gathering proceeded without incident until around nine-thirty, when Kim's troublesome houseguest, Guy Burgess, returned to the house. He had been drinking, as usual, and was in a peculiar mood. William Harvey's wife, Libby, a little tipsy by now herself, struck up a conversation with Guy Burgess. She had heard that he was a gifted artist who often drew amusing cartoons, and asked him to sketch a caricature of her. For reasons unknown to anyone but Burgess, he proceeded to draw a most offensive portrait. Depending on the version of the story (and there are several), her caricature was either terribly unflattering, or outright obscene.[15]

Libby Harvey stormed out of the house, furious. She was followed by her enraged husband, and a contrite Kim Philby, desperately explaining that it was only a joke. Aileen, her elegant dinner party ruined by her husband's idiot friend, retreated to the kitchen in tears. Cicely Angleton and Miriam Mann followed, attempting to comfort her, as their husbands stepped outside for some air. Guy Burgess, pleased that he had taken William Harvey down a peg, poured himself a drink, smiling like that cat who caught the canary. Wilfred Mann came back inside to find Philby sitting in a darkened room, weeping into his hands. The party, which had previously been going well, broke up in the awkwardness. Although the guests were certainly embarrassed for Kim and Aileen, the catastrophic evening did not cast any aspersions onto Kim Philby. If anything, he was pitied for his victimisation by the antics of Guy Burgess.

Back in London, Donald Maclean resumed his mission of self-destruction. December 1950 had offered the hope of redemption for his work, his marriage, and his family. January 1951 threatened to dash it all.

Philip Toynbee reappeared in Maclean's life like a stubborn rash. His tenure in Cairo complete, he returned to London, where he promptly disrupted Maclean's brief streak of sobriety. They attended a party together, where both men resumed their familiar pattern of binge drinking. Another guest, writer and anti-communist Humphrey Slater, began deriding communism, spurring Maclean to anger. Offended, Maclean raised his voice at Slater, proclaiming that he himself was a Party member, and had been for years.[16]

This outburst was as false as it was reckless. Maclean had never officially joined the Communist Party of Great Britain. Slater repeated the anecdote to his cousin, Patience Pain, who worked in the Foreign Office. Pain reported the incident to the personnel office, and a note was placed in Maclean's file. Curiously, the concern was chiefly over the fact that Maclean was drinking again, ignoring his professed communism. This oversight was especially egregious considering the ongoing search within the Foreign Office for the spy called HOMER.

Maclean continued to frequent the Gargoyle Club, where he felt at home among the intellectual and creative set, and he was largely free to imbibe in peace, without being spotted by his Foreign Office colleagues. Goronwy Rees, who had maintained his friendship with Guy Burgess despite his own disavowal of communism, was also a member of the club. Rees was approached there one evening by a staggering Maclean, whom he had not seen in fifteen years. Maclean leaned close and hissed, 'I know all about you. You used to be one of us, but you ratted'. He then fell to the floor.[17]

Rees was alarmed by this reminder that he had indeed been recruited by Burgess, before bowing out of the espionage business. He had not, however, 'ratted', being kept on a short leash by his ongoing friendship with Burgess.

In another revealing episode, an inebriated Maclean challenged his friend, Mark Culme-Seymour, 'What would you do if I told you I was a communist agent?'

Culme-Seymour, who had been the best man at Donald's wedding, was stunned into silence.

'Well', insisted Maclean, 'Wouldn't you report me?'

'I don't know', stammered Culme-Seymour. 'Who to?'

'Well, I am', asserted Maclean, defiantly. 'Go on, report me.'[18]

Donald's friends were inclined to give him the benefit of the doubt when he offered up these outrageous confessions. They correctly attributed his statements to his intoxication, but wrongly diagnosed them as an attempt to shock them, or to test their loyalty. In reality, Donald Maclean was crushed by the weight of his many secrets, and drinking provided his only release. While under the influence of alcohol, he felt free to confess his true self and his real ideology.

The fateful reunion between Donald Maclean and his closest friend, Philip Toynbee, was not to last. Their long friendship came to an end over a disagreement about another diplomatic spy, Alger Hiss.

Hiss, a Soviet agent at a high level in the US State Department, had been exposed by the journalist, Whittaker Chambers, who had been his courier during the 1930s. Chambers had broken with the Soviets and gone into hiding during the Great Purge of the late 1930s. In 1948, Chambers was called to testify before the House Committee for Un-American Activities (HUAC). Under subpoena, Chambers corroborated some of the allegations made by former spy runner, Elizabeth Bentley. Though the statute of limitations had expired on charges of espionage, Hiss was convicted on two charges of perjury. He appealed the conviction, but his appeal was denied in March 1951.

Toynbee published an article in *The Observer* in March 1951, giving a surprisingly balanced commentary on the sensational trial of Alger Hiss, which had sharply divided Americans along political lines.[19] A former communist himself, Toynbee sympathised with Hiss' 1930s-era communism, though he agreed with the court's findings that Hiss had given State Department secrets to the Soviets. He went so far as to presume that Hiss could not stop spying once he became trapped under the thumb of the KGB. Toynbee went on to criticise the liberals who attempted to destroy the career of Whittaker Chambers in their defence of Alger Hiss.

Having read the article, Donald Maclean confronted Toynbee in the Gargoyle Club. He was enraged that his good friend would defend Chambers. Perhaps Toynbee had hit a nerve when, sympathetically, he theorised that the Soviets must have had 'an unbreakable hold' on Alger Hiss. In his drunken rage, Maclean, still holding his pint glass, swung at Philip, sending his dearest friend tumbling into the band.[20]

'I am the English Hiss', Maclean said, walking away.[21]

They never saw one another again.

Meanwhile, Guy Burgess, not content simply to embarrass Kim Philby, ratcheted up his own efforts at self-sabotage. He had begun an ill-advised relationship with Philby's personal secretary, Esther Whitfield. Kim had already engaged in an extramarital affair with Whitfield while in Turkey. Kim had moved Esther into a room in the attic of the house on Nebraska Avenue, much to Aileen's annoyance. Whitfield developed strong feelings for Burgess, despite his homosexuality.

Upon his arrival in the United States, Burgess purchased a convertible Lincoln Continental, which he proudly drove like a maniac. In February 1951, the Citadel, a military college in South Carolina, asked the British Embassy to send a speaker to appear at its annual three-day conference for the South Eastern Regional International Relations Club. The original speaker had to back out at the last minute, and Guy Burgess was the only officer available with enough expertise on the subject to fill in. The selection of Burgess was risky, but not totally out of the question. In spite of Guy's recent troubles, he had escorted Deputy Prime Minister Anthony Eden during his official visit to Washington the previous November. Except for Guy's misplacement of his car keys, the visit had gone very well.

On 28 February, Burgess hopped into the Lincoln for the 500 mile trip to Charleston. He brought with him a companion, James Turck, a local homosexual in his twenties. Burgess was pulled over in Woodbridge, Virginia, for driving ninety miles per hour. Burgess claimed diplomatic immunity, and was let go with a warning. Sixty miles later, in Richmond, he was stopped a second time while attempting to pass an army convoy at eighty miles per hour. Again, he received a warning. The two men stopped for lunch, where Burgess had a few beers. Turck took over driving. He had been urged by Burgess to speed to make up the time lost during their two traffic stops. Turck, who happened to be black, easily caught the eye of the Virginia state patrol while driving a flashy convertible in the still segregated American south. The two men were pulled over for the third time that day near St Petersburg.

Burgess attempted to cover for Turck, insisting that he was his chauffer, and was thereby covered under Guy's diplomatic immunity. The patrolman disagreed, and Turck was arrested. Burgess cashed a check at a nearby hotel to secure his boyfriend's fifty-five dollar bail. While waiting, Turck signed a sworn affidavit affirming that it was, in fact, their third traffic stop of the day, and that Burgess had told him to speed, reassuring him that it was permitted by Guy's diplomatic immunity.[22]

The remainder of the drive went off without incident, but Turck's affidavit was forwarded to the Governor of Virginia, who eventually passed it along to the British Embassy.

The following evening, Burgess gave his talk at the Citadel. His purpose, ostensibly, was to defend Great Britain's recognition of communist China, in contrast with the American position of non-recognition. He made a terrible impression, showing up in a wrinkled suit and slurring his words. His presentation was incoherent and hostile; he spent most of his time attacking American foreign policy. After his speech, Guy returned to his place at the head table, and promptly fell asleep in his chair.

Over the next few weeks, James Turck's affidavit, as well as an official complaint from the State of Virginia, slowly made its way back to the Foreign Office. Virginia Governor, John Battle, wrote to the US State Department, lambasting Guy's disregard for Virginia's traffic laws, and his abuse of diplomatic privilege. The complaint was forwarded to British Ambassador Oliver Franks, who summoned Burgess to his office on 14 April. Burgess was suspended, pending an investigation by the disciplinary board in London. A few days later the US State Department was notified that Burgess was being recalled. His job performance had been lacklustre, and his drinking problem disruptive, just as everyone had predicted. The incident with the speeding tickets was simply the final straw.

Michael Straight, the erstwhile American Cambridge spy, described a strange meeting with Burgess that spring in Washington. Straight claimed that he was driving away from the embassy, when he happened to see Burgess hailing a cab. Straight pulled over, and Burgess climbed in. The two men proceeded to get into an argument over the Korean War, and Straight threatened to turn him in on charges of espionage.[23] Though Michael Straight claimed it was a chance encounter, he may have been sent to deliver Burgess a warning. Anthony Blunt had sent a copy of his latest book, *The Nation's Pictures*, to Washington along with one of his boyfriends, John Blamey. Blamey allegedly gave the book to Straight, who then passed it along to Burgess.[24] This seems like a rather circuitous method for sending a present. It is possible that a message was hidden inside the book, warning Burgess to leave the United States.

As the binge drinking and reckless driving finally caught up to Guy Burgess, the Venona cables finally caught up to Donald Maclean.

Ever since MI5 and the Foreign Office had been notified of the mysterious spy named HOMER, they had been searching in all of the wrong places. They began by investigating the cipher clerks, then moved on to janitorial workers and to lower level officers. Only later did investigators take a look at high level diplomats. Kim Philby did his best to sabotage the investigation. Despite his efforts, the investigation began to zero in on Donald Maclean by April 1951.

Robert Mackenzie, Head of Security at the Washington Embassy, began to make the connection once Meredith Gardner concluded that G, MATERIAL G, and GOMER were probably three names for the same person. He also took another look at the testimony of Soviet defector Walter Krivitsky, which Kim Philby had brought to his attention (in an effort to deflect suspicion from himself). Mackenzie reviewed embassy records from 1944, when the first cables were sent to Moscow. A short list of suspects was compiled, at which Maclean was at the bottom. Rather than narrowing the search, Walter Krivitsky's tips muddied the waters; his clues were inconsistent, and read more like a composite of Maclean, Cairncross, and possibly Burgess.

A cable sent from New York to Moscow on 28 June 1944, planted the seed for Maclean's eventual unmasking. The message was sent by Vladimir Pravdin after meeting Maclean for the first time. Maclean had just moved to Washington, and Melinda, pregnant, was staying in New York with her family. Large portions of the message were decoded, though not all of it. The message, in part, read:

> *To VIKTOR*
>
> *SERGEJ's meeting with GOMMER took place on 25 June. GOMMER did not hand anything over. The next meeting will take place on 30 July in TYRE (code name for New York). It had been made possible for G. to summon SERGEJ in case of need. SIDON's (London's) original instructions have been altered...*
> *...(thirty-four groups unrecoverable)...*
> *...travel to TYRE where his wife is living with her mother while awaiting confinement.*[25]

Donald Maclean was the only Foreign Office diplomat to whom these phrases could be applied. He arrived in Washington in the summer of 1944, he was at first unable to find family housing in Washington, his wife was pregnant (awaiting confinement), and she was living with her mother in New York. After two years of searching for HOMER, the Foreign Office believed they had finally found him.

As part of the effort to apprehend HOMER, Kim Philby was notified of MI5's intent to interrogate Maclean. Some historians have speculated that

Guy Burgess orchestrated his own ouster from Washington for the purpose of warning Maclean.[26] It is certainly plausible.

Philby and Burgess met for dinner at Peking Restaurant, a noisy place where they could discuss plans for the exfiltration of Donald Maclean to the Soviet Union, without fear of being overheard.

'Don't you go, too', warned Philby, only half-joking.[27] He could weather the disappearance of Maclean, to whom he had only tenuous connections. Burgess, however, was one of his closest friends, and until recently, had lived in his home. A defection by Guy Burgess would lay suspicion squarely at the feet of Kim Philby.

Chapter Fourteen

The Flight
A Daring Escape to Moscow

After his discussion with Kim Philby, Guy Burgess left Washington to spend a few days in New York, where he stayed at the apartment of Alan Maclean, Donald's brother. On the night before Guy was to sail for London, a small group of friends gathered for a going-away party. Burgess was not his usual jovial self; he was in a melancholy state. He asked his friend, Norman Luker, who worked for the BBC in Rockefeller Centre, if he could borrow his tape recorder. Burgess then recounted to the party guests the story of how he had once met Winston Churchill. Guy delighted the party goers with a hilarious impersonation of Churchill, and it was all recorded for posterity. Burgess was a compulsive name-dropper, who could never resist reminding people of his important connections.

After sailing on the *Queen Mary*, Burgess was met at the docks at Southampton by Anthony Blunt. The old friends went back to Blunt's apartment at the Courtauld Institute, where Burgess told him what he had learned from Philby. The Foreign Office knew that Maclean was the mysterious HOMER mentioned in the cables decoded by Venona, and it was only a matter of time before he would be picked up by MI5.

The following morning, Blunt met with his handler, Yuri Modin. Modin put a message in to the Centre, asking for the exfiltration of Donald Maclean. Moscow responded quickly in agreement. Only one question remained – how could Maclean slip out of the country, when he was already under suspicion?

The matter was certainly urgent, but the spies were aided by the procrastination of MI5. The Venona transcripts, though definitive, could never be used as evidence in an espionage trial. The US government considered the KGB cables so valuable to its national interest that their existence could not be revealed, lest the Soviets find out and stop sending telegrams (unbeknownst to the Americans, the KGB had already stopped, thanks to Kim Philby). If Maclean was to be prosecuted, corroborating evidence, or else a confession, would have to be obtained.

Though Kim Philby was promptly informed of the Foreign Office's identification of Maclean as their suspect, the FBI was not. While Guy Burgess was sailing home to London, the heads of MI5 met with senior officials at the Foreign Office to discuss strategy. At first, it was agreed that they would tell the FBI about their suspicion, but would ask them to stay quiet until they had the chance to interrogate Maclean. Realising that the Americans weren't in a patient mood, they changed course. Robert Lamphere, from the FBI, was meeting with MI5's Washington representative, Geoffrey Paterson, almost daily, and Paterson was finding it increasingly difficult to keep the secret. The FBI was still chafing over the matter with Klaus Fuchs; they blamed lax British security for allowing Fuchs, a British physicist turned communist spy, to infiltrate the Manhattan Project. Agent Robert Lamphere, in particular, was growing impatient with the British foot-dragging. The investigators at MI5 didn't want to be rushed by the FBI. They decided that the FBI would be told about Maclean as soon as he was picked up for questioning.

Donald Maclean was officially identified as a suspect, and wiretaps were placed on his phone at the Foreign Office. He was followed by MI5's surveillance unit, Branch A4. For the first time, he was issued a code name by MI5: CURZON.[1]

The A4 'watchers', as they were known, were selected based on their good vision and hearing. Though they aimed to blend in with the general public, the watchers were comically conspicuous. They wore raincoats and trilby hats, even when it was warm outside. Maclean certainly noticed their presence. The KGB officers at the London Rezidentura noticed too, having seen these same characters pacing the sidewalk in front of the Soviet Embassy for many years. They casually deployed their own counter-surveillance; in effect, the KGB began watching the watchers.

The Soviets noted that the watchers did not follow Maclean on nights or weekends, owing to MI5's restrictions on overtime. They would not board the train with Donald; surely he would notice a new face among the regular commuters. They also did not follow him home to the rural village of Tatsfield, where a stranger in a raincoat would certainly raise eyebrows. Yuri Modin identified these gaps in surveillance as opportunities.

Though he realised that he was being followed, Donald Maclean remained ignorant of the Venona exposure and the subsequent investigation. It was time to let him in on the secret.

On 14 May, Burgess called Donald Maclean at his office, suggesting they meet for lunch at the Reform Club the following day. They started off with drinks, before deciding to move to the Royal Automotive Club, where the dining room was not so full. As they walked over together, Maclean remarked that he had been followed lately. Burgess confirmed Maclean's suspicions; MI5 had figured him out, and his only option was to defect to Moscow.

Maclean sighed, dejectedly. He could not bear the thought of leaving his children, nor Melinda, who was seven months pregnant. Maclean also knew that he could not hold up under interrogation. He was in such a frail state that he was actually relieved to unburden himself to Burgess. He had seen the consequences play out for Alan Nunn May, and for Klaus Fuchs. Perhaps he could get a light sentence for himself, too. Maclean insisted that he would stay in London.

After lunch, Maclean returned to work, and Burgess reported the conversation to Modin. Modin sent a cable to Moscow Centre. Within one hour, Moscow cabled back: 'HOMER *must* agree to defect'.[2] The Centre could not risk a confession by their most valuable spy. He simply knew too much.

While trying to convince Maclean that leaving was the best option, Burgess was asked to accompany him on the journey. While it would suit the interests of Kim Philby for Burgess to stay in London, the Centre saw things differently. Though not yet exposed as a spy, Guy's utility to the KGB was rapidly diminishing. His drinking was out of control, which might loosen his tongue, leading to some dangerous revelations. Also, Burgess was about to lose his job at the Foreign Office, which would cut off his access to any useful material, anyway. According to Yuri Modin, Burgess was assured that he could come back to London once Maclean was spirited safely away to Moscow.[3]

If this was ever true, there is no indication that Burgess believed it. In fact, his own defection with Maclean may well have been Guy's idea. All of his actions pointed to a man bent on permanent escape. Since the moment his ship docked in Southampton, Guy had been conducting a farewell tour, of sorts. He visited his family, and many of his old friends – Goronwy

Rees, Victor Rothschild, Quentin Bell, Cyril Connolly, and Peter Pollock, among others. He attended the annual Apostles dinner at Cambridge, where the easy charm and charisma of his youth gave way to sarcasm and aggression, making the other guests uncomfortable. He spent his evenings making drunk phone calls to old friends and associates. Most damning of all, when Guy returned to the house that he shared with Jack Hewit, Jack found several bundles of cash while unpacking Guy's luggage.[4]

While making the rounds among his many London contacts, Burgess received correspondence from America, too.

Guy received a letter from Kim's secretary, Esther Whitfield, asking what should be done with his Lincoln. In a heartfelt postscript, she gently turned down his earlier marriage proposal. She expressed a great deal of affection for him, but feared that he would be unhappy in a heterosexual relationship.[5]

Guy also received mail from Kim Philby, who was getting nervous. Kim had seen a telegram from MI5 sent to their embassy representative, Geoffrey Paterson. The cable inquired about an interview with a cipher clerk who had worked in the embassy in 1944, about a matter concerning the HOMER telegrams. Hoping to rush the matter along, Philby sent a cryptic letter to Burgess, reminding him that he had left his car at the embassy, and needed to take care of the matter soon. Philby also remarked that it was getting very 'hot' in Washington.[6]

Things were getting 'hot' in London, too. Having heard the voice of Guy Burgess through the wiretap on Maclean's phone, MI5 began tracking Burgess, as well. He was issued the code name BERKELY. On 15 May, plans were finalised for the arrest and interrogation of Donald Maclean. On 21 May, a second meeting was held. Percy Sillitoe, Head of MI5, wanted to inform FBI chief J. Edgar Hoover of Maclean's impending arrest, but was dissuaded by Dick White, Head of Counter-Intelligence. White wanted to wait, in case Maclean decided to confess on his own.

In order to build a stronger case against Maclean, MI5 decided to search Donald's home. Melinda had a scheduled Caesarean section in mid-June, and they planned to search the house while Melinda was in the hospital and while Donald was at work. This strategy pushed back their timeline by nearly a month.

The Cambridge spies had a plan, too. The idea came from Anthony Blunt. He knew of weekend pleasure cruises into France, where boats would briefly

The Flight

dock, and their passengers could take in meals or some shopping. They were very popular with philandering married men and their mistresses, to which the French could certainly relate. Passports were not typically checked on either side of the channel. Maclean could board a cruise under a false name, and could then be spirited away to the Continent with no record of his passage. If he and Burgess left on a weekend, they would not be spotted by the watchers, who would be clocked out by Friday evening.

Yuri Modin urged Anthony Blunt to defect, as well. Blunt, comfortable in his role as a highly regarded art historian, flatly refused. He enjoyed the career he had made for himself, which garnered the respect of the art community and the admiration of his students. He later admitted that he had no desire to live in the Soviet Union, and, if exposed, he would have simply committed suicide.[7] Though Blunt could not be forced to defect, the Centre could no longer work with Blunt in London. Modin knew that once Burgess left with Maclean, Blunt would fall under suspicion, too. He would no longer be useful as an agent. Anthony Blunt's career with the KGB officially came to an end, to his great relief.

Burgess made two more brief meetings with Maclean to confirm the plan, and to convince him to follow through. Melinda, despite her late stage of pregnancy, encouraged Donald to go. He finally acquiesced, knowing deep down that it was for the best. After all, Donald had written to Moscow from Cairo only a year prior, desperately asking to be exfiltrated.

On the morning of Friday 25 May, Guy Burgess booked a cabin on a boat called the *Falaise* for a weekend cruise to St Malo. The reservation listed himself and Bernard Miller, whom he had sailed with on board the *Queen Mary* a few weeks earlier. Miller knew nothing of this ruse. Miller was an American student on his way to Switzerland to study medicine, and Burgess had promised to put him in touch with some people in London who could help him in his career. He was used by Burgess to cover his plans for Maclean.

After booking the cruise, Burgess then rented a car, an Austin A-40. He stopped by the Courtauld to see Anthony Blunt before having lunch at the Reform Club. Guy then met up with Bernard Miller, the unwitting shill in his misdirection scheme, and the two men went shopping. Burgess bought a suitcase, clothes, and an umbrella. He returned home to pack. In his suitcase, Burgess packed a tweed suit, a dinner jacket, shoes, socks, and the complete works of Jane Austen, without which he never travelled.

Donald Maclean, meanwhile, spent that Friday celebrating his 38th birthday. Having accepted his fate, he was strangely calm. The burden of carrying so many secrets, and keeping his true self under wraps, was nearly over. Upon arriving at work, he rang his mother to invite her to lunch. She already had plans to lunch with a friend, and regretfully declined. He then called his old friends, Robin and Mary Campbell, whom he had known since his days studying for the Foreign Office exam at Scoones. They picked him up at his office to take him for a birthday lunch at Wheeler's oyster bar. They chatted excitedly about the upcoming arrival of the new baby, and made plans for Donald to stay with the Campbells while Melinda was in the hospital.

After lunch, they ran into Donald's Foreign Office colleague, Cyril Connolly, who was pleased to see a cheerful and sober Donald Maclean. Their last meeting, two weeks earlier, had involved Connolly serving a glass of Alka Seltzer to Maclean after finding him passed out on his doorstep.

Maclean stopped by the Travellers Club on his way back to the office, where he cashed a cheque and phoned his colleague, Geoffrey Jackson. He asked Jackson if he would look after the office on Saturday; Maclean had scheduled off the next day, Saturday, some weeks ago. He had planned to pick up his sister, Nancy, and her new husband, Bob Oetking, who were coming to town for a visit.

After meeting with the Argentinian Minister-Counsellor (it was Argentinian National Day), Maclean was careful to let his colleagues know that he wouldn't be in to work the following day. Sir Roger Makins, Deputy Under-Secretary of State, was the last person to see Maclean at the Foreign Office that Friday afternoon. They passed each other in the courtyard as Maclean was leaving. Maclean reminded Makins that he wouldn't be in the office the next morning.[8]

Makins, who the previous day had attended yet another meeting with MI5 representatives on when to interrogate Maclean, quickly returned to the office to verify whether Maclean had indeed scheduled the day off. He looked for George Carey-Foster, Head of Security, but he had already left for the day. Knowing that Maclean was under surveillance, Makins decided to let the matter go. He was not aware that Maclean's watchers would not follow him home, since it was now the weekend. The MI5 watchers, getting ready to end their work week, logged their final entry soon afterwards. After a drink, Maclean boarded his usual train at Charing Cross, alone, at 6:10 pm.

Maclean arrived home to a modest birthday celebration. The children had come down with measles, and Melinda, pregnant and exhausted, had prepared a special ham for Donald's birthday dinner. Guy Burgess arrived soon after Donald, and introduced himself as Roger Styles. After a pleasant dinner, Maclean announced that he and 'Mr Styles' had some business to attend to, which might take the whole night. Maclean packed pyjamas and some toiletries into a Gladstone bag, and said goodbye to his two sons. He hopped into the rented car with Burgess and departed at some point between nine and ten o'clock.

Having said their goodbyes, they sped off on their ninety mile journey to Southampton, taking the back roads to avoid being seen. They arrived at the dock just before midnight, as the gangplank of the *Falaise* was about to be raised. Abandoning the vehicle with the keys in the ignition, Burgess and Maclean ran to board the departing vessel.

The *Falaise* docked at St Malo, France, at nine o'clock the next morning. Burgess and Maclean slept in, and had a late breakfast before disembarking, leaving their luggage behind in the cabin. Their leisurely morning kept them from being seen by the other passengers, but it also caused them to miss the 11:20 train to Paris. They quickly hailed a taxi. The taxi driver sped to the next city, Rennes, where they caught up with the train at a quarter past one. They had dinner and drinks in Paris before heading to Bern, Switzerland, where they were issued forged passports by the Soviet Embassy. The pair went on to Zurich, where they boarded a flight to Stockholm, Sweden. The flight stopped in Prague, Czechoslovakia, where Burgess and Maclean stepped off. Now safely within the East Bloc, Burgess and Maclean stayed for a week before they were collected by KGB agents, and transported to Moscow. They were not seen again for five years.

Unbeknownst to the two fugitives, they were spotted leaving the dock at Southampton on Friday. An immigration official recognised Maclean, whose name had been placed on a watch list. The official called MI5 headquarters in London. An alert was issued to British Intelligence across Europe, but, in an effort to keep the embarrassing matter under wraps, the French police were not notified.

Melinda Maclean, who knew full well what her husband was up to, orchestrated a sophisticated cover up in order to buy him enough time to slip away.[9]

Donald had told his colleagues that he had scheduled that Saturday off to pick up his visiting sister from the dock. On the contrary, his sister, Nancy, drove with her husband to the Maclean's house from the dock in their own vehicle. Wiretaps on the Maclean house recorded no phone calls on Saturday until eight o'clock that evening, when Nancy called to say that she and her husband, Bob Oetking, had stopped in Ashford on their way from Dover, and would be there by nine-thirty. When they arrived, Melinda told them that Donald had called to say he was running late, and to start dinner without him. Donald and Nancy's mother, Lady Maclean, called around ten o'clock to make plans for lunch the next day. Melinda suggested dinner instead, to give their guests time to rest up from their trip.

On Sunday morning, Melinda stunned Nancy with the news that Donald had disappeared. Nancy and Bob went to London without Melinda, where they broke the news to Lady Maclean that her favourite son had gone missing. She was upset and regretful that she had turned down his lunch invitation on Friday.

An inexplicable denial took hold of Donald Maclean's family, as well as his colleagues.

Nancy, a former SIS officer, ignored her own training and assumed that Donald was just on another drinking binge and would turn up soon. Donald's history of weekend benders gave him plenty of cover, at least for the first few days.

The MI5 wiretaps recorded a call to Melinda from Lady Maclean on Monday morning, asking if Donald had returned home yet. Melinda, according to the reports, sounded 'very upset'.[10] She could not have been *too* upset, because she did not call the office looking for him until Tuesday, nor did she notify the police.

When Maclean failed to show up for work on Monday morning, George Carey-Foster asked Roger Makins about him. Makins, remembering that Maclean took the day off on Saturday, wondered aloud if he hadn't scheduled off Monday as well.

Robert Cecil, Maclean's deputy, was returning from a week-long trip in France. He was surprised when his passport was checked at the airport in Paris, then confused when his co-workers expressed relief that he had actually returned to work. When he learned that Maclean had failed to show up the office, and that Guy Burgess had also disappeared, Cecil assumed, like nearly everyone else, that the pair had gone off on a drinking binge together.

As the Foreign Office scrambled to locate Maclean, Jack Hewit noticed that Guy Burgess had failed to return Sunday night from his weekend cruise, allegedly with Bernard Miller. He called Anthony Blunt, who denied knowledge of his whereabouts. Hewit offered to call Miller's hotel, but Blunt told him not do so. Blunt told Hewit that he was certain that Burgess would be home soon and there was no point in calling around and upsetting people. Hewit did not immediately contact Miller, but he did call Guy's close friend, Goronwy Rees.

Upon hearing the news of Guy's disappearance, Goronwy feared the worst. He placed a call to David Footman, Burgess' old MI6 contact, and told him his suspicion – that Guy Burgess must have defected to the Soviet Union. Next, he called Anthony Blunt. The following morning, Monday, 28 May, Blunt paid Rees a visit at his home. According to Rees, Blunt tried to discourage Rees from spilling what he knew about Burgess and his espionage work.[11] Rees, who had never liked Anthony Blunt, was disinclined to take orders from him. In any case, he had already spoken with David Footman, who immediately went to Guy Liddell.

Witnesses at the dock reported seeing Burgess and Maclean board the ship together on Saturday, and Burgess' rental car was soon found, abandoned in the nearby car park. Dick White and Guy Liddell from MI5 were dumbfounded. Just as the Foreign Office could not have imagined that an upstanding figure like Maclean could ever be a spy, MI5 could not believe that a reprobate like Guy Burgess could be one, either.

Anthony Blunt spoke with his old friend, Guy Liddell, and did his best to act surprised. He had a key to Guy's house, and offered to let Liddell in to search it. Blunt told Jack Hewit to leave town for a little while, which he did. Before meeting Liddell, Blunt likely made a sweep of his own to remove any incriminating evidence. Unfortunately, he overlooked something.

When Guy Liddell searched Guy's home, he found a guitar case filled with letters. There was a postcard from Kim Philby, an old letter from John Cairncross, and even a few letters from Blunt. Nonetheless, Anthony Blunt did a masterful job convincing his old chums at MI5 of his own innocence, despite his close ties with Burgess, despite the suspicions of people like Cyril Connolly, and despite the outright accusations by Goronwy Rees.

By the time Melinda called the office looking for Donald on Tuesday, 29 May, the pieces of the puzzle were falling into place. All of the Western European embassies were notified, and were instructed to enlist the help of the local police. The Swiss Embassy, however, was discouraged from involving their local police force, in the hopes of keeping Moscow out of the loop. The spies having escaped through Switzerland, this was a dreadful miscalculation on the part of the SIS.

The incompetence and inconceivable delays continued. Melinda was not interviewed by MI5 until 30 May, and by then, the Foreign Office had advised her to say nothing. Alan Maclean was recalled to London and questioned about his missing brother, but knew nothing of his whereabouts. On 2 June, a full week after their disappearance, a bulletin with the mugshots of Burgess and Maclean was issued to the embassies, along with a directive to confiscate their passports if they were seen. On 6 June, the embassies of Latin America, Africa, and the Middle East were notified. The FBI, still unaware that Maclean had been identified as HOMER, were not informed of the disappearance of the two diplomats. They would find out soon enough.

On 7 June 1951, a headline splashed across the front page of the London *Daily Express*: 'Yard Hunts Two Britons'.[12] The Paris bureau chief, Larry Solon, had received a tip from George Gherra, a reporter from the French paper *France-Soir*. Gherra informed Solon that the French police had been searching for two missing British diplomats. They were not named in the news story, but clearly, the game was up.

The Foreign Office, its attempts at secrecy now blown, was forced to issue a press release:

> *Two members of the Foreign Service have been missing from their homes since 25 May. One is Mr D.D. Maclean, the other Mr G.F. de M. Burgess. All possible enquiries are being made. It is known that they went to France a few days ago. Mr Maclean had a breakdown a year ago owing to overstrain, but was believed to fully have recovered. Owing to their being absent without leave, both have been suspended with effect from 1 June.*[13]

A media frenzy ensued, resulting in the harassment of the families of Maclean and Burgess. Melinda was forced to close the gates to the property, but that did not prevent her 6-year-old son, Fergus, from the bullying of his classmates. Guy's mother and stepfather, Colonel and Mrs Bassett, were mobbed by reporters. Anthony Blunt, due his close friendship with Burgess, was hounded by the press, and took shelter in his apartment at the Courtauld.

Guy's stepfather, Colonel Bassett, and Alan Maclean were summoned by Detective Jim Skardon to Waterloo station to collect the clothes left behind on the boat by Burgess and Maclean, respectively. Embarrassed laughs were shared when neither man wanted to claim a pair of torn pyjamas, nor a stiff and filthy pair of socks. Both items were trashed.

Guy Burgess had placed a call to Goronwy Rees from the Reform Club in his final days in London. He had instead reached his wife, Margie. Guy never paid the charges for the call, and a notice was tacked to the bulletin board at the club, along with the phone number. Reporters saw this, and immediately flocked to the home of Goronwy Rees. The Rees children, who had been given presents by Burgess upon his return from the United States, now received chocolates from journalists hoping to get a scoop. Margie Rees was allegedly approached by a reporter who said, 'It's all right to talk to me, Mrs Rees. I'm bisexual, myself'.[14]

Reassuring, but cryptic, telegrams arrived for the families. Guy's mother received a short note from Guy, claiming he was on a long holiday. Donald's family received a similar telegram, signed with his childhood nickname, Teento, to assure them it was really him.

While the media circus continued in London, the American diplomatic and intelligence agencies in Washington bitterly processed the news, which they learned from the London *Daily Express*, like everyone else. The US State Department received so many cables inquiring about the incident on 7 June that they ran out of paper. It is not clear whether it was arrogance, embarrassment, or perhaps a little of both, that kept MI5, MI6, and the Foreign Office from briefing their American counterparts on the disappearance of the two diplomats.

Kim Philby learned of the defection at the end of May. When he was told that Burgess defected along with Maclean, which he had specifically asked him *not* to do, Philby came close to panic. He packed his camera and other spy tools into the trunk of his car and drove out to the woods, where he buried them. He was right to be worried.

Kim Philby was recalled to London by MI6, and was interrogated over several days beginning 12 June. Kim's fears that Burgess' disappearance would implicate him were confirmed. There had been nothing linking Philby with Maclean, until Burgess disappeared with him. Over the course of three days of questioning, Philby's interrogators made every attempt to determine how Burgess might have learned about HOMER's real identity. Neither Burgess nor Maclean had access to the top secret Venona transcripts. Kim Philby, however, had access to all of them.

Percy Sillitoe, director of MI5, flew to Washington with investigator, Arthur Martin, to brief J. Edgar Hoover on Maclean and Burgess. Arthur Martin, a tenacious detective, first became suspicious of Philby after the botched defection of Konstantin Volkov in 1945. After watching Kim do everything in his power to thwart Volkov's defection, Martin began to dig into Philby's record. He first checked Philby's MI6 employment forms from 1940. Philby had falsely claimed that he was married to Aileen Furse (though living together, Kim was still legally married to Litzi Friedmann). With a quick perusal of public records, Martin discovered that Kim and Aileen were not married until 1946. Martin then stumbled upon Kim's 1934 marriage to Litzi, as well as their divorce, in 1946. Some further digging uncovered Litzi's extensive communist connections, which should have been disclosed to his new employer, and may have disqualified him for work in the SIS. The simple act of lying about his marriage was enough to bar him from service.

Once Philby's friend and houseguest, Guy Burgess, disappeared with Donald Maclean, Martin realised that Kim's communist ex-wife, his sabotage of the Volkov case, and his close friendship with a suspected Soviet agent were likely not a coincidence.

The Americans were furious about the British cover up, especially after the Klaus Fuchs affair. Given Maclean's previous unlimited access to the headquarters of the US Atomic Energy Commission, it appeared that the British had let an atomic spy slip through their fingers. Martin personally apologised to Robert Lamphere, who had been hot on the trail of HOMER since Meredith Gardner had found mention of him in the KGB cables. Nonplussed, Hoover ordered his own investigation of Burgess and Maclean, as well as Philby.

Twenty days after the disappearance of her husband, Melinda Maclean gave birth to a baby girl, whom she named Melinda. To distinguish her from her mother and grandmother (both also named Melinda), the baby was nicknamed 'Pink Rose'. Melinda was accompanied in the hospital by her mother and her steadfastly dependable sister, Harriet. Toward the end of the summer, Melinda's mother, Mrs Dunbar, received two cashier's cheques in the mail at the Maclean home in Tatsfield. The cheques were drafted from two different Swiss banks, both signed by a mysterious Mr Robert Becker, and were each made out in the amount of £1000. Days later, Melinda received a letter from Donald himself, postmarked from a town near Tatsfield. He explained that the cheques made out to Mrs Dunbar were actually intended for Melinda. He expressed his delight in the birth of his daughter, affection for his young sons, grief for his absence, and his abiding love and appreciation for Melinda.[15]

In an effort to shield Melinda from prying reporters, Mrs Dunbar arranged to bring Melinda and the children on a month long holiday to the south of France, where Melinda's sister, Catherine, had rented a house near St Tropez. Melinda was glad to get away. Once the cheques had arrived at her home, MI5 investigators stopped treating the new mother with kid gloves. They began to suspect that Melinda knew of Donald's espionage and of his whereabouts.

John Cairncross was questioned briefly about the matter in June, as part of a canvassing of former Cambridge communists. He had already been coached by Yuri Modin, who expected MI5 to come poking around. Given that he knew little about Burgess' espionage activities, and nothing at all about Maclean's, Cairncross could not be of much help to investigators anyway. However, once John's letter was found hidden in the guitar case in Guy's flat, Cairncross was facing more careful scrutiny. The letter was a fourteen-page handwritten synopsis of the Foreign Office's position on Nazi appeasement, written after the invasion of Czechoslovakia. He had given the notes to Burgess after having lunch with some of his old Foreign Office colleagues; a luncheon suggested by Burgess. Cairncross was now linked, undeniably, with Guy Burgess.

John's exposure could not have come at a worse time. He had just married Gabrielle Oppenheim earlier that spring at the Kensington Registry. He was anxious to begin his new married life and to finally pursue his academic ambitions. John was again hoping to break away from his work for the Soviets, though Yuri Modin, with approval from the Centre, had paid for his honeymoon at Graham Greene's vacation home in Italy.

Cairncross was visited at work the following March by Jim Skardon. Skardon, a skilled interrogator, had famously managed to extract confessions from both Alan Nunn May and Klaus Fuchs. He hoped to repeat his success with John Cairncross. Midway through the interview, Skardon slid the damning letter across the table to Cairncross, who visibly blanched at the sight of own handwriting.

Cairncross maintained that the letter was part of the regular friendly policy conversations he had with Burgess, whom he knew only casually. He expressed surprise that Burgess had kept the letter all of this time, and denied that he had written it for any nefarious purpose. In the absence of more incriminating evidence, Skardon did not arrest Cairncross that day. He did, however, inform John's supervisor of the ongoing investigation. Cairncross was immediately suspended.

Cairncross met again with Skardon on 2 April, this time at the War Office. Having had a few days to prepare himself, John gave carefully worded statements about his dalliance with communism at Cambridge, working at the Foreign Office with Donald Maclean, and his acquaintance with Guy Burgess. John claimed that he and Guy had many conversations about current events and foreign policy, which led to his letter. Cairncross showed a great deal of concern over his reputation, and hoped to resolve the matter without a great deal of publicity.

Skardon scheduled a third meeting with Cairncross to take place the following week. Panicked, Cairncross sought an emergency meeting with Modin in the interim. Before they could make contact, though, both Cairncross and Modin realised that they were each being followed by Special Branch surveillance. The meeting was aborted by Cairncross. The non-smoker lit a cigarette as he stood in Gunnersbury Park, signalling to Modin that the meeting was cancelled.[16]

When Skardon later asked Cairncross what he was doing alone in the park, John claimed that he was meeting with a married woman. As Skardon further probed his relationship with Burgess, Cairncross gave all of the right answers. Still, Skardon's intuition nagged at him. He was sure Cairncross was hiding something. At the end of the interview, Skardon asked Cairncross about his summer plans, and John mentioned that he and Gabrielle planned a visit to Italy. Inexplicably, Skardon did not seize his passport. Cairncross quietly resigned from the Treasury, made one brief meeting to break contact with Modin (who agreed that any further contact was now unwise), and headed to Italy with Gabrielle.

He would not return to Great Britain for another forty years.

Kim Philby, meanwhile, never fully shook off the suspicion surrounding him. Though he had endured days of interrogations by officials at MI5, Kim never broke. In spite of the circumstantial evidence brought forth by Arthur Martin, there was so far no hard evidence implicating Kim Philby. Criminal charges would have required a confession, and Kim was unwilling to give it. However, Martin had compiled a long enough list of Philby's problematic behaviour, which now included his communist associations at Cambridge and his misleading memo about the HOMER investigation, that his employment at the SIS was no longer tenable. In July 1951, Sir Stewart Menzies, Head of MI6, asked for Kim's resignation. In lieu of his pension, Philby was issued a generous severance payment of £4000.

Chapter Fifteen

The Fallout
After the Flight

While defectors from the Soviet Union were becoming increasingly common in the west, defectors *to* the Soviet Union were vanishingly rare. Moscow had no official protocol to receive them and no purpose for them once they arrived. If Burgess and Maclean were expecting a hero's welcome, the reality fell somewhat short.

Their first night in Moscow was pleasant enough, with dinner served on the balcony of their hotel, which provided a stunning view of the Kremlin. Maclean and Burgess, relieved that their clandestine travelling had come to an end, celebrated in their customary fashion: they drank Russian vodka until three in the morning. After a few days, the spies were moved to a small town on the Volga River called Kuybyshev, where they endured endless debriefings. Kuybyshev, a manufacturing hub for the Soviet defence industry, was a closed city, patrolled by the military and inaccessible to foreigners and most Soviet citizens. The industrial city was dirty, dreary, and lonely.

Burgess and Maclean, who had little in common, were forced to live together in a small flat overlooking the river. Having escaped imprisonment in the west, they were now subjected to house arrest in the Soviet Union. Armed guards patrolled outside and a personal agent accompanied them around town, as if they had anywhere to run.

Donald Maclean got busy learning Russian, while Burgess drank and practised piano. To prevent leaks to the western media, they took pseudonyms. Maclean became Mark Petrovich Frazer, and Burgess became Jim Andreyevitch Eliot.

The KGB, already suspicious by nature, was driven to outright paranoia by Joseph Stalin, who was in the throes of his own delusions. In failing health, the increasingly isolated Stalin saw enemies everywhere. He came to believe his own doctors were trying to kill him, which triggered a purge on intellectuals, particularly Jewish intellectuals. In this tense environment, the KGB feared that Burgess and Maclean had come to the Soviet Union to work as double agents for the British. Their endless debriefings escalated into interrogations.

Back in London, Kim Philby's resignation from SIS failed to absolve him of suspicion. A judicial inquiry into the Burgess-Maclean affair was opened that November and Philby was summoned to testify. He was questioned by the King's Counsel, Helenus 'Buster' Milmo, a ruthless interrogator with a reputation for cracking his most resistant targets. Though nervous, Kim held fast. As long as Milmo had no new evidence, Philby could not be prosecuted. He was not criminally charged that day, but he was ordered to hand over his passport.

Jim Skardon resumed his investigation of Kim Philby. He phoned and visited the Philby home periodically. Although his style was less forceful than Buster Milmo's, Skardon had a way of gently keeping the pressure on his suspect, eventually chipping away at their resistance. He had broken Klaus Fuchs in this persistent manner and hoped to do the same with Kim Philby.

At home, Aileen Philby was reaching her breaking point with Kim. After all of his secrecy, his numerous affairs, his poor choice in friends, and his periodic binge drinking, he was now unemployed and under investigation. She berated Kim and threatened to expose him as a spy. It's not clear how much, if anything, Aileen knew, but she did in fact call the Foreign Office, telling them that Kim was planning to escape to Moscow with Burgess and Maclean. Kim, in turn, blamed Aileen's behaviour for his inability to find work. Kim called her insane, and later claimed that she tried to kill him. This may or may not be true, but Kim did begin sleeping in a tent in the yard.[1]

Kim tried in vain to find employment. His applications were rejected time and again when the Foreign Office refused to give him a reference. Philby managed to secure a book deal to write a history of the Spanish Civil War, but the deal fell apart when the publisher learned that it was illegal for a former intelligence officer to write that kind of book. He finally took an entry level position at an import and export firm, but his meagre salary did not quite cover the bills. For over two years, Kim and his family were kept afloat through the generous financial help of St John Philby.

During this period, Yuri Modin did not have contact with Philby. With Jim Skardon always keeping an eye on him, it was simply too dangerous. Philby did his best to lay low and avoid the police, as well as the press. By 1953, the officials at Moscow Centre became concerned about him. Word of his financial troubles had reached the Rezidentura, and, according to Yuri Modin, the Centre wanted to help the agent who had done so much for the Soviet Union over the course of his career. Modin was ordered to check in with Kim Philby and give him some money to help make ends meet.

Not having a current address for Philby, Modin solicited the help of Anthony Blunt. The KGB had officially ended its relationship with Blunt in 1951, when he refused to defect with Burgess and Maclean. There were no hard feelings; Anthony would no longer be of much use to Moscow after the sensational scandal of the missing diplomats, one of which, Burgess, was Anthony's close friend. For his part, Anthony was ready to bow out of a game that he had never wanted to play in the first place. He had settled into a long term relationship with John Gaskin, a jewellery salesman twelve years his junior, and published a new book, *Art and Architecture in France*.

In trying to contact Blunt after all of this time, Modin had to be careful. Anthony Blunt was somewhat famous now; he was highly regarded as the director of the Courtauld Institute, and was well known as the Surveyor of the Queen's Pictures (formerly Surveyor of the King's Pictures, George VI having died in early 1952). Modin relied on their previous signal to request a meeting – he crushed a piece of chalk on the pavement outside Anthony's door. When Blunt failed to show up at their old meeting point, Modin changed tactics. He watched the society pages of the newspapers for scheduled appearances by the esteemed professor. He finally found an advertisement for an event at the Courtauld, where Anthony Blunt would be a featured speaker.

During his speech at the Courtauld event, Blunt failed to recognise the thick-set foreigner with the black hair and heavy eyebrows sitting in the front row. It was Yuri Modin, and he approached Blunt after his talk, handing him a postcard of a Renaissance painting.

'Excuse me', Modin sputtered, in his Russian accent. 'Do you know where I can find this picture in the museum?'

'Yes', answered Blunt, now remembering his old Soviet handler. Blunt flipped over the postcard, where Modin had written, *Tomorrow, 8 PM, Ruislip.*

'Yes', Blunt repeated deliberately, nodding and tucking the postcard into his pocket.

Modin and Blunt met the following evening at a pub near the Ruislip tube station, as scheduled. Modin asked after Kim Philby and Anthony confirmed that his financial situation was as dire as Modin had feared. They set up a second meeting, so that Modin could give Anthony some money to pass along to Kim.

When Modin next saw Blunt, he brought with him £5000 in cash. As the two men walked through the streets, Modin realised that they were being followed. He raised his concern quietly to Blunt, who laughed. Blunt explained that their stalker was Kim Philby. Blunt smiled as he pointed to a shadowy figure in the distance. He offered to invite Philby over to join them. Modin refused. The risk was too great, for all three of them. Kim, lonely and disappointed, was nonetheless grateful to receive the money.[2]

Melinda Maclean, without her husband and now under suspicion herself, descended into a deep depression. Mrs Dunbar worried for her daughter's mental health and suggested that she spend some time living abroad with the children. A change of scenery might be refreshing and she could regain some privacy outside of the media's blistering spotlight. On her mother's advice, Melinda moved out of the family home and rented an apartment in Switzerland. Mrs Dunbar came along to help with the children, and the boys, Fergus and little Donald (nicknamed 'Beany'), were enrolled in a school in Geneva. Melinda finally explained to the children what had happened to their father. Though she framed his actions in noble terms, the children were not reassured. They now worried that their mother might leave them, too.

On 5 March 1953, Soviet Leader, Joseph Stalin, died two days after suffering a massive stroke. Melinda, who had not heard from Donald in nearly two years, began to show signs of cautious optimism, hoping that the closed Soviet society would soon open up a little. By summer, Melinda's mother noted a marked change in Melinda's mood. She had emerged from her hopelessness, and was now excited to plan a summer holiday with the children. They left for the Spanish island of Majorca on 23 July.

Melinda reportedly gave away a large amount of her clothes and makeup to the maid at the house where she stayed; Fergus and Beany allegedly told other children that they would soon be going away, but they didn't know where.

Upon their return to Geneva, Melinda came home from shopping one day and told her mother that she had run into an old friend from Cairo, Robin Muir. Muir had invited her and the children to stay at their villa for the weekend. Mrs Dunbar offered to watch the children at home while Melinda visited with her friend, but Melinda brushed her off. The Muirs had a nanny, she said, and it wouldn't be a problem. Melinda had also cashed a cheque that morning and purchased some new clothes for baby Melinda, now known as 'Mimsie'. Melinda and the children left the house at three in the afternoon on Friday. When they hadn't returned by Monday afternoon, Mrs Dunbar called the British Consul.[3]

Though everyone concluded that Guy Burgess and Donald Maclean had gone to the Soviet Union, nobody knew for sure until April 1954. A KGB colonel named Vladimir Petrov defected from his post at the Soviet Embassy of Australia. In exchange for asylum and £5000, Petrov offered to hand over every document that he could carry out of the embassy.

Of prime interest to MI6 was information related to Guy Burgess and Donald Maclean. Petrov provided information from his colleague, Filip Kislytsin, who had worked as a cipher clerk in London's Soviet Embassy from 1945 through 1948. Kislytsin was then transferred to Moscow Centre, where he was in charge of the files that were collected by Burgess and Maclean. The two spies had brought in so much material that most of it was never even read.

Kislytsin's files confirmed what MI5 had suspected. Burgess and Maclean had been recruited as Soviet agents while at Cambridge. Their 1951 disappearance had been facilitated by the KGB. Both were alive and well and were living in a town called Kuybyshev. While a Royal Commission was established to investigate the new information, Petrov published a memoir, *Empire of Fear*. He recounted the many occasions when, according to Kislytsin, Burgess walked out of the Foreign Office with a briefcase full of documents. He would give them to his handler, who brought them to the Soviet Embassy to be photographed or copied. Petrov also relayed the details of Burgess and Maclean's escape from Great Britain, beginning at the docks at Southampton and ending at the airport in Prague. Petrov claimed the duo escaped with the help of an unnamed third man.

When a weekly newspaper, *The People*, began serialising excerpts of Petrov's book, the British government was forced to publicly address

Petrov's claims. A whitepaper was commissioned by Foreign Secretary, Harold Macmillan, and the cabinet convened to discuss it on 21 September. The whitepaper, released to the public in October, downplayed the role of the Foreign Office in covering up the scandal, as well as MI5's numerous failures in the days leading up to the defection. Outrageously, it stated that Guy Burgess had been a satisfactory diplomat and Donald Maclean had no access to any sensitive information.[4]

In Washington, FBI director J. Edgar Hoover seethed in anger. He knew better than most the extent of the duo's damage, and he was certain of Kim Philby's involvement. Hoover retaliated against the British cover up by planting a story, through a friendly reporter, in the New York *Sunday News*, implicating Kim Philby as the mysterious third man in the Burgess-Maclean affair.

The 23 October story caused a sensation in the London papers. Harold Macmillan, eager to put the matter to rest, refused to be bated. Instead of ordering an official inquiry into Kim Philby, he appeared before parliament on 7 November, and proclaimed Philby's innocence. Philby, even more anxious to kill the story, held a press conference in his mother's apartment the following day. His characteristic stutter was curiously absent, as he confidently addressed a small crowd of reporters. An American reporter, NBC's Ed Newman, questioned Philby as cameramen recorded the interview.

Philby, unblinking, boldly told one lie after another. He denied being the third man, and refused to comment when asked if there even was a third man. He claimed that when he was asked to resign from the Foreign Office, it was only because of his 'imprudent' friendship with Guy Burgess. Kim asserted that the last time he had knowingly spoken with a communist was in 1934, and Burgess gave him no idea whatsoever that he was a communist, or a spy.

Though his brazen performance didn't convince everyone, MI5 had no choice but to drop the matter. The case against Philby was effectively closed with Macmillan's exoneration.

Notwithstanding Kim's confident performance, before Macmillan's rescue, Kim was mentally at the end of his rope. He was preparing to defect to the Soviet Union, as Aileen had predicted. Fearing that Kim would take the children with him, Aileen had written to St John, begging him to talk some sense into his son. As usual, St John treated Aileen dismissively.

He later confided to Dora that he worried about Aileen's influence on her children.

Aileen, though she was right about Kim, *had* become very unstable. She had spent numerous stints in a mental hospital and was prone to burst into tears at any moment. Unable to live together, the couple finally separated, though they remained married. Aileen stayed with the five children in a house rented by her mother. She wrote a letter to Kim's mother, Dora, complaining that Kim was not financially supporting the family. When Dora asked Kim about this, he became defensive, claiming that they had an arrangement whereby Aileen would pay the household bills and send Kim the receipts. He would then reimburse her the money she had spent. Kim gave Aileen no money, because she had sent him no receipts. If this wasn't bad enough, Kim had begun having an affair with Constance Ashley-Jones, a family friend of Tim Milne.[5]

Meanwhile, Kim's father, St John Philby, was having troubles of his own. His old friend, King Ibn Saud, had passed away in 1953. Ibn Saud's son and successor, King Saud, did not have the patience for St John's anti-American diatribes, especially when he was trying to cultivate friendly relations with the United States. When St John ran afoul of King Saud one too many times, he was forced into exile. Instead of returning to London, St John settled in Lebanon. Meanwhile, Dora, still legally married to St John, discovered that her husband had been married to an Arab woman since 1945 and had two children with her. On being discovered, St John suggested that Dora move to Lebanon with him in a polygamous arrangement with his new family. Dora understandably chose to stay in London.

Though Kim didn't know it yet, his father was about to help him once more.

The Middle East was emerging as a critical region in global Cold War diplomacy during this period. As the Soviet Union and the United States jockeyed for influence in the oil rich, yet tumultuous area, the old colonial order was falling apart. In 1952, Egypt's King Farouk, the tenth ruler in Egypt's Muhammad Ali dynasty, was toppled in a coup d'état. He was eventually replaced by Gamal Abdel Nasser, the leader of the Free Officer's Movement, a revolutionary group within Egypt's military.

Though Egypt had not been officially under British occupation since 1922, the British maintained control of the Suez Canal, a key waterway for commerce, and kept their troops stationed in Egyptian cities. The British government had maintained friendly relations with King Farouk, though the Egyptian people were increasingly agitated by the presence of British soldiers in their allegedly independent country. Nasser and his Free Officers Movement vowed to expel British forces from Egypt forever.

The British were horrified to discover that the United States, through the CIA, had given financial support to the insurgent Free Officers Movement. American intelligence agencies were not inclined to share information with the British after the Burgess and Maclean fiasco, fearing their security was irreparably compromised. The exoneration of Kim Philby further exacerbated their concerns. The 'special relationship' between British and American intelligence was clearly damaged, and might never fully recover.

The need for intelligence in the Middle East was pushed to the forefront for the British government. St John Philby, now the most respected British Arab expert, was living in Beirut. His son, Kim Philby, had been fully cleared of any wrongdoing in the Burgess and Maclean affair, and was now looking for work. Reprising his role in Kim's hiring by MI6, St John once again helped his son obtain a posting in the Secret Intelligence Service, albeit indirectly. In a shocking change of heart, MI6 rehired the suspected Soviet agent that had been fired less than five years prior. Kim Philby was once again an MI6 agent. He was stationed in Beirut, Lebanon, where he could be close to the world's most prominent Middle East Expert: his father.

Things appeared to be getting back on track for the Cambridge Five.

John Cairncross, after writing part time for *The Economist* and *The Observer*, left Italy for Switzerland, where he took up work as a United Nations translator to supplement his modest income. In 1956, Cairncross finally published his first book on his favourite play write. Titled *New Light on Molière*, his first publication was met with complimentary reviews.

In 1957, Cairncross became the UN's chief editor for its Economic Commission for Asia and the Far East (ECAFE). The promotion required him to relocate to Bangkok, Thailand. He and Gabrielle moved into a large home, complete with two servants. Gabi took a job at a tourism office, where she enjoyed meeting new people and learning about the history of Thailand.

Anthony Blunt's esteem rose in the art world, as he received a knighthood in 1956 for his work as Surveyor of the Queen's Pictures. Though he complained about the dull nature of court life, he enjoyed giving interviews to the press about the Royal Art Collection.

In Russia, Burgess and Maclean were afforded a little more freedom after Stalin died in 1953. Guy Burgess took a job in the Foreign Language Publishing House, where he tried to convince them to translate and publish more English literature. In addition to Guy's publishing job, he allegedly wrote a guidebook of espionage tradecraft for aspiring Soviet agents on behalf of the KGB.[6] The book, if it exists, has not surfaced in the west. According to the defector Anatoliy Golitsyn, Burgess was used as a homosexual 'honey trap' in Peking in 1954, in an attempt to seduce and blackmail a diplomat from the British mission.[7]

Burgess never fully assimilated to Russian culture. Despite his commitment to communism, he loved England, and never ceased to be an Englishman. He missed London terribly; the parties, the gossip, and his wide circle of friends. There was no gossip in the Soviet Union; it was risky for people to share too much with the wrong person.

Donald Maclean, on the other hand, managed to assimilate quite well. He began his new life by entering a sobriety clinic. He took a job in a local school, teaching English, just as he had planned to do after graduating from Cambridge, so many years ago. He was pleased that his family had come to join him. The children were placed in Soviet schools and the family moved into their own apartment, across the hall from Burgess. By 1955, they were all deemed fully 'rehabilitated', in Soviet lingo, and were permitted to move to Moscow.

The communism of Donald's youth was not just a passing fancy; it was one of the few things that stayed constant throughout his life. Now that he lived in the Soviet Union, his reality aligned, for once, with his own beliefs. Though he had to live under a Russian pseudonym to avoid being located by the western press, he experienced a truth within himself that he had never known.

On 11 February 1956, four reporters were summoned to the National Hotel in Moscow. Two correspondents were from the Soviet papers, *Tass* and *Pravda*, and the other two were British correspondents, representing Reuters news service and *The Sunday Times*. The missing diplomats, Guy Burgess and Donald Maclean, walked into the room and sat at a table, making their first public appearance in nearly five years. They read a prepared statement, which began:

> *It seems to us doubts and speculation as to our present whereabouts and our former activity may represent a small but*

significant factor which has hitherto been used by opponents of Anglo-Soviet understanding. In view of these considerations we though it better to publish this statement:

We arrived in the Soviet Union in order to make our contribution to a policy aimed at achieving greater mutual understanding between the Soviet Union and the West.[8]

The statement went on to declare that both had been communists while attending Cambridge, but that they ceased their political activity upon entering the Foreign Office. The statement described both of their careers, and put forth their reasons for leaving. The statement flatly denied that either had ever been Soviet agents. The statement reiterated that they had come to Moscow to advance the cause for peace, and concluded with the declaration that:

Our life in the Soviet Union has convinced us that we took at that time the correct decision.

Maclean and Burgess, having read their statement, left without taking questions.

The press conference came at an important moment in history, though the western newspapers could not have known it at the time. A little over a week later, on 25 February, Soviet Premier, Nikita Khrushchev, addressed a closed session of the Twentieth Congress of the Communist Party of the Soviet Union, to which journalists were not invited. In his 'secret speech', as it later became known, Khrushchev began by denouncing Stalin's cult of personality, which contradicted the Marxist ideal of collective leadership. He criticised Stalin's management of the Red Army during the Second World War, and his break with Yugoslavia. He condemned Stalin's most brutal action, the Great Purge of the late 1930s. Khrushchev called for a return to Leninist policies, which rejected the glorification of individual power.

The text of Khrushchev's ground breaking address was declassified shortly afterward, when Khrushchev ordered that it be read at local party meetings. It was eventually leaked to the west and published in *The New York Times* the following June. The address, giving voice to Stalin's terrors, led to a new, slightly more liberalised period in the Soviet Union, later known as Khrushchev's Thaw.

Around the time of their press conference, Guy Burgess and Donald Maclean were allowed to leave Kuybyshev, and they moved to Moscow. Burgess settled into a flat on the sixth floor of a classical Stalin era building. The Maclean family settled into a large flat overlooking the Moscow River. They had some personal furnishings pulled out of storage and shipped from London, giving their new Russian home an English feel. Both Burgess and the Macleans were given the use of country dachas, reserved for those in the Party's good graces.

With their public breaking of silence, along with Khrushchev's Thaw, both men began to reopen correspondence with their friends and families. After exchanging a few letters, they even received visitors. Burgess was visited by his brother, Nigel, and he took his mother on holiday to Sochi. Maclean first wrote to his brother, Alan, whom he asked for the address of Mrs Dunbar, on behalf of Melinda.

Guy eagerly gave interviews to British reporters, just to have someone familiar to talk with. He kept regular correspondence with his friends and family back home, and often asked them to send tokens of comfort that were unavailable to him in Moscow – books, silk pyjamas, suits from Savile Row, and, of course, Old Etonian bow ties.

Burgess was contacted by journalist Tom Driberg, who asked permission to visit and interview Guy for a biography. Burgess, who was always excited to see a familiar British face, agreed to speak with his friend Driberg, who was a former Labour MP, and a fellow homosexual. Driberg made two visits to Moscow before publishing a sympathetic hagiography of Burgess, in which Burgess insisted that he was innocent of the charges against him, and would someday come home to England and prove it.

The book caused a sensation in London, as journalists and intelligence officers scoured its pages for any new revelations. Driberg's book, *Guy Burgess: A Portrait with Background*, was widely regarded as old news. There were no bombshells and no hard-hitting journalism.

Burgess eventually found companionship in the person of Tolya Chishekov, a short and stalky young electrician who had a cheerful disposition and was interested in music. The story of their first meeting was decidedly unromantic. While visiting Guy in Moscow, Guy's biographer, Tom Driberg, a barely closeted homosexual, discovered a public urinal which served as a secret meeting place for men seeking clandestine trysts with one another. Driberg enthusiastically shared his discovery with

Burgess. There Guy met Tolya, who became his long term partner for the rest of his life.[9]

While the Cambridge Five all seemed to be moving on with their lives, Goronwy Rees began waging a personal vendetta. He wrote a five part series of anonymous articles for the tabloid magazine, *The People*, the first of which appeared on 11 March, 1956.[10] Salaciously titled, *Guy Burgess Stripped Bare,* the series breathlessly delved into the seedy personal life of Burgess, as well as his work for the Soviets. Identifying himself only as Guy's 'closest friend', Rees described the debauchery on display at a typical party at the old house on Bentinck Street. He named several people in their circle of friends, including Jack Hewit and Victor Rothschild. Rees recounted his confrontation by Donald Maclean in the Gargoyle club, and hinted at the complicity of Anthony Blunt, though he didn't name Blunt explicitly. It is possible that the knighting of Anthony Blunt, for whom Rees harboured an unreasonable hatred, pushed him over the edge. Rees may also have been worried that Guy Burgess, no longer in hiding, might reveal Rees' own activities on behalf of the KGB. Rees was also suffering some financial difficulties, and the £2700 paid by *The People* for the story was hard to resist.[11]

Whatever Rees' intentions, his bombshell story backfired spectacularly. London society was a small world at that time, and diligent reporters had no trouble figuring out who Guy's 'closest friend' was. Goronwy Rees was soon exposed as the author of the scandalous articles in *The Daily Telegraph*. Many of their mutual friends were horrified that Rees would turn on his friends in this manner, and disgusted at the fact that he did it anonymously. In addition to losing some friends, Rees was forced to resign from his position as principal at the University College of Wales at Aberystwyth. Meanwhile, Anthony Blunt, though unnerved by the articles, suffered no consequences from their publication.

Kim Philby arrived in Lebanon in August 1956. He was met at the airport by St John, looking elegant in a white linen suit, blue eyes peeking out from beneath his traditional Saudi *keffiyeh*. In those days, Beirut was known as the Paris of the Middle East, characterised by its French architecture and vibrant cosmopolitan culture. Kim was admired there as something of a celebrity – partly because of his famous father, and partly due to his own fox-like cunning; Kim had fooled both the Americans and the British, and he had gotten away with it. Upon his arrival, Kim stayed with St John and Rozy, his second wife, in their house in the village of Ajaltun, tucked into the mountains outside of Beirut. Despite the peaceful environment, the household was somewhat chaotic. When St John wasn't busy writing his nineteenth book, he argued with Rozy. Rozy spent much of her time attempting to wrangle Kim's little brothers, Khalid and Faris.

Kim Philby could no longer use the Foreign Office as cover for his work for the SIS, after all of the scandal of the previous few years. He instead went back to his roots: journalism. His old friend from MI6, Nicholas Elliott, who had arranged for Aileen's hospitalisation in Switzerland all those years ago, set Kim up with a job as the Beirut correspondent for both *The Observer* and *The Economist*. Elliott had been one of Kim's most steady supporters. He had never believed the accusations of espionage, and he had kept Kim's children in good schools during Kim's years of financial difficulty.[12]

The Middle East was boiling with tension during the 1950s. As the slow and painful process of decolonisation met with the rising popularity of Arab nationalism, the competing interests of the United States and the Soviet Union added another layer of complexity to the changing region. Complicating matters further, the United States and Great Britain did not always see eye to eye on these matters. Sometimes they cooperated – like in the joint US-British backed overthrow of Iranian Prime Minister, Mohammad Mosaddegh. Other times, their interests were opposed, like in the Egyptian revolution. In general, the Americans were pro-nationalist and anti-communist. If democracy was possible, they supported it, though it wasn't required. The British, though also anti-communist, tended to favour monarchies, and preferred to hang on to at least some of their old protectorates, particularly where oil rights were concerned.

Located in the centre of all of this intrigue was Beirut. An agent like Kim Philby was right where he needed to be. With the help of St John, an Arab expert with four decades of experience in the Middle East, Kim was in good hands. He received a crash course from St John in all the nuances and entanglements of the region, and introduced Kim to his broad circle of contacts in the city.

Philby's reinstatement by MI6 was not without controversy. He was hired after the retirement of the legendary Stewart Menzies, and during the brief tenure of Sir John Sinclair. Shortly after Kim's assignment to Beirut, Sinclair resigned as chief of SIS, and was replaced by Dick White, upon his retirement as Director General of MI5. Dick White now holds the distinction of being the only person to have headed both MI5 and MI6 – back-to-back, no less.

The hiring of White presented a possible problem for Kim Philby. While Kim's former colleagues at MI6 had been inclined to sweep his suspected espionage under the rug, White's detectives at MI5 had been eager to prosecute him, and were dumbfounded at his exoneration by Harold Macmillan. White's first inclination might have been to fire Philby and cut off contact. White, however, saw a more promising opportunity. As one of the masterminds behind Operation Double Cross, he conspired to double cross Kim Philby.

White concluded that it would only be a matter of time before Philby was back to his old ways. It shouldn't be long before Kim established contact with a Soviet courier in the intelligence hotbed of Beirut. When that day came, Kim could be fed some phony intelligence, and he could then be caught red-handed passing it to the Soviets. White would then, finally, have the spy brought to justice.

It wasn't long before St John Philby patched things up with King Saud and moved back to Riyadh with his young family. Kim moved out of St John's mountain villa and into a flat in the city, where he could be close to the action. He began hanging around his father's old haunts, like the Normandy Hotel, and the St George Hotel, where British and American expats would often stop for drinks. Before long, Kim reconnected with a *New York Times* reporter named Samuel Pope Brewer, whom he had met in Washington. Brewer was living in Beirut with his wife, Eleanor. He socialised frequently with the American couple, who introduced him to people in the intelligence community.

Kim's first act of treachery in his new city was to seduce Sam Brewer's wife. Brewer was frequently out of town on assignment, and Eleanor quickly succumbed to Philby's charms. When he wasn't sneaking Eleanor into secluded cafes, or slipping her charming love notes, he continued to play the role of backslapping friend and fellow journalist to Sam. Philby used the friendship to access not just Eleanor, but important American contacts, as well.

The most consequential of these was Wilbur Crane 'Bill' Eveland, a CIA agent operating in the Middle East. Eveland was an important player for the CIA during its period of covert actions in the 1950s. He worked closely with CIA director Allen Dulles, negotiated with Egyptian leader Abdel Nasser, and was involved in plans to overthrow the communist backed government in Syria.[13] He later admitted to rigging elections in Lebanon.[14]

Under diplomatic cover by the US State Department, Eveland was stationed at the embassies of both Beirut and Damascus, Syria. When he arrived in Beirut in the autumn of 1956, Eveland heard rumours that Kim Philby was once again working for British Intelligence. Eveland had, of course, heard of St John Philby, and hoped to learn some things from his son. Over many drinks at the Brewers' house, Eveland attempted to cultivate Kim as an informant.

It didn't work out that way.

For the many covert operations that failed in the Middle East during that tumultuous decade, much of the blame was laid at the feet of Bill Eveland. Years later, the CIA came to believe that Eveland, wittingly or not, had shared many of its clandestine plans with Philby. Eleanor Brewer, under interrogation by the CIA, admitted in 1965, '…all (Kim) had to do was to have one evening with Bill Eveland in Beirut, and before it was over he would know all of his operations'.[15]

In May 1957, Kim was devastated to learn that his mother, Dora, had died in her sleep. Even St John, upon hearing the news, was badly shaken by her passing. She had always stood by him, and he had taken her for granted. Kim conceded that Dora had, in her sorrow, drank herself to death. Dora's passing dragged up Kim's complicated feelings toward his father. Kim privately blamed St John for Dora's steady decline, though he did not tell him so.

The following winter brought more tragic news from London. On 12 December 1957, Aileen Philby was found dead in her bedroom by her daughter, Josephine. Aileen's friends, witnessing her fragile state, suspected suicide. Aileen's psychiatrist, unhelpfully, floated the idea that Kim Philby may have had her murdered for knowing too much. The coroner ruled her death one as one by natural causes; namely, congestive heart failure brought on by influenza.

When word of Aileen's death reached Beirut, Kim felt a burden lifted from his shoulders. He was in love with Eleanor and was now free to marry her. Of course, there was still the matter of Eleanor's husband. Kim and Eleanor sat down with Sam at a bar, and over drinks, confessed their love for each other and their desire to marry. Sam and Eleanor were divorced soon afterward, and by 1959, Kim and Eleanor were married.

The CIA attempted, in vain, to trap Kim Philby. In 1958, the new Head of Station in Beirut, Edgar Applewhite, learned that the notorious Kim Philby was in town. He too, befriended the charming Brit, and kept a file on all of their interactions. Applewhite concluded, correctly, that it would be no use for him to recruit, or to entrap, the clever Kim Philby. Applewhite was overmatched.

James Angleton, still stung by Philby's betrayal of their friendship in Washington, enlisted the help of Miles Copeland,[16] a business executive and partner of the public relations firm, Copeland and Eichelberger. In addition to his cover business, Copeland was instrumental in CIA operations in support of, and later against, Abdel Nasser. Angleton encouraged Copeland to befriend and watch Kim Philby, and to report any sign that Philby was spying for the Soviets. Miles Copeland's wife, Lorraine, was already good friends with Eleanor; they had met when Miles and Sam Brewer were stationed in Syria.

Miles and Lorraine invited Philby and Eleanor to their dinner parties, and occasionally brought the couple boating off the Lebanese coast. The two couples went on regular family outings together (the Copelands had four children, and Eleanor had a daughter, Annie). Though they became good friends, Copeland paid a small network of local cab drivers and street merchants to follow Philby and report on his activities. Though Philby sometimes ventured to places well off the beaten path, he typically eluded his followers. Copeland, too, failed to catch Philby in the act.

In 1960, Kim's good friend, Nicholas Elliott, arrived in Beirut, taking over as Head of Station. He would now be Kim's supervisor and case officer.

Soon afterward, St John Philby returned to visit Beirut. He and Kim spent a few days drinking and watching belly dancers, and were so inebriated by the end of the night that Eleanor had to help them both to bed. St John was invited to lunch at the home of Nicholas Elliott and his wife, Elizabeth. They were joined by their houseguest, Humphrey Trevelyan, British Ambassador to Iraq. After many glasses of wine, Kim and St John headed over to a large party hosted by John Fistere, the new western advisor to King Hussein of Jordan. At some point that evening, St John stepped out onto a balcony to take a break from the noisy crowd. A young American teacher was outside chatting with St John when he suddenly clutched his chest and fell to the ground.

John Fistere's panicked wife, Isobel, screamed, 'God! I've poisoned him!' Her unfortunate outburst triggered rumours in Beirut of St John's poisoning for weeks.

None of the tipsy party guests called an ambulance. Kim, intoxicated in another part of the house, was eventually summoned to attend to his father. Kim brought St John back to his hotel, where a doctor confirmed that he had suffered a heart attack. He was not taken to the hospital until the next morning, when he suffered a second heart attack. Arriving at the hospital unconscious, St John briefly awakened in the afternoon.

'God, I'm bored', he sighed, before closing his eyes again. St John Philby was pronounced dead by five o'clock that evening, 30 September 1960.[17]

St John had converted to Islam many years ago, so Kim arranged for a Muslim burial. He was interred under his Islamic name, Haji Abdullah, in the Muslim cemetery in Beirut. Islamic law required his immediate burial, so very few mourners attended his simple graveside service. Kim later had his headstone inscribed, 'Greatest of All Arabian Explorers'.

Kim Philby's drinking, which was already excessive, spun out of control with the death of his father. His behaviour began to resemble that of his compatriots, Burgess and Maclean, in the months leading up to their defections. Kim was hauled out of at least one embassy party for his intoxication, and had urinated on the tile floor of a home he was visiting in Tehran.[18]

In the spring of 1961, Philby, already unstable, was rattled again. News broke in the SIS Beirut station that a Soviet agent had penetrated its ranks, and he was in Beirut. George Blake, a Dutch born naturalised British citizen, had been attending the Middle East College for Arabic Studies (MECAS), located outside of Beirut. MECAS was established by the British Foreign Office for the training of diplomats and intelligence officers. Blake was a highly regarded intelligence agent, who had worked as a case officer in Berlin, recruiting Soviet officers as double agents for the British.

Earlier that year, a Polish defector named Michael Goleniewski came forward with information exposing George Blake as a Soviet agent.[19] Blake was suspected of leaking to the KGB details of Operation Gold, in which tunnels were dug into East Berlin to tap Soviet phone lines.

Nicholas Elliott was instructed to send Blake home to London to interview for a promotion. Upon his arrival, Blake was arrested and interrogated. On his third day of questioning, Blake confessed to spying for the Soviet Union.

Meanwhile, on the other side of the world, another Soviet defection threatened Philby's security. A KGB operative named Anatoliy Golitsyn contacted a CIA officer stationed in Helsinki, Finland, requesting asylum. Golitsyn arrived in the United States on 18 December 1961, where he was questioned by James Angleton. Arthur Martin of MI5 travelled to Washington in 1962 for his own interview. Among other revelations, Golitsyn told Martin that the KGB had recruited a ring of five British spies from Cambridge University in the 1930s. Though unable to identify Philby by name, he provided enough information that Martin could easily figure it out. Golitsyn's testimony was the first to specify a ring of five,[20] leading to an urgent search for its fourth and fifth members. It also turned a spotlight back onto Kim Philby. In an effort to get serious about Philby, MI6 called Nicholas Elliott, Kim's old friend, back to London, and replaced him with Peter Lunn.

In August 1962, new evidence materialised from the most unlikely of places. Victor Rothschild, the former Cambridge Apostle and MI5 officer, had contacted MI5 officer Peter Wright with big news. Rothschild had been to Israel, where he met Flora Solomon, the woman who had introduced Kim to Aileen so many years ago. Solomon, a committed Zionist, had read some of Philby's dispatches in *The Observer*. She was offended, reported Rothschild, at the pro-Arab, anti-Israel bias in Philby's news reports. She then revealed to Rothschild that she knew Philby had been a Soviet agent, because he had once tried to recruit her.[21]

Flora Solomon said that she had been good friends with Philby in the 1930s, and that he had told her all about his work for the Soviets during the Spanish Civil War. He had asked her if she would help with his secret and important work for the Comintern. She refused, already busy assisting Jewish refugees who had fled the Continent.

Flora Solomon was a respected society lady, well-educated with a long history of activism and charity work. People might believe her testimony, Rothschild thought. At the urging of investigator Arthur Martin, Rothschild persuaded the reluctant Solomon to repeat her comments under oath.

Dick White, Head of MI6, finally felt that he had enough evidence to take down Kim Philby. Rather than recall Philby to London, as they had with Blake, White chose to interrogate Philby in Beirut. The decision was pushed by now prime minister, Harold Macmillan, who had publicly exonerated Philby in 1955. Macmillan was not eager to stage a public spectacle over Philby, naturally. He hoped that, perhaps, a confession might quietly be extracted from Philby, far away in Lebanon. White considered sending Arthur Martin to question Philby, but soon reconsidered. Kim was a wily prey, who had eluded capture for twenty years. White chose instead to send someone whom Philby trusted. He sent Nicholas Elliott. Angry at Kim's betrayal, after all he had done for him, Elliott readily agreed.

It is possible that Kim received some kind of warning. According to CIA records, Yuri Modin paid a visit to Lebanon in September 1962.[22] Modin had come straight from Pakistan, suggesting that he may have brought with him a Pakistani passport for Kim, who was born in Ambala.[23] In December 1962, just weeks before Elliott's arrival, Anthony Blunt visited Beirut. He told the embassy that he came to search the mountains of Lebanon for a rare orchid.[24] This story seems unlikely; Blunt was neither a hiker nor a floral enthusiast.

Elliott's flight arrived in Beirut on 10 January 1963. He checked in to a modest hotel, and tried to keep a low profile. From an MI6 safe house, he phoned Kim Philby, and told him to come over immediately. When he arrived, it was Kim who spoke first.

'I rather thought it would be you', Philby muttered, ominously.[25]

Elliott was taken aback by Philby's appearance. He had recently fallen down drunk in his own bathroom and injured his head, which was now taped up with bloody bandages. Both of his eyes were blackened in the accident and his face was swollen. Recovering, Elliott confronted Philby with the accusation by Flora Solomon. Kim, who had never seen reason to confess before, was not about to start now. He denied Elliott's charges and stood up to leave.

'You had to choose between Marxism and your family, and you chose Marxism', said Elliott, raising his voice. 'I once looked up to you. My God, how I despise you now.'[26]

He reminded Kim of the consequences of defying the National Secrets Act, which Kim surely knew already. The maximum penalty was fourteen years, but recently, George Blake had been sentenced to fourteen years for each instance of his violation, landing him a sentence of forty-two years in prison.

Elliott then offered Kim a lifeline. If Kim was willing to cooperate, Elliott was prepared to offer him immunity. Kim had twenty-four hours to decide. Elliott ordered him to report back to the safe house the following afternoon.

To Elliott's surprise, Kim returned at four o'clock the next day as promised. He brought with him two typewritten pages, confessing to spying on behalf of the Soviet Union, up until 1949. They met several more times in the next few days as Kim gave more information to Elliott.

Nicholas Elliott closed his visit by inviting Kim and Eleanor to dinner, and he brought with him a woman from the SIS station. Eleanor, who knew nothing of Kim's espionage, let alone his confession, felt a strange energy between the two men. She knew they were keeping something from her.

In a move that has baffled historians ever since, Elliott returned to London. He brought with him Kim's signed confession, but not Kim. He triumphantly handed the pages to Dick White, before heading to the Congo to begin his new posting as head of the MI6 station in Africa.

The existence of Philby's confession remained an official state secret until 1993, and only selected excerpts were released to the public in 2019, over fifty years later. A very small number of CIA officers were permitted to read it sooner.

Back in Beirut, the Philbys continued their daily lives as usual. Two of Kim's children were visiting from London, and Kim and Eleanor were invited to dinner at the home of an embassy official. After a few drinks at the bar in the St George Hotel, Kim phoned Eleanor to tell her that he was running late and to go ahead to the dinner without him. He said he would catch up later. He never arrived.

On the night of 23 January 1963, Kim Philby vanished.

Chapter Sixteen

The End of the Road
Life after Espionage

During Kim Philby's time in Beirut, Anthony Blunt attempted to continue his life as usual. Though he became nervous with every public revisiting of the Cambridge Spy scandal, he continued to work, to lecture, and to write. In 1959, Blunt published *The Art of William Blake,* and collaborated with Phoebe Pool on *Picasso: The Early Years*. He wrote numerous articles about artists, both classical and contemporary, during the 1950s and 1960s. He tended to be attracted to artists and architects who were complicated, misanthropic, or misunderstood in their time. Perhaps he could relate.

In 1960, Anthony curated the first exhibition featuring the work of his favourite artist, Poussin, at the Louvre in Paris. Attended by dignitaries of the art world, old friends, and former students, the exhibition was the apex of Blunt's career. Having introduced the world to Poussin from early on in his career, the splashy event served to firmly establish Poussin's importance to the classical period, and established Anthony Blunt as his foremost expert.

Blunt's tireless devotion to the Courtauld Institute bore fruit with his growing renown. Once an obscure centre of study, it became a respected and sought-after college. By 1961, the Courtauld had expanded to accommodate the increasing number of student applicants, taking over two neighbouring buildings.

Ironically, as his esteem grew, Blunt retreated, becoming more reclusive and mysterious with each passing year. He was never able to put rumours of his espionage fully to rest. The public recognition of his work, which he so desperately craved, inevitably led to curiosity about his inner life. His secretive nature, meanwhile, only fuelled the rumour mill. Hidden in the acknowledgements of his 1940 book, *Artistic Theory in Italy*, Blunt had credited Guy Burgess with 'the stimulus of constant discussion and suggestions on all the more basic points at issue'.[1] Blunt never removed the inscription in subsequent editions, and his students often wondered why he hadn't done so, considering Guy's later infamy. The mild mannered professor was rumoured to throw wild parties with his homosexual friends. Most revealing, Blunt gave a lecture, every year, about communism during the 1930s, which sounded oddly sympathetic in the Cold War of the 1960s.

In 1963, Blunt was approached by a journalist named Douglas Sutherland while having a drink at the Traveller's Club. Sutherland was collaborating with Anthony Purdy on a book about Guy Burgess. Sutherland directly accused Anthony Blunt of being the legendary 'Third Man' in the Cambridge Spy Ring. Blunt, visibly shaken, denied the accusation, and threatened Sutherland with legal action if his name was mentioned in the forthcoming book. He then hastily left the club.[2] Sutherland had been working with Blunt's nemesis, Goronwy Rees. Though Rees had recently been hospitalised for a nervous breakdown, he refused to let go of his mission to expose Anthony Blunt. The book, *Burgess and Maclean*, was published that May, and while it did not directly name Anthony Blunt, it did make oblique references to a homosexual former MI5 officer.

Meanwhile, John Cairncross had found his quiet life in Bangkok to be quite rewarding. His workday at the UN ended by four o'clock, leaving him plenty of time for any number of pursuits. He began a research project into the history of seventeenth-century Siam, which he never finished. He published a translation of Racine's *Phaedra*, which literary experts had previously considered untranslatable. He published a volume of poetry, *By a Lonely Sea*, which included translations of German, French, Spanish, and Italian poetry, along with some original poems of his own.

The death of John's mother, Elizabeth, in 1958, just when his gifts were beginning to bear fruit, came with an added sorrow for John. Elizabeth had been the earliest and strongest supporter of his intellectual pursuits, and he lost her just as he had begun to achieve them.

By 1961, John and Gabrielle were ready to move back to Rome. He published another book on Molière, this one in French. *Molière: Bourgeois et Libertin*, focused on Molière's radicalism, particularly his mocking of religious constraints and his sympathy for the limited role of women in seventeenth-century French society.

Though his professed respect for women was an ongoing theme in Cairncross' life and writing (he dedicated his first book to his mother, and a later book to his wife), he was growing restless in his marriage to the intelligent and capable Gabrielle. He had already entertained a brief dalliance with a married woman during their time in Asia, and it was clear to Gabrielle that he was pursuing other relationships in Rome.[3]

Their marriage was beginning to falter on other fronts, too. He was becoming so engrossed in his work that the couple barely spent time together. He also began to revert to his characteristic defensiveness, refusing to hear any constructive criticism of his work. Gabrielle, an accomplished woman in her own right, grew weary of simply being his cheerleader. When Cairncross was offered a temporary position on the Pakistan Planning Commission in 1963, he travelled to Karachi without Gabrielle. Their separation would be permanent, though the couple stayed legally married. John later cited his concern about her financial security as the reason they never divorced.

While in Karachi, Cairncross was notified of an opening for a position as Chair of the Romance Languages department at Western Reserve University in Cleveland, Ohio. With a reference from his old friend, Graham Greene, Cairncross enthusiastically accepted the offer. After spending his entire life pining for a respected academic career, he finally would have it. Cairncross arrived in Cleveland in February 1964.

Both John Cairncross and Anthony Blunt were in the midst of stellar careers when the 1963 defection of Kim Philby once again ripped open the case of the missing diplomats.

Though Philby vanished in January 1963, the story didn't break until July.

When Kim failed to turn up at the dinner party in Beirut on that last rainy night in January, Eleanor at first worried that he may have drank too much, fallen from the waterfront outside the St George Hotel, and been washed out to sea. Miles Copeland thought otherwise. He quickly notified both the CIA and SIS stations of Philby's disappearance, and cables soon alerted both of their headquarters. The following morning, the CIA was asked by the SIS to aid in the worldwide search for Kim Philby.

After three days of searching the city with the help of Miles Copeland, Eleanor received a letter, postmarked in Cairo. It was from Kim. He reassured Eleanor that he was alright, and would be in touch soon. A second letter arrived on 4 February, and a third one two weeks later. On 2 March, she received a telegram, again from Cairo, wishing her a happy anniversary.

He took pains to express his love and devotion to Eleanor, and to give the impression that he was simply chasing down a news story somewhere in the Middle East, just in case the SIS got hold of his letters.[4]

Finally, in April, Eleanor answered a knock at the door of her Beirut apartment. A strange man silently handed her an envelope, then turned abruptly and ran down the stairs. It was a three page typewritten letter from Kim, instructing her to book a flight to Prague. He told her to go to an alley with a piece of chalk, and write her flight information on a wall.

It wasn't that simple. Eleanor was often followed by the press, and she was still under the watchful eye of Nicholas Elliott, who had returned to Beirut to follow up on the Philby case. Furthermore, Kim's son Harry was still staying with her and he did not have his own passport (he had travelled to Beirut on Kim's). Instead of flying to Prague, Eleanor went to London, bringing Harry and her daughter, Annie. She soon met with Dick White, who brought her up to speed on the pending charges of espionage against Kim.

The news of Kim's disappearance finally made headlines in July, nearly six months after he was last seen. A small story had appeared in the *Beirut Daily Star* when Kim went missing, and a few western correspondents picked up the story and sent dispatches to London and New York, but they were not printed. Nicholas Elliott had arrived on the scene in Beirut quickly, and ordered the British press to kill the story. Prime Minister Harold Macmillan himself was not notified of Philby's disappearance until 19 February, twenty-seven days after he vanished. Finally, a Russian paper spilled the beans.

On 1 July 1963, the Soviet newspaper, *Izvestia*, featured an article headlined, 'Hello, Mr Philby!' Unlike the five-year period of secrecy surrounding the whereabouts of Burgess and Maclean, the Soviet Union proudly announced the arrival of Kim Philby, only seven months after his defection. He was officially welcomed to Moscow, and granted Soviet citizenship.

The Foreign Office was forced to issue an official statement. Kim Philby, it said, was known to have been a Soviet agent since 1946.[5] After giving two brief interviews to British reporters in Moscow, which stressed his commitment to fight against fascism and imperialism, Kim Philby issued no more statements for the next ten years.

Philby's triumph was followed swiftly by tragedy.

Kim's old friend, Guy Burgess, was admitted to the hospital for hardening of the arteries on 20 August 1963. He died there ten days later of acute liver failure. Kim never saw Burgess once he got to Moscow, according to Yuri Modin. Modin claimed that Kim refused to see Guy, having harboured a grudge since Burgess' defection in 1951, which had set his own downfall into motion.[6] As late as 1987, Kim Philby maintained that he would have liked to see him, but was prohibited by the KGB.[7] On the other hand, Eleanor Philby insisted that Kim had visited Guy during his final days in the hospital, and an ITN television report about Burgess' death seems to confirm this. In an audio recording phoned in by Moscow correspondent Jeremy Wolfenden, a mysterious visitor, matching Philby's description, reportedly visited Burgess on his deathbed.[8]

Burgess' final years had been rough. Cigarettes and liquor were cheap in Moscow and Burgess had indulged in them freely, while eating very little. His health, long subjected to fast living, now deteriorated with equal velocity. He suffered from ulcers, and underwent two operations to treat them. In a forgotten 1959 TV interview with the Canadian Broadcasting Company (CBC), a bloated and pallid Burgess, clearly intoxicated, slurred through his flippant answers to questions about his defection.

In sharp contrast to his atheism and his hedonistic lifestyle, Burgess was strangely drawn to an Orthodox monastery, which he could see from the window of his high-rise apartment. In his later years, he often attended Mass there, enchanted by the ceremony and the organ music.

In 1962, grimly aware of his failing health, Burgess sent a letter to Esther Whitfield, Kim's former secretary and Guy's erstwhile girlfriend. He instructed Whitfield to divide his savings, still deposited at Lloyd's in London, four ways. Guy asked that one quarter of the funds each be given to herself, Anthony Blunt, Tolya Chishekov, and Kim Philby.[9]

When Burgess passed away on 30 August 1963, his mother was too frail to travel to Moscow for his funeral. Guy's brother, Nigel, came on her behalf. Also in attendance were a few reporters, Guy's colleagues from the publishing house, and Donald and Melinda Maclean. Kim Philby was absent, prohibited from attending by the KGB. Donald Maclean, despite not being close with Burgess, delivered a eulogy. It was oddly fitting. Due to their notorious defection together, their names would forever be linked in the pages of history.

While the story of Guy Burgess after the defection was largely a tragic one, Maclean fared somewhat better. Unlike Burgess and Philby, Maclean took no satisfaction in the thrill of espionage. He treated it like a job; it was unpleasant and dirty, but it had to be done. He did it because he believed in communism and felt it a necessary task to move the revolution forward. Though he was innately wired to compartmentalise, and to keep secrets, it was exactly this practice that had nearly destroyed him. Once he was in the Soviet Union, Maclean was finally free to be himself. In 1956, after the Khrushchev Thaw had begun, Donald Maclean finally joined the Communist Party. He worked for a while as a magazine correspondent, then took a posting at the Institute of World Economics and International Relations (IMEMO) in 1961. He became a respected researcher and teacher for the institute, and wrote articles for their magazine. It was a perfect fit for Maclean, who still maintained his interest in foreign policy.

The Maclean children joined the Young Pioneers, and worked on collective farms in the summer. Melinda, who had hated living in Kuybyshev, found a measure of happiness in their roomy Moscow flat. Their standard of living was better than most; their home had a television, and a housekeeper. They had the use of their dacha for weekend getaways, and they were permitted to shop in stores reserved for favoured Party members. Things were going well, until Kim Philby arrived.

Unlike Donald, Kim waited less than a year to be reunited with his wife. Like Melinda, Eleanor Philby gave up everything to follow the man that she loved. After learning of Kim's treachery (courtesy of Dick White at MI6), Eleanor walked into the Soviet Embassy in London, seeking passage to Moscow. She left her stepchildren in the care of Kim's sister, Patricia, and sent her daughter, Annie, to the United States to live with her father, Sam Brewer. Eleanor was given money to purchase warm clothes and instructed to go to the airport two days later. She arrived at London Airport by taxi on 27 September 1963. She was met at the curb by a Russian man, who led her to an airport bar where she waited. Skipping customs and passport checks, he walked her across the tarmac, where she boarded an Aeroflot plane bound for Moscow.[10]

Philby met her at the airplane when she arrived. His journey had been tougher than hers. He had escaped from Beirut the previous January by sneaking aboard a Soviet freighter and sailing to Odessa. About a week after settling in to their apartment, Kim introduced Eleanor to Donald and

Melinda Maclean. Beyond their work for the KGB, and their American wives, Philby and Maclean didn't have a great deal in common. Still, Donald and Melinda received Eleanor warmly, if only due to their curiosity about news from the west. The couples began seeing each other two or three nights a week for drinks, or dinner, or to play cards.

The harmony soon dissipated. Eleanor went to visit her daughter in the United States in the summer of 1964. Due to her living in the Soviet Union, and her marriage to notorious Soviet agent Kim Philby, Eleanor's passport was confiscated upon her arrival. She was stranded in America for several months as she was questioned by the FBI, and taken to court by her ex-husband for legal custody of their daughter.[11] Melinda Maclean, who still had money in a bank account in New York, graciously paid Eleanor's living expenses while she waited. When Eleanor finally returned to Moscow in November, the mood was different. Kim was distant, irritable, and drinking more than usual. He criticised Eleanor for not trying harder to learn Russian, and seemed agitated with her for no real reason. Kim revealed that he had recently had a terrible argument with Donald Maclean, who accused Kim of being a double agent.[12]

The secret soon came out that Donald had started binge drinking again. Melinda confessed to Eleanor that they, too, were going through a rough patch, and had recently begun sleeping in separate rooms. The two couples spent a positively wretched holiday together at the Macleans' dacha, where Donald and Melinda bickered, and an intoxicated Kim fell down and broke his wrist. Eleanor couldn't help but notice that Kim was very concerned and sympathetic toward Melinda.

When Eleanor confronted Kim about her growing suspicion, he confessed that he had begun an affair with Melinda Maclean while Eleanor was in America, and the two were now in love. His betrayal of Eleanor was compounded by his offer to allow her to stay in Moscow, with him and his new paramour; the same offer that St John made to Dora from Beirut. Outraged, Eleanor made plans to leave. By May 1965, she was gone.

With Eleanor out of the picture, Melinda moved in with Kim, while the children stayed with Donald. Melinda stayed for the next three years, until Kim fell for a Russian woman twenty years his junior. Kim Philby had now succeeded in betraying everyone who trusted him.

When her relationship with Kim ended, Melinda returned to Donald. After two years of trying to piece things back together, Melinda relented, moving into her own apartment nearby. Their long marriage finally broke beneath the cumulative weight of their history.

As the personal drama of the Macleans and Philbys played out behind the Iron Curtain, the past deeds of Anthony Blunt and John Cairncross were catching up to them.

Anthony Blunt received news of the death of his oldest friend, Louis MacNeice, on 3 September 1963. He died only two weeks after Guy Burgess. These back to back personal losses came on the heels of Kim Philby's defection and the ongoing attempt by Goronwy Rees to expose him. The weight of his losses, on top of his secrets, were exacting their toll. Anthony distracted himself with a trip to Rome, followed by the purchase of a recently discovered painting by Poussin, at the staggering price £12,000.

Meanwhile, trouble was brewing across the pond. Michael Straight, the former Cambridge spy, was facing a troubling decision. American President John F. Kennedy had created the new Advisory Council on the Arts, and appointed Straight as a member. To administer this new government agency, Kennedy established the National Endowment for the Arts, and Michael Straight was on the short list of consideration for chairman. Straight, who had left his position as publisher of *The New Republic* magazine in 1956 to write novels, was concerned when offered the position. The appointment would surely be preceded by a background check. Not wanting his past espionage activity to be publicly exposed, Straight decided to come clean about his past, and get ahead of any surprises. Straight first approached his friend, Art Schlesinger, who was special assistant to the president. Schlesinger put Straight in touch with the Deputy Director of the FBI, William Sullivan.

The interview was relatively friendly. The hysteria of the McCarthy years were long since over, with the fall from grace and subsequent death of Senator McCarthy himself in the mid-1950s. Furthermore, the ten year statute of limitations for espionage had long since come and gone. Straight confessed to his work for the KGB during the Roosevelt administration and gave the names of some old KGB contacts in America, all of them either dead or out of the country.[13] His appointment as Chair of NEA was temporarily derailed, not by Straight's confession, but by the November assassination of President Kennedy.

Arthur Martin from MI5 had some questions for Michael Straight, too. Upon his notification of Straight's confession, Martin flew to Washington to have a word with him in late January 1964. Straight revealed to Martin that he had been recruited by Anthony Blunt, and he was willing to say so under oath in a British court.[14]

It was a busy American visit for Arthur Martin. When John Cairncross arrived on 11 February in the United States, days after Martin, to begin his new job, he was notified by customs officials that he would be contacted for questioning once he reached Cleveland. Unlike the adversarial relationship between the CIA and the SIS, the FBI and MI5 were now working hand in hand to finally reign in the last of the Cambridge spies.

Cairncross was visited by Martin on 16 February 1964. Though he had finally reached the pinnacle of his academic career, Cairncross was tired of running. Confronted with Martin's newfound evidence against Anthony Blunt, Cairncross concluded that the game was up. He agreed to give a full confession, conducted with Martin over the course of several weeks, in between his lectures at the university.[15]

John Cairncross was never offered immunity, but the British government was content to let him stay in the United States. They were reluctant to stir up yet another spy scandal by prosecuting an inactive agent who no longer posed a threat, and his crimes did not fall under Great Britain's extradition treaty with the United States, anyway. The Americans, however, were not keen to harbour a confessed Soviet agent on their soil. The FBI ordered Cairncross to leave the country by 29 June 1964. He complied, and was escorted onto an Air France flight by FBI agents two days shy of the deadline. He was met in Paris by Arthur Martin and Peter Wright for a further interview, before Cairncross moved on to Italy. Though never convicted of espionage, he would endure periodic interviews by Martin and Wright for the next ten years. He was even roped into a meeting with his old friend James Klugmann, in a failed scheme devised by Peter Wright to extract a confession.[16]

Anthony Blunt was another story. The potential for a public scandal and further embarrassment to the British Intelligence Services was much greater, particularly due to Blunt's knighthood, and his employment by the Crown. While John Cairncross had quietly left the country and lived a private life in the wake of the Burgess and Maclean scandal, Anthony Blunt was still living in London thirteen years later, and living well.

Arthur Martin paid Anthony Blunt a visit at his flat in the Courtauld on 23 April 1964. When Martin asked to record their conversation, Blunt agreed, doing his best to act surprised. When Martin announced that he had evidence that Blunt had acted as a Soviet agent during the Second World War, Anthony denied it. When presented with the testimony of Michael Straight, he still wouldn't budge. When Martin finally told him that he was authorised to offer him immunity for his confession, Anthony silently poured himself a drink, stared out the window, and sighed, 'It is true'.[17]

Over monthly interviews over the remainder of 1964, Blunt told Martin about his recruitment by Guy Burgess, gave him details about what he had shared with the KGB, as well as what he knew about Kim Philby and Donald Maclean. He admitted his recruitment of Leo Long and Michael Straight, as well as his knowledge about Cairncross.

Blunt's confession was kept secret from the press, and from all but the most necessary of government officials. Queen Elizabeth was not informed until 1973, almost nine years later. She never spoke about the matter, publicly or privately. A consensus was reached within MI5 that Anthony Blunt was no longer a threat, and he was permitted to continue his life as usual, excepting the periodic interviews by Arthur Martin and later, Peter Wright, which continued for another eight years.

It was beginning to look like Anthony might take his secret to his grave, when, in 1979, journalist Andrew Boyle published his blockbuster book about the Cambridge Spy Ring, *Climate of Treason*. Boyle implicated a 'fourth man' in the Cambridge Spy ring, referring to him only by the pseudonym 'Maurice', hoping to avoid a defamation lawsuit by the *real* fourth man, Anthony Blunt. Blunt had, in fact, tried to halt publication of Boyle's book when he first heard rumours of its impending revelations. Blunt's attempt was leaked by the publisher to *Private Eye* magazine. When excerpts from *Climate of Treason* were published in *The Observer* that November, *Private Eye* ran a story naming Blunt as the real Maurice. Andrew Boyle refused to confirm the assertion, saying that was the government's responsibility, not his.[18]

Prime Minister Margaret Thatcher, a staunch anti-communist, gladly took up Boyle's challenge. On 15 November, in the House of Commons, during Question Time, Labour MP Ted Leadbitter inquired about Anthony Blunt. His question had been pre-arranged to set up an opportunity for Thatcher to address the matter. Thatcher rose, and read a prepared statement:

> *In the early part of last week, Professor Blunt was publicly identified as having been a suspect Soviet agent. This disclosure*

> *understandably gave rise to grave concern… Professor Blunt has admitted that he was recruited for Russian intelligence when he was at Cambridge before the war. In 1940 he joined the Security Service.*[19]

Thatcher went on to lay out some of the details of Blunt's work for the Soviets, followed by the course of his investigation by MI5, and the granting of his immunity by the Attorney General in 1964. Moments after the conclusion of Thatcher's address, Buckingham Palace announced that Blunt would be stripped of his knighthood.

In the immediate buzz following Thatcher's revelations, John 'Jock' Colville, former personal secretary to Winston Churchill, spoke to reporters about a 'Fifth Man' in the Cambridge Spy Ring. John Cairncross used to lunch with Colville at the Traveller's Club before the war. Following the disappearance of Burgess and Maclean, Colville had helped MI5 to identify the incriminating letter found in Burgess' apartment as belonging to John Cairncross. In his statements to a group of breathless reporters, he bragged of his role in leading investigators to the fifth spy. Colville did not identify Cairncross by name, but let slip sufficient details that journalist Barry Penrose was quickly able to connect the dots.[20] Penrose flew to Rome with his colleague, Simon Leitch, on Friday night, and by Saturday morning, they were knocking on the door of John Cairncross. Cairncross reluctantly granted an interview, and the story was posted just in time for the Sunday edition. Just weeks after Blunt was publicly named by Thatcher, *The Sunday Times* ran the story naming John Cairncross as the fifth man in the Cambridge spy ring.[21]

All five of the Cambridge spies were now publicly identified. Though the central question of the mystery surrounding the initial disappearance of two diplomats in 1951 was now put to rest, the resolution was oddly unsatisfying. The Cambridge Five were possibly the most damaging spies in British history, and certainly the most productive. The great spy hunt, beginning with the revelations of defector Walter Krivitsky, had spanned nearly four decades, yet none of the Cambridge spies were ever prosecuted.

Anthony Blunt stepped away from the spotlight after his public unmasking. He continued to study art history and began to write his memoirs. He later abandoned the project in frustration, having burned his diaries years earlier. Though many of his titles and academic fellowships were withdrawn, he maintained the support of a small circle of friends, as well as many of his students. He passed away in Westminster on 26 March 1983, at the age of 75.

In 1982, John Cairncross was charged with currency smuggling in Italy after he was caught near the Swiss border carrying 52 million lire in cash (worth around £22,000). Though he avoided prison time, he was forced to forfeit the money and pay a fine.[22]

Two years later, at the age of 71, he met an American named Gayle Brinkerhoff, who was 28 at the time. They remained together for the rest of his life, though he was still legally married to Gabrielle. John later retired in the south of France, where his life was relatively uneventful, barring the occasional visit from journalists. After Gabrielle died in 1995, Cairncross returned to England and finally married Gayle. He suffered a stroke and died later that year, at the age of 82.

Donald Maclean, once a high level diplomat in the British Foreign Office, stayed true to his form and became a high level Foreign Policy analyst with the Soviet government. He was finally able to give up drinking, which left time for his other addiction, his work. He published a book in 1970, *British Foreign Policy Since Suez,* which was highly regarded in both the Soviet Union and the United Kingdom. Melinda left Moscow for New York, where she lived until her death in 2010. All three of their adult children eventually moved to England with their Russian spouses. Donald Maclean died alone in Moscow at the age of 69 on 6 March 1983.

Unlike the reclusive Donald Maclean, Kim Philby was eager to tell his story and shape his own legacy. He published a memoir, *My Silent War,* in 1968. He granted a series of interviews to journalist Phillip Knightly in the late 1980s, leading to the 1988 release of a ground breaking biography, *The Master Spy.* After a few years, he was permitted to do some consulting work for the KGB. Kim enjoyed his final years in the company of his fourth wife, a Russian woman named Rufina Pukhova, and was allowed the occasional visit by his children, or an old friend. Philby never abandoned his commitment to communism, though he became disillusioned with its Soviet implementation. Like many believers, he chose to blame those in power, rather than communism itself, for its failing. He passed away on 11 May 1988 at the age of 76.

Philby was forever tainted with the same distrust by the KGB that had doggedly followed him since the purge of the late 1930s. Kim's Moscow apartment, with its unlisted address and phone number, was bugged, and he never left the house without the clearance of his personal KGB security detail. Though Kim Philby had worked tirelessly for the advancement of communism since 1933, spied for the Soviet Union since 1936, and was awarded the Order of the Red Banner, the KGB never stopped watching him.

Bibliography

Andrew, Christopher. *Defend the Realm: The Authorized History of MI5* (Vintage, New York, 2010).

Andrew, Christopher and Gordievsky, Oleg. *KGB: The Inside Story* (Harper Collins, New York, 1990).

Andrew, Christopher and Mitrokhin, Vasili. *The Sword and the Shield: The Mitrokhin Archive and the Secret History of the KGB* (Basic Books, New York, 1999).

Andrews, Geoff. *Agent Moliére: The Life of John Cairncross, the Fifth Man of the Cambridge Spy Circle* (Bloomsbury, London, 2020).

Andrews, Geoff. *The Shadow Man: At the Heart of the Cambridge Spy Circle* (Bloomsbury, London, 2015).

Bethel, Nicholas. *The Great Betrayal: The Untold Story of Kim Philby's Final Act of Treachery* (Hodder and Stoughton, London, 1984).

Blum, Howard. *In the Enemy's House: The Secret Saga of the FBI Agent and the Code Breaker Who Caught the Russian Spies* (Harper, New York, 2018).

Borovik, Genrikh with Knightly, Phillip. *The Philby Files: The Secret Life of Master Spy Kim Philby* (Little, Brown and Company, London, 1994).

Boyle, Andrew. *The Climate of Treason: Five Who Spied for Russia* (Hutchinson, London, 1979).

Cairncross, John. *The Enigma Spy* (Century, London, 1997).

Carter, Miranda. *Anthony Blunt: His Lives* (Macmillan, London, 2001).

Cave Brown, Anthony. *Treason in the Blood: H. St. John Philby, Kim Philby, and the Spy Case of the Century* (Houghton Mifflin, New York, 1994).

Cecil, Robert. *A Divided Life: A Biography of Donald Maclean* (Bodley Head, London, 1988).

Connolly, Cyril. *The Missing Diplomats* (Queen Anne Press, London, 1952).

Copeland, Miles. *Without Cloak or Dagger: The Truth about the New Espionage* (Simon and Schuster, New York, 1974).

Costello, John and Tsarev, Oleg. *Deadly Illusions: The KGB Orlov Dossier Reveals Stalin's Master Spy* (Crown, New York, 1993).

Davenport-Hines, Richard. *Enemies Within: Communists, the Cambridge Spies, and the Making of Modern Britain* (William Collins, Glasgow, 2018).

Earl Haynes, John and Klehr, Harvey. *Venona: Decoding Soviet Espionage in America* (Yale University Press, New Haven, 1999).

Eveland, Wilbur Crane. *Ropes of Sand: America's Failure in the Middle East* (W.W. Norton, New York, 1980).

Hanning, James. *Love and Deception: Philby in Beirut* (Corsair, London, 2021).

Harrison, Edward. *The Young Kim Philby: Soviet Spy and British Intelligence Officer* (University of Exeter Press, Exeter, 2012).

Holtzman, Michael. *Donald and Melinda Maclean: Idealism and Espionage* (Chelmsford, Briarcliff Manor, 2014).

Holtzman, Michael. *Guy Burgess: Revolutionary in an Old School Tie* (Chelmsford, Briarcliff Manor, 2013).

Holtzman, Michael. *Spies and Traitors: Kim Philby, James Angleton, and the Betrayal that Would Shape the Cold War* (Weidenfeld and Nicolson, London, 2023).

Kipling, Rudyard. *Kim* (Macmillan, 1901, London).

Knightly, Phillip. *The Master Spy: The Story of Kim Philby* (Vintage Books, New York, 1988).

Lownie, Andrew. *Stalin's Englishman: The Lives of Guy Burgess* (Hodder and Stoughton, London, 2015).

Macintyre, Ben. *A Spy Among Friends: Kim Philby and the Great Betrayal* (Crown, New York, 2015).

Milne, Tim. *Kim Philby: A Story of Friendship and Betrayal* (Biteback Publishing, London, 2014).

Modin, Yuri. *My Five Cambridge Friends* (Headline Book Publishing, London, 1994).

Morley, Jefferson. *The Ghost: The Secret Life of CIA Spymaster James Jesus Angleton* (St Martin's Press, New York, 2017).

Newton, Vernon W. *The Cambridge Spies: The Untold Story of Maclean, Philby, and Burgess in America* (Madison Books, Lanham, 1991).

Penrose, Barry and Freeman, Simon. *Conspiracy of Silence: The Secret Life of Anthony Blunt* (Grafton, London, 1986).

Perry, Roland. *Last of the Cold War Spies: The Life of Michael Straight* (Da Capo Press, Boston, 2005).

Philby, Kim. *My Silent War* (Grove Press, New York, 1968).

Philby, Rufina. *The Private Life of Kim Philby: The Moscow Years* (St Ermine's Press, London, 1999).

Philipps, Roland. *A Spy Named Orphan: The Enigma of Donald Maclean* (W.W. Norton and Company, New York, 2018).

Purvis, Stewart and Hulbert, Jeff. *Guy Burgess: The Spy Who Knew Everyone* (Biteback Publishing, Hull, 2015).

Rees, Goronwy. *A Chapter of Accidents* (The Library Press, New York, 1972).

Romerstein, Herbert and Breindel, Eric. *The Venona Secrets: The Definitive Exposé of Soviet Espionage in America* (Regnery History, Washington DC, 2014).

Smith, Chris. *The Last Cambridge Spy: John Cairncross, Bletchley Park Mole and Soviet Agent* (The History Press, Cheltenham, 2022).

West, Nigel. *MI6* (Grafton Books, London, 1988).

West, Nigel and Tsarev, Oleg. *The Crown Jewels: The British Secrets at the Heart of the KGB Archives* (Yale University Press, New Haven, 1999).

Wright, Peter. *Spy Catcher: The Candid Autobiography of a Senior Intelligence Officer* (Viking, New York, 1987).

Notes

Chapter One

1. Andrew, C. and Mitrokhin, V., *The Sword and the Shield: The Mitrokhin Archive and the Secret History of the KGB* (Basic Books, New York, 1999) p.57.

Chapter Two

1. Cave Brown, A., *Treason in the Blood* (Houghton Mifflin, New York, 1994) p.118.
2. Ibid., p.133.
3. Milne, T., *Kim Philby: The Unknown Story of the KGB's Master Spy* (Biteback Publishing, Hull, 2014) p.2.
4. Knightley, P., *The Master Spy: The Story of Kim Philby* (Vintage Books, NY, 1988) p.28.
5. Cave Brown, A., *Treason in the Blood* (Houghton Mifflin, New York, 1994) p.134.
6. Knightley, P., *The Master Spy: The Story of Kim Philby* (Vintage Books, NY, 1988) p.29.
7. Philby, K., *My Silent War* (Grove Press, NY, 1968) Introduction, p.xxx (30).
8. Knightley, P., *The Master Spy: The Story of Kim Philby* (Vintage Books, New York, 1988) p.36.
9. Ibid., p.45.
10. Ibid.
11. Borovik, G., and Knightley, P., *The Philby Files: The Secret Life of Master Spy Kim Philby* (Little, Brown and Company, Toronto, 1994) p.27.
12. Ibid., p.29.

Chapter Three

1. Phillips, R., *A Spy Named Orphan: The Enigma of Donald Maclean* (W. W. Norton and Company, New York, 2018) p.12.
2. Ibid., p.13.
3. *Granta*, Cambridge, 11 July 1933.
4. Philipps, R., *A Spy Named Orphan: The Enigma of Donald Maclean* (W. W. Norton and Company, New York, 2018) p.42.
5. Lownie, A., 'New Revelations on the Cambridge Spy Ring', *History Today* (17 October 2016). Retrieved 2 August 2024, historytoday.com/new-revelations-cambridge-spy-ring.
6. Cecil, R., *A Divided Life: A Biography of Donald Maclean* (The Bodley Head Ltd, London, 1988) p.47.
7. *The Silver Crescent*, (Cambridge, Lent, 1934).
8. Borovik, G. and Knightly, P., *The Philby Files: The Secret Life of Master Spy Kim Philby* (Little, Brown, and Company, Toronto, 1994) p.46.
9. Philipps, R., *A Spy Named Orphan: The Enigma of Donald Maclean* (W. W. Norton and Company, New York, 2018) p.54.
10. Ibid., p.45.
11. Borovik, G. and Knightly, P., *The Philby Files: The Secret Life of Master Spy Kim Philby* (Little, Brown, and Company, Toronto, 1994) p.42.
12. Cecil, R., *A Divided Life: A Biography of Donald Maclean* (The Bodley Head Ltd, London, 1988) p.70.

Chapter Four

1. Borovik, G. and Knightly, P., *The Philby Files: The Secret Life of Master Spy Kim Philby* (Little, Brown, and Company, Toronto, 1994) p.48.
2. Lownie, A., *Stalin's Englishman: The Lives of Guy Burgess* (Hodder and Stoughton, London, 2015) p.9.
3. Ibid., p.13.
4. Purvis, S. and Hulbert, J., *Guy Burgess: The Spy Who Knew Everyone* (Biteback Publishing, Hull, 2016) p.15.
5. Lownie, A., *Stalin's Englishman: The Lives of Guy Burgess* (Hodder and Stoughton, London, 2015) p.14.
6. Ibid., p.26.

7. Ibid., p.21.
8. Purvis, S. and Hulbert, J., *Guy Burgess: The Spy Who Knew Everyone* (Biteback Publishing, Hull, 2016) p.55.
9. Ibid., p.38.
10. Modin, Y., *My Five Cambridge Friends* (Headline Book Publishing, London, 1994) p.72.
11. Lownie, A., *Stalin's Englishman: The Lives of Guy Burgess* (Hodder and Stoughton, London, 2015) p.49.
12. Ibid., pp.49–50.
13. Carter, M., *Anthony Blunt: His Lives* (Macmillan, London, 2001) p.160.
14. Borovik, G. and Knightly, P., *The Philby Files: The Secret Life of Master Spy Kim Philby* (Little, Brown, and Company, Toronto, 1994) p.48.
15. Carter, M., *Anthony Blunt: His Lives* (Macmillan, London, 2001) p.161.

Chapter Five

1. Philipps, R., *A Spy Named Orphan: The Enigma of Donald Maclean* (W. W. Norton and Company, New York, 2018) p.70.
2. Holzman, M., *Guy Burgess: Revolutionary in an Old School Tie* (Chelmsford Press, Briarcliff Manor, 2013) pp.80-81.
3. Borovik, G. and Knightly, P., *The Philby Files: The Secret Life of Master Spy Kim Philby* (Little, Brown, and Company, Toronto, 1994) p.173.
4. Lownie, A., *Stalin's Englishman: The Lives of Guy Burgess* (Hodder and Stoughton, London, 2015) p.57.
5. Purvis, S. and Hulbert, J., *Guy Burgess: The Spy Who Knew Everyone* (Biteback Publishing, Hull, 2016) p.95.
6. Holzman, M., *Guy Burgess: Revolutionary in an Old School Tie* (Chelmsford Press, Briarcliff Manor, 2013) pp.93-94.
7. Cave Brown, A., *Treason in the Blood* (Houghton Mifflin, New York, 1994) p.186.
8. Philby, K., *My Silent War* (Grove Press, NY, 1968) pp.4–6.

Chapter Six

1. Carter, M., *Anthony Blunt: His Lives* (Macmillan, London, 2001) p.10.
2. Ibid., p.29.

3. Ibid., p.39.
4. Ibid., p.113.
5. Ibid., p.151.
6. Ibid., p.165.
7. Ibid., p.179.
8. Perry, R., *Last of the Cold War Spies* (De Capo Press, Boston, 2005) p.67.
9. Ibid., p.93.

Chapter Seven

1. Cairncross, J., *The Enigma Spy* (Century, London, 1997) p.33.
2. Ibid., p.37.
3. Ibid., p.38.
4. Ibid., p.51.
5. Ibid., p.12.
6. Andrews, G., *The Shadow Man: At the Heart of the Cambridge Spy Ring* (Bloomsbury, London, 2015) p.63.
7. Cairncross, J., *The Enigma Spy* (Century, London, 1997) p.70.
8. Andrews, G., *Agent Molière* (Bloomsbury, London, 2020) p.69.
9. Ibid., p.72.
10. Cairncross, J., *The Enigma Spy* (Century, London, 1997) p.74.
11. Andrew, C. and Mitrokhin, V., *The Sword and the Shield: The Mitrokhin Archive and the Secret History of the KGB* (Basic Books, New York, 1999) p.65.
12. Cairncross, J., *The Enigma Spy* (Century, London, 1997) p.77.
13. Andrews, G., *The Shadow Man: At the Heart of the Cambridge Spy Ring* (Bloomsbury, London, 2015) p.119.
14. Ibid., pp.119–120.
15. Cairncross, J., *The Enigma Spy* (Century, London, 1997) p.84.

Chapter Eight

1. Andrew, C. and Mitrokhin, V., *The Sword and the Shield: The Mitrohkin Archive and the Secret History of the KGB* (Basic Books, New York, 1999) p.80.

2. Lownie, A., *Stalin's Englishman: The Lives of Guy Burgess* (Hodder and Stoughton, London, 2015) p.94.
3. Neville Chamberlain, number10.gov.uk, retrieved 3 August 2024.
4. Lownie, A., *Stalin's Englishman: The Lives of Guy Burgess* (Hodder and Stoughton, London, 2015) p.104.
5. Carter, M., *Anthony Blunt: His Lives* (Macmillan, London, 2001) p.243.
6. Philipps, R., *A Spy Named Orphan: The Enigma of Donald Maclean* (W. W. Norton and Company, New York, 2018) pp.105–107.
7. Cairncross, J., *The Enigma Spy* (Century, London, 1997) pp.96–97.
8. Cecil, R., *A Divided Life: A Biography of Donald Maclean* (The Bodley Head Ltd, London, 1988) p.93.
9. Philipps, R., *A Spy Named Orphan: The Enigma of Donald Maclean* (W. W. Norton and Company, New York, 2018) p.117.

Chapter Nine

1. Public Domain.
2. Cave Brown, A., *Treason in the Blood* (Houghton Mifflin, New York, 1994) pp.237–238.
3. Purvis, S. and Hulbert, J., *Guy Burgess: The Spy Who Knew Everyone* (Biteback Publishing, Hull, 2016) p.177.
4. Cave Brown, A., *Treason in the Blood* (Houghton Mifflin, New York, 1994) pp.254–255.
5. Purvis, S. and Hulbert, J., *Guy Burgess: The Spy Who Knew Everyone* (Biteback Publishing, Hull, 2016) pp.179–180.
6. Smith, C., *The Last Cambridge Spy* (The History Press, Cheltenham, 2022) p.53.
7. Philipps, R., *A Spy Named Orphan: The Enigma of Donald Maclean* (W. W. Norton and Company, New York, 2018) p.130.
8. Carter, M., *Anthony Blunt: His Lives* (Macmillan, London, 2001) p.265.
9. Cave Brown, A., *Treason in the Blood* (Houghton Mifflin, New York, 1994) p.266.
10. Philipps, R., *A Spy Named Orphan: The Enigma of Donald Maclean* (W. W. Norton and Company, New York, 2018) p.129.
11. Holzman, M., *Guy Burgess: Revolutionary in an Old School Tie* (Chelmsford Press, Briarcliff Manor, 2013) p.180.

Chapter Ten

1. Philby, K., *My Silent War* (Grove Press, NY, 1968) p.46.
2. Ibid., pp.60–62.
3. Cave Brown, A., *Treason in the Blood* (Houghton Mifflin, New York, 1994) pp.286–287.
4. Andrew, C. and Mitrokhin, V., *The Sword and the Shield: The Mitrokhin Archive and the Secret History of the KGB* (Basic Books, New York, 1999) p.84.
5. Ibid.
6. Smith, C., *The Last Cambridge Spy* (The History Press, Cheltenham, 2022) p.67.
7. Ibid., p.72.
8. Holzman, M., *Spies and Traitors* (Weidenfeld and Nicolson, London, 2023) pp.85–87.
9. Knightley, P., *The Master Spy: The Story of Kim Philby* (Vintage Books, New York, 1988) pp.109–110.
10. Cave Brown, A., *Treason in the Blood* (Houghton Mifflin, New York, 1994) p.318.
11. Phillips, R., *A Spy Named Orphan: The Enigma of Donald Maclean* (W. W. Norton and Company, New York, 2018) pp.133–134.

Chapter Eleven

1. Lownie, A., *Stalin's Englishman: The Lives of Guy Burgess* (Hodder and Stoughton, London, 2015) pp.145–146.
2. Ibid., p.148.
3. Smith, C., *The Last Cambridge Spy* (The History Press, Cheltenham, 2022) p.80.
4. Philby, K., *My Silent War* (Grove Press, NY, 1968) pp.94–98.
5. Ibid., (Foreword by Graham Greene, pp.xix–xx).
6. Lownie, A., *Stalin's Englishman: The Lives of Guy Burgess* (Hodder and Stoughton, London, 2015) p.148.
7. Carter, M., *Anthony Blunt: His Lives* (Macmillan, London, 2001) p.311.
8. Ibid., p.319.

9. Cave Brown, A., *Treason in the Blood* (Houghton Mifflin, New York, 1994) p.363.
10. Philipps, R., *A Spy Named Orphan: The Enigma of Donald Maclean* (W. W. Norton and Company, New York, 2018) pp.168–169.
11. Ibid., p.172.
12. Ibid., p.176.

Chapter Twelve

1. Philipps, R., *A Spy Named Orphan: The Enigma of Donald Maclean* (W. W. Norton and Company, New York, 2018) p.191.
2. Andrews, G., *Agent Molière* (Bloomsbury, London, 2020) p.152.
3. Ibid., p.155.
4. Ibid., p.159.
5. Philipps, R., *A Spy Named Orphan: The Enigma of Donald Maclean* (W. W. Norton and Company, New York, 2018) pp.148–149.
6. Ibid., p.162.
7. Lownie, A., *Stalin's Englishman: The Lives of Guy Burgess* (Hodder and Stoughton, London, 2015) p.165.
8. Modin, Y., *My Five Cambridge Friends* (Headline Book Publishing, London, 1994) pp.155–156.
9. Lownie, A., *Stalin's Englishman: The Lives of Guy Burgess* (Hodder and Stoughton, London, 2015) p.166.
10. Ibid., p.171.
11. Ibid., p.174.
12. Ibid., p.175.
13. Milne, T., *Kim Philby: The Unknown Story of the KGB's Master Spy* (Biteback Publishing, Hull, 2014) p.173.
14. Holzman, M., *Spies and Traitors* (Weidenfeld and Nicolson, London, 2023) pp.127–128.
15. Philipps, R., *A Spy Named Orphan: The Enigma of Donald Maclean* (W. W. Norton and Company, New York, 2018) pp.210–212.
16. Cecil, R., *A Divided Life: A Biography of Donald Maclean* (The Bodley Head Ltd, London, 1988) p.144.
17. Lownie, A., *Stalin's Englishman: The Lives of Guy Burgess* (Hodder and Stoughton, London, 2015) p.188.

18. Ibid., pp.188–189.
19. Carter, M., *Anthony Blunt: His Lives* (Macmillan, London, 2001) p.333.
20. Ibid.
21. Philipps, R., *A Spy Named Orphan: The Enigma of Donald Maclean* (W. W. Norton and Company, New York, 2018) pp.223–226.
22. Lownie, A., *Stalin's Englishman: The Lives of Guy Burgess* (Hodder and Stoughton, London, 2015) p.193.

Chapter Thirteen

1. Modin, Y., *My Five Cambridge Friends* (Headline Book Publishing, London, 1994) p.187.
2. Philipps, R., *A Spy Named Orphan: The Enigma of Donald Maclean* (W. W. Norton and Company, New York, 2018) pp.237–238.
3. Ibid., p.239.
4. Lownie, A., *Stalin's Englishman: The Lives of Guy Burgess* (Hodder and Stoughton, London, 2015) pp.190–191.
5. Philipps, R., *A Spy Named Orphan: The Enigma of Donald Maclean* (W. W. Norton and Company, New York, 2018) p.243.
6. Toynbee, P., 'Maclean and I', *The Observer* (London, 15 October 1967) p.21. newspapers.com/images/258893432; retrieved 6 August 2024.
7. Philipps, R., *A Spy Named Orphan: The Enigma of Donald Maclean* (W. W. Norton and Company, New York, 2018) p.245.
8. Toynbee, P., 'Maclean and I', *The Observer* (London, 15 October 1967) p.21. newspapers.com/images/258893432; retrieved 6 August 2024.
9. Philipps, R., *A Spy Named Orphan: The Enigma of Donald Maclean* (W. W. Norton and Company, New York, 2018) pp.245–247.
10. Lownie, A., *Stalin's Englishman: The Lives of Guy Burgess* (Hodder and Stoughton, London, 2015) pp.194–195.
11. Central Intelligence Agency. (1951). OIR Contribution to NIE-42: The Situation in Albania, with Particular Reference to Greek, Yugoslav, and Italian Interest and Pretensions. (CIA-RDP79R01012A001200030001-3).
12. Cave Brown, A., *Treason in the Blood* (Houghton Mifflin, New York, 1994) p.419.

13. Lownie, A., *Stalin's Englishman: The Lives of Guy Burgess* (Hodder and Stoughton, London, 2015) p.207.
14. Ibid., pp.210–212.
15. Purvis, S. and Hulbert, J., *Guy Burgess: The Spy Who Knew Everyone* (Biteback Publishing, Hull, 2016) p.354.
16. Philipps, R., *A Spy Named Orphan: The Enigma of Donald Maclean* (W. W. Norton and Company, New York, 2018) p.285.
17. Rees, G., *A Chapter of Accidents* (The Library Press, New York, 1972) p.191.
18. Connolly, C., *The Missing Diplomats* (Queen Anne Press, London, 1952) p.31.
19. Toynbee, P., 'Alger Hiss and His Friends', *The Observer* (London, 18 March 1951) p.4. newspapers.com/images/258853247/; retrieved 6 August 2024.
20. Toynbee, P., 'Maclean and I', *The Observer* (London, 15 October 1967) p.23. newspapers.com/images/258893432 retrieved 6 August 2024.
21. Cecil, R., *A Divided Life: A Biography of Donald Maclean* (The Bodley Head Ltd, London, 1988) p.177.
22. Lownie, A., *Stalin's Englishman: The Lives of Guy Burgess* (Hodder and Stoughton, London, 2015) pp.218–219.
23. Ibid., p.222.
24. Perry, R., *The Last of the Cold War Spies* (Da Capo Press, Boston, 2005) p.239. (John Blamey is referred to by an alias, Alan Baker.)
25. National Security Agency (28 June 1944) A KGB Meeting with Donald Maclean. Venona, (reissue, T-83,1973) https://www.nsa.gov/portals/75/documents/news-features/declassified-documents/venona/dated/1944/28jun_kgb_mtg_donald_maclean.pdf.
26. Cave Brown, A., *Treason in the Blood* (Houghton Mifflin, New York, 1994) p.429.
27. Philby, K., *My Silent War* (Grove Press, NY, 1968) p.171.

Chapter Fourteen

1. Phillips, R., *A Spy Named Orphan: The Enigma of Donald Maclean* (W. W. Norton and Company, New York, 2018) p.297.
2. Modin, Y., *My Five Cambridge Friends* (Headline Book Publishing, London, 1994) p.202.

3. Ibid., p.204.
4. Lownie, A., *Stalin's Englishman: The Lives of Guy Burgess* (Hodder and Stoughton, London, 2015) p.227.
5. Ibid., p.234.
6. Cecil, R., *A Divided Life: A Biography of Donald Maclean* (The Bodley Head Ltd, London, 1988) p.198.
7. Carter, M., *Anthony Blunt: His Lives* (Macmillan, London, 2001) p.336.
8. Cecil, R., *A Divided Life: A Biography of Donald Maclean* (The Bodley Head Ltd, London, 1988) p.205.
9. Philipps, R., *A Spy Named Orphan: The Enigma of Donald Maclean* (W. W. Norton and Company, New York, 2018) p.320.
10. Ibid., p.322.
11. Rees, G., *A Chapter of Accidents* (The Library Press, New York, 1972) pp.207–209.
12. Purvis, S. and Hulbert, J., *Guy Burgess: The Spy Who Knew Everyone* (Biteback Publishing, Hull, 2016) p.375.
13. Uncredited Reporter., 'Foreign Office Name Two Missing Chiefs', *The Evening Standard* (7 June 1951) p.1. newspapers.com/image/720838939/; retrieved 6 August 2024.
14. Rees, G., *A Chapter of Accidents* (The Library Press, New York, 1972) p.214.
15. Philipps, R., *A Spy Named Orphan: The Enigma of Donald Maclean* (W. W. Norton and Company, New York, 2018) p.345.
16. Andrew, C., *The Defence of the Realm* (Allen Lane, London, 2009) p.428.

Chapter Fifteen

1. Cave Brown, A., *Treason in the Blood* (Houghton Mifflin, New York, 1994) pp.447, 450.
2. Modin, Y., *My Five Cambridge Friends* (Headline Book Publishing, London, 1994) pp.231–232.
3. Philipps, R., *A Spy Named Orphan: The Enigma of Donald Maclean* (W. W. Norton and Company, New York, 2018) p.351.
4. Cave Brown, A., *Treason in the Blood* (Houghton Mifflin, New York, 1994) pp.456–454.

5. Milne, T. *Kim Philby: The Unknown Story of the KGB's Master Spy* (Biteback Publishing, Hull, 2014) p.187.
6. Lownie, A., *Stalin's Englishman: The Lives of Guy Burgess* (Hodder and Stoughton, London, 2015) p.291.
7. Ibid., p.292.
8. Driberg, T., *Guy Burgess: A Portrait with Background* (Weidenfeld and Nicolson, London, 1956) p.121.
9. Lownie, A., *Stalin's Englishman: The Lives of Guy Burgess* (Hodder and Stoughton, London, 2015) p.279.
10. Rees, G, anonymously. 'Guy Burgess Stripped Bare', *The Sunday People* (11 March 1956) p.3. newspapers.com/images/811508605/; retrieved 6 August 2024.
11. Purvis, S. and Hulbert, J., *Guy Burgess: The Spy Who Knew Everyone* (Biteback Publishing, Hull, 2016) p.471.
12. Cave Brown, A., *Treason in the Blood* (Houghton Mifflin, New York, 1994) p.469.
13. Eveland, W., *Ropes of Sand: America's Failure in the Middle East* (W.W. Norton, New York, 1980) p.234.
14. Ibid., pp.248–249.
15. Knightley, P., *The Master Spy: The Story of Kim Philby* (Vintage Books, New York, 1988) p.211.
16. Copeland, M., *Without Cloak or Dagger: The Truth about the New Espionage* (Simon and Schuster, New York, 1974) p.146.
17. Cave Brown, A., *Treason in the Blood* (Houghton Mifflin, New York, 1994) p.495.
18. Hanning, J., *Love and Deception: Philby in Beirut* (Corsair, London, 2022) p.162.
19. Wright, P., *Spy Catcher: The Candid Autobiography of Senior Intelligence Officer* (Viking Penguin, New York, 1987) p.129.
20. Costello, J., *Mask of Treachery* (William Morrow, New York, 1988) pp.582–583.
21. Wright, P., *Spy Catcher: The Candid Autobiography of Senior Intelligence Officer* (Viking Penguin, New York, 1987) pp.172–173.
22. Ibid., p.193.
23. Cave Brown, A., *Treason in the Blood* (Houghton Mifflin, New York, 1994) p.502.
24. Hanning, J., *Love and Deception: Philby in Beirut* (Corsair, London, 2022) pp.228–229.

25. Cave Brown, A., *Treason in the Blood* (Houghton Mifflin, New York, 1994) p.507.
26. Boyle, A., *Climate of Treason: Five Who Spied for Russia* (Hutchinson, London, 1979) p.437.

Chapter Sixteen

1. Blunt, A., *Artistic Theory in Italy:1450–1600* (Oxford University Press, London, 1940).
2. Carter, M., *Anthony Blunt: His Lives* (Macmillan, London, 2001) p.440.
3. Andrews, G., *Agent Molière* (Bloomsbury, London, 2020) p.197.
4. Cave Brown, A., *Treason in the Blood* (Houghton Mifflin, New York, 1994) p.521.
5. Ibid., p.527.
6. Modin, Y., *My Five Cambridge Friends* (Headline Book Publishing, London, 1994) p.256.
7. Knightley, P., *The Master Spy: The Story of Kim Philby* (Vintage Books, New York, 1988) p.223.
8. Purvis, S. and Hulbert, J., *Guy Burgess: The Spy Who Knew Everyone* (Biteback Publishing, Hull, 2016) p.547.
9. Lownie, A., *Stalin's Englishman: The Lives of Guy Burgess* (Hodder and Stoughton, London, 2015) p.316.
10. Hanning, J., *Love and Deception: Philby in Beirut* (Corsair, London, 2022) p.253.
11. Ibid., pp.264–265.
12. Philipps, R., *A Spy Named Orphan: The Enigma of Donald Maclean* (W. W. Norton and Company, New York, 2018) p.374.
13. Perry, R., *Last of the Cold War Spies* (Da Capo Press, Boston, 2005) pp.291–292.
14. Ibid., pp.297–298.
15. Smith, C., *The Last Cambridge Spy* (The History Press, Cheltenham, 2022) p.98.
16. Cairncross, J., *The Enigma Spy* (Century, London, 1997) pp.176–178.
17. Penrose, B. and Freeman, S., *Conspiracy of Silence: The Secret Life of Anthony Blunt* (Grafton, London, 1986) p.416.
18. Carter, M., *Anthony Blunt: His Lives* (Macmillan, London, 2001) p.471.

19. Thatcher, M., [transcript from House of Commons] Hansard HC [974/402-10] margaretthatcher.org/document/104175; retrieved 7 August 2024.
20. Cairncross, J., *The Enigma Spy* (Century, London, 1997) pp.184–185.
21. Penrose, B. and Freeman, S., *Conspiracy of Silence: The Secret Life of Anthony Blunt* (Grafton, London, 1986) p.525.
22. Smith, C., *The Last Cambridge Spy* (The History Press, Cheltenham, 2022) p.107.

Index

Abwehr (German Military Intelligence) xv, 95–96, 98, 103, 105
Albania 72, 145–146, 213
Angleton, James viii, xiii, 104–105, 137–138, 146, 148, 185, 187
Apostles xiii, 29, 36, 48, 49, 132, 158
Archer, Jane (nee Sissmore) 77
Arlington Hall 121, 135, 139
Ashton, Harry 59
Austria 3, 4, 11–14, 15, 57, 58, 69, 82, 84, 123

Bassett, Evelyn (nee Burgess) xi, 25, 32, 50, 139, 165, 180, 194
Bassett, Colonel John xi, 32, 110, 165
Beirut, Lebanon xiii, 177, 181–189, 190, 192, 193, 195, 196
Bell, Julian xiii, 31, 41, 49, 53, 67
Bentinck Street 89, 100, 127, 181
Bentley, Elizabeth 120, 121, 137, 150
Beria, Lavrenty 78
Berlin, Isaiah 31, 126
Bletchley Park 94, 95, 96, 101–105, 125
Bloomsbury Group 48, 49
Blunt, Anthony vi, viii, x, xi, xii, xiii, xvi, 5, 6, 29, 40, 43, 44–53, 55, 59, 60, 63, 64, 67, 70, 71, 73, 75, 76, 78, 79, 80, 82, 87, 88, 89, 99–101, 103, 104, 108, 109, 110, 111, 114, 116–118, 124, 132, 152, 155, 158, 159, 163, 165, 172–173, 177, 181, 188, 190–191, 192, 194, 197, 198–200
British Broadcasting Company (BBC) xiii, 5, 40, 41, 42, 72, 84, 89–90, 100, 106–107, 111, 124, 155
British Security Coordination (BSC) 96
Brooman-White, Dick 91
Burgess, Guy vii, viii, x, xi, xii, xiii, xvi, 5, 6, 19, 24–34, 36–37, 38, 39, 40–41, 42, 43, 44, 49, 50, 52, 53, 55, 63–64, 67, 69, 70–74, 76–79, 82–84, 87–90, 99–100, 103, 106–107, 110–113, 116, 118, 124, 127–129, 131–132, 134, 135, 137, 139–140, 143–144, 146, 148–149, 150–152, 153–168, 170–172, 174–175, 177–180, 186, 190, 191, 193–195, 197–200
Burgess, Nigel xi, 25, 26, 27, 32, 50, 180, 194

Caffrey, Jefferson 142–143
Cairncross, Sir Alexander 'Alec' xii, 55, 56, 57, 59, 87, 124

Cairncross, Alexander 54–55, 56
Cairncross, Elizabeth (nee Wishart) 54, 55, 191
Cairncross, Gabrielle (nee Oppenheim) xii 124, 167, 168, 177, 191–192
Cairncross, Gayle (nee Brinkerhoff) xii, 201
Cairncross, John vii, viii, x, xi, xii, xiii, xvi, 5, 6, 53, 54–66, 69–71, 74, 77–80, 87–89, 101–104, 109–111, 113, 116–117, 124–125, 153, 163, 167–168, 177, 191, 192
Cairo, Egypt xiv, 118, 119, 127, 129–130, 132–134, 140–143, 147, 148, 149, 174, 192
Cambridge University vii, xiii, xiv, 1–5, 8, 10, 11, 15, 18, 20, 22, 29, 30–32, 36, 40, 47–53, 55, 56, 59, 60, 62–65, 67, 70, 75, 76, 78, 82, 89, 91, 95, 100–103, 110, 120, 132, 158, 167–169, 174, 178, 179, 187, 200
Campbell, Ronald 130, 131, 134, 143–143
Canaris, Admiral William 98, 105, 108
Carey-Foster, George 160, 162
Central Intelligence Agency (CIA) viii, ix, xiii, 134, 137, 138, 144, 145, 148, 177, 183, 184, 185, 187, 188, 189, 192, 198
Chamberlain, Neville 69, 71, 88
Chambers, Whittaker 120, 150
Churchill, Clarissa xiii, 127
Churchill, Winston xiii, 71, 81, 87, 88, 101, 115, 116, 125, 127, 155, 200

Colville, John 'Jock' xiii, 200
Communist International (Comintern) 3, 11, 12, 21, 32, 41, 58, 62, 64, 70, 74, 79, 187
Connolly, Cyril vii, xiii, 158, 160, 163
Copeland, Lorraine 185
Copeland, Miles Jr xiii, 185, 192
Cornford, John xiii, 31, 41, 50, 51, 52, 53, 60, 67
Courtauld Institute 50, 116, 117, 124, 155, 159, 165, 172, 190, 198
Cowgill, Felix xiii, 91, 94, 95, 96, 97, 98, 114, 115
Curry, Jack xiii, 99, 113

Dartmouth College 24, 25, 26–27, 40
De Gaury, Gerard 83
Deladier, Édouard 37
Deutsch, Arnold x, xi, xiii, 1, 3–5, 14–15, 19, 21–22, 33, 34, 35–36, 38–39, 41, 51, 52, 59, 63, 64–66, 68, 69, 70, 74, 87, 110
Dobb, Maurice xiii, 10, 11, 30, 31
Donovan, William 96–97
Double Cross, or 'XX' 95, 101, 103, 105, 109, 183
Dunbar, Melinda xii, 143, 167, 173, 174, 180

Eitingon, Leonid 70
Elliott, Nicholas xiii, 105, 129, 182, 185, 186, 187, 188–189, 193
Eton College 25, 26, 27–28, 29, 32, 77, 78
Eveland, Wilbur 183–184

Index

Federal Bureau of Investigation (FBI) ix, xv, 31, 96, 120, 121, 122, 135, 136, 137, 147, 148, 155, 156, 158, 164, 175, 196, 197, 198

Footman, David xiii, 40–41, 103, 163

Foreign Office vii, xii, xiii, xiv, 6, 21, 22, 33, 35, 38, 43, 61, 63, 65, 66, 69, 77, 78, 82, 84, 85, 86, 92, 98, 103, 107, 109, 112, 113, 118, 124, 128, 130, 131, 136, 138, 140, 141, 143, 144, 146, 146, 147, 149, 152, 153, 156, 157, 160, 164, 165, 167, 168, 171, 174, 175, 179, 182, 186, 193, 201

Franco, General Francisco 41, 42, 43, 52, 62, 72, 77, 95, 96, 98, 138, 140

Gardner, Meredith xv, 121, 122, 134, 135, 153, 166

Gaskin, John xii, 172

Glenalmond 94, 97

Great Purge 62, 67, 73, 77, 109, 110, 150, 179, 202

Green, Frederick 102, 103

Greene, Graham xiii, 96, 103–104, 114, 115, 124, 167, 192

Gresham's School xi, 17, 18, 70

Gorsky, Anatoly xi, 68, 74, 78, 87, 88, 100, 101, 102, 103, 104, 112, 120, 121, 137

Gouzenko, Igor 119–120, 123

Gubbins, Collin 84–85

Guest, David Haden xiii, 11, 30, 31, 41, 50, 51, 60, 67

Hankey, Maurice 87–88, 101

Harris, Kitty xi, 68, 69, 70, 73, 77, 79, 80

Harris, Tomás xiv, 91, 108

Hess, Rudolph 91–92

Hewit, Jack xii, 40, 89, 99, 131, 158, 163, 181

Hiss, Alger 131, 150

Hoover, J. Edgar 158, 166, 175

Istanbul, Turkey 105, 118, 119, 122, 128

Jebb, Gladwyn xii, 84, 144, 146

KGB (Soviet Secret Intelligence) viii, ix, x, xv, xvi, 3, 4, 14, 15, 21, 36, 62, 63, 64, 68, 69, 70, 74, 77, 78, 87, 88, 91, 94, 99, 103, 109, 110, 111, 112, 115, 117, 118, 119, 120, 121, 127, 130, 134, 137, 139, 150, 155, 156, 157, 159, 161, 166, 170, 171, 172, 174, 178, 181, 186, 187, 194, 196, 197, 199, 201, 202

Kessler, Erich xi, 99

Keynes, John Maynard 10, 26, 29, 30, 48, 59

King, John Herbert 78

Kislytsin, Filip 174

Klugmann, James viii, xi, 18, 21, 31, 50, 51, 53, 60, 64–65, 70, 79, 117–118, 198

Koestler, Arthur 62, 65, 73

Kreshin, Boris x, 100, 104, 108, 112, 113, 116, 118, 120

Krivitsky, Walter xv, 77, 78, 88, 109, 120, 138, 139, 153, 200

Lamphere, Robert xv, 135, 148, 156, 166

Lees, Jim xiv, 10, 30

Lenin, Vladimir 15, 85
Liddell, Guy xiv, 82, 99, 100, 114, 140, 143, 163
Lockers Park School 25, 26
Lockhart, Robert Bruce 85
Long, Leo xi, 100, 117, 199
Lyndsay-Hogg, Lady Frances Doble 42

Mackenzie, Robert xv, 139, 148, 153
Maclean, Alan xii, 17, 112, 146, 155, 164, 165, 180
Maclean, Donald vii, viii, ix, x, xi, xii, xiii, xiv, xv, xvi, 5, 6, 15, 16–23, 24, 31, 33, 34, 35–36, 37–38, 43, 52, 55, 61, 62, 63, 65, 66, 68–70, 73, 76, 77, 78, 79, 80, 85–86, 87, 88, 89, 92, 103, 107, 109, 110, 112, 113, 118, 120, 121, 122, 123, 124, 125, 126–127, 129–131, 132–134, 135, 136, 137, 139, 143–143, 146–147, 148–150, 152–154, 155–157, 158–165, 166, 167, 168, 170–171, 172, 174, 175, 177, 178–181, 186, 191, 193, 194–195, 196–197, 198, 199, 200, 201
Maclean, Lady Gwendolyn xii, 17, 18, 19, 20, 22, 143, 146, 147, 160, 161
Maclean, Melinda (nee Marling) xii, 76–77, 80, 86–87, 107, 112, 123, 126–127, 130–131, 132–133, 141–143, 146–147, 153, 157, 158, 159, 160, 161–162, 164, 166–167, 173,–174, 180, 194, 195–197, 201
Makins, Roger 123, 160, 162
Maly, Theodore x, 36, 41, 67, 68, 78

Marling, Harriet xii, 76, 133, 141, 142, 143, 167
Martin, Kevin 76
Martin, Arthur xv, xvi, 166, 169, 187, 188, 197–199
Maxse, Marjorie 82, 83
Mayall, Lees xiv, 133–134
Mayor, Tess xiv, 88–89
McNeil, Hector xiv, 124, 127, 128
Menzies, Stewart xiv, 91, 96, 97, 98, 114, 118, 169
MI5 (Security Service) ix, x, xiii, xiv, xv, xvi, 77, 78, 82, 87, 88, 91, 95, 99, 100, 103, 108, 113, 114, 116, 118, 120, 124, 136, 140, 143, 147, 152, 153, 155, 156, 157, 158, 160, 161, 162, 163, 164, 165, 166, 167, 169, 174, 175, 182, 183, 187, 191, 197, 198, 199, 200
MI6 (Secret Intelligence Service, or SIS) ix, x, xiii, xiv, xv, xvi, 36, 39, 40, 41, 43, 72, 78, 82, 84, 87, 89, 90, 91, 92, 94, 95, 96, 97, 98, 102, 103, 104, 105, 106, 107, 108, 109, 110, 113, 114, 115, 116, 118, 119, 120, 137, 140, 147, 162, 163, 164, 165, 166, 169, 171, 174, 177, 182, 183, 186, 187, 188, 189, 192, 193, 195, 197
Miller, Bernard xiv, 159, 163
Milne, Tim xiv, 9, 11, 96, 98, 115, 128, 176
Modin, Yuri xi, 124, 125, 127, 132, 135, 155, 156, 157, 159, 167, 168, 172–173, 188, 194
Modrzhinskaya, Elena 110, 111
Molotov, Vyacheslav 72, 73, 93, 127
Montgomery, Peter xii, 48

Index

Moscow, Soviet Union ix, xi, 3, 6, 15, 21, 32, 34, 38, 40, 41, 51, 53, 64, 66, 67–68, 69, 70, 71, 72, 76, 80, 86, 87, 88, 92, 109, 111, 113, 119, 121, 122, 134, 136, 139, 141, 143, 153, 155, 157, 159, 161, 164, 170, 171, 172, 174, 178, 179, 180, 193–196, 201–202

Muggeridge, Malcolm xiv, 89, 96

Nicolson, Harold xiv, 36–37, 40
Nunn May, Alan 120, 157, 168

Orlov, Alexander xi, 33, 34, 37, 38, 68
Oxford University 10, 11, 31, 32, 37, 40, 47, 70, 77, 78, 95

Paris, France xi, 6, 11, 21, 37, 45, 46, 58, 59, 63, 64, 66, 69, 70, 71, 73, 76, 78, 79, 80, 85, 86, 109, 130, 140, 141, 147, 161, 162, 164, 190, 198
Pearson, Norman Holmes 104
Petrov, Vladimir xv, 174–175
Pfeiffer, Edouard 37
Philby, Aileen (nee Furse) xii, 74–75, 82, 89, 94, 106, 123, 128–129, 137, 144, 147, 148, 150, 166, 171, 176–176, 182, 184, 187
Philby, Dora xii, 7, 8, 9, 13, 90, 106, 176, 184, 196
Philby, Eleanor (nee Brewer) xii, 183, 184, 185, 189, 192–193, 194, 195–196
Philby, Kim vii, viii, x, xii, xiii, xiv, xv, xvi, 4–5, 6, 7–15, 18, 19, 21–22, 24, 30, 31, 33, 34, 36, 37, 38–40, 41–43, 52, 55, 56, 62, 64, 74–75, 76, 78, 79, 80, 82–83, 84–85, 87, 88, 89, 90, 91, 92, 94, 95, 96, 97–99, 103, 104–106, 108, 109–110, 111, 113–115, 118–119, 120, 123, 128–129, 135, 137–139, 143, 144, 146, 147–148, 150, 152, 153–154, 155, 156, 157, 158, 163, 165–166, 167, 171–173, 175, 176, 177, 181–189, 190, 192–194, 195–196, 197, 199, 201–202
Philby, Litzi (nee Friedmann) xi, xiii, 12, 13, 14, 42, 82, 123, 166
Philby, Rufina (nee Pukhova) xii, 201
Philby, St John xii, 4, 7, 8, 9–10, 13–14, 15, 38, 39, 40, 41–42, 83–84, 90–91, 104, 106, 110, 171, 175, 176, 177, 181, 182, 183, 184, 185–186, 196
Pollock, Peter xii, 89, 99, 127, 132, 158
Prae Wood 97, 110
Pravdin, Vladimir xi, 112, 153
Proctor, Dennis xiv, 76, 100

Rawdon-Smith, Patricia xiv, 89, 127
Redgrave, Michael 29
Regent's Park 4, 14, 65
Rees, Goronwy xi, 31, 40, 70, 73, 89, 132, 149, 158, 163, 165, 181, 191, 197
Reich, Dr Wilhelm 4, 59
Revoi (or Revai), Andrew xi, 99
Ribbentrop, Joachim von 39, 72, 73, 93
Ridsdale, William 107, 112–113, 141
Rothschild, Victor xiv, xv, 36, 49, 53, 82, 88, 103, 158, 181, 187
Rylands, George 'Dadie' 29, 48

Saud, King Ibn 8, 9, 83, 176
Sillitoe, Percy 158, 165
SIS, or Secret Intelligence Service *see* MI6
Skardon, Jim xv, 165, 167–168, 171, 172
Solomon, Flora xv, 74, 187, 188
SOS (Special Operations Executive) 84–85, 90, 96, 97, 104, 105, 117–118, 144
Spain 3, 10, 35, 41, 42, 51, 52, 53, 62, 63, 65, 68, 69, 71, 74, 77, 91, 95–96, 98–99, 108, 131, 138, 139, 143, 146
Stalin, Joseph 62, 67, 68, 69, 73, 74, 77, 92, 106, 107, 115, 116, 125, 126, 144, 145, 170, 173, 178, 179
Stephenson, William 97, 120
Strachey, John 89
Strachey, Lytton 30, 48
Strachey, Oliver 96
Straight, Michael viii, xi, 53, 132, 152, 197–198, 199
St Albans 94, 97, 103, 104
St George Hotel 183, 189, 192

Taylor, Eunice 142, 143
Toynbee, Philip xv, 37, 80, 140–142, 148, 150
Trinity College 1, 4, 5, 6, 8, 9, 10, 18, 29, 30, 32, 41, 47, 49, 51, 59, 64, 99

Trinity Hall 5, 18, 22
Triplex 99
Trotsky, Leon 99
Tube Alloys 134
Tudor Hart, Edith xiii, 14
Turck, James 151, 152
Tyrell-Martin, Eric 133, 134

University of London 3, 116

Venona xv, 121, 122, 134, 135, 137, 138, 143, 147, 148, 152, 155, 157, 166
Vermehren, Erich xv, 105–106, 108
Vivian, Colonel Valentine xv, 41, 90–91, 114, 115
Volkov, Konstantin xvi, 118–119, 120, 166

Warner, Fred 131
Washington, DC, United States xi, xv, 97, 107, 112, 122, 123, 125–126, 129, 132, 135–136, 137–138, 143–144, 147, 151, 152, 153, 154, 155, 156, 158, 165, 166, 175, 183, 185, 187, 197
Westminster College xiv, 8, 9, 11, 38, 42, 96
White, Dick xv, 91, 100, 147, 158, 163, 182, 187, 193, 195
Wright, Peter xvi, 187, 198, 199
Wylie, Thomas 38–39